My Fight For Nothing Less

FIERCE

Marian Washington
In their words...

"We have a tendency to forget where things started and who opened doors for us. And we must not do that. We need to educate ourselves because the more you know, the more you can impact others and share knowledge. That's why this is an important book.

"Coach Washington has a presence about her. She's very charismatic and she doesn't have to say a word. You know you stand among greatness because of that. She's known who she is for a very long time and doesn't need anyone to justify her legacy. I'm glad she wrote this book that gives us a glimpse of what greatness looks like, what a legacy looks like, that tells us what we don't know but need to know. The lessons unpacked in this book are incredible. I'm glad she has given us her flowers while we can still smell them."

— **Dawn Staley,** Naismith Basketball Hall-of-Famer, Olympian and NCAA championship coach

"I felt really fortunate that Marian wanted to be part of my Olympic staff in 1996. We wanted to win. And I wanted to hire the person who would help us win. Marian is a very humble woman. She went about how she did things in a humble way. She had a great rapport with everyone on the team. She had the ultimate respect of all the coaches. It was a wonderful time we spent, and Marian did a fabulous job."

— **Tara VanDerveer,** retired Stanford coach, 1,216 career victories

Marian E. Washington
with Vicki L. Friedman

My Fight For Nothing Less

FIERCE

Foreword by Kathleen Sebelius • Afterword by Lynette Woodard

ASCEND BOOKS

Requests for permission should be addressed to: Ascend Books, LLC, Attn: Rights and Permissions Department, 11722 West 91st Street, Overland Park, KS 66214

First Edition
10 9 8 7 6 5 4 3 2 1

ISBN: print book 979-8-9863584-2-0
Ebook ISBN: 979-8-9863584-6-8
Library of Congress Control Number: 2023950095

Publisher: Bob Snodgrass
Editor: Jim Marchiony
Publication Coordinator: Molly Gore
Sales and Marketing: Lenny Cohen
Dust Jacket and Book Design: Rob Peters
All photos courtesy of Marian E. Washington unless otherwise indicated.

Publisher's Note: The goal of Ascend Books is to publish quality works. With that goal in mind, we are proud to offer this book to our readers. Please notify the publisher of any erroneous credits or omissions, and corrections will be made to subsequent editions/future printings. Please note, however, that the story, experiences, and the words are those of the authors alone.

Printed in Canada

ASCEND BOOKS

www.ascendbooks.com

"I think we've done a good job in women's basketball of telling Pat Summitt's story. But I don't think we've done a good job telling the stories of some of the other pioneers, including Coach Washington, who was following a parallel path to Coach Summitt's but doing it as an African American head coach. Now is the perfect time to tell these stories about people who certainly should have been celebrated more but for whatever reason have been overlooked. We need to look back and understand the time she spent at Kansas, the success that she had there, the great players she produced and what she means as one of the originals in women's college basketball."

— **Rebecca Lobo,** Naismith Hall-of-Famer,
basketball analyst and Olympic gold medalist

"When I first started coaching at Tennessee, Pat Summitt arranged for me to go to the Black Coaches Association convention in Florida. I walked in, and there sat Marian Washington, Vivian Stringer, John Chaney and Nolan Richardson, the Mount Rushmore of Black coaches all at one table. As a player, I watched Marian Washington and Vivian Stringer and the success they had. They were icons and role models."

— **Carolyn Peck,** broadcaster and the first
African American coach to win a women's
basketball national title (Purdue 1999). Peck was
an assistant to Pat Summitt at Tennessee

"They should give Coach Washington her flowers because there is no Dawn Staley without Coach Washington before her. That's her legend to me."

— **Venus Lacy,** National Player of the Year
in 1990 and Olympic gold medalist

"Marian is something special. Not only as a player and a coach, but also as a person. Being the first to do something, the first Black woman to go into a white school and coach, you go through a lot that people don't know about, and she did that. And as long as she was there — wow — her teams were always tough."

— **Ann Meyers Drysdale,** among the first women to be inducted into the Naismith Hall of Fame

"You feel the power of her presence immediately. That never leaves you and you want more of it somehow. The players who have come through her program revered and admired everything about her. When you're that coach who your players never want to get away from, there's definitely magic there. She's got that Maya Angelou voice. When she speaks, nobody's talking. That's how powerful, how special Coach Washington is."

— **Teresa Edwards,** a 4-time Olympic gold medalist

"Whether the world calls your name, if you've got belief inside, nobody can stop you. That's the inner strength Coach Washington gave her players. She's walked it, lived it and earned a legacy that will never be matched."

— **Lynette Woodard,** Naismith Hall-of-Famer, held Division I women's basketball scoring record for 43 years

"Marian E. Washington has impacted the growth of women's sports in immeasurable ways throughout her lifetime. She was a national champion collegiate athlete, a world-class track and field performer, one of the first two Black women to represent the U.S. in international basketball competition, and the first Black woman hired as head women's basketball coach, athletic director and track coach at a predominantly white institution. She recruited and mentored some of the best women to ever play the game. She endured sexism and racism but triumphed to serve as head coach of the University of Kansas women's basketball program for 31 years and influenced important policies within USA Basketball. A champion for women overall and a role model for women of color, her impact will be felt for generations. It's time that more people know about the historic contributions of Coach Marian E. Washington."

— **Brenda VanLengen,** Emmy Award-winning broadcaster and executive producer of "If Not for Them," a project recognizing the pioneers of women's basketball

"Marian came to our program my senior year at Kansas. We knew she could play the game and coach the game. It was like a breath of fresh air and brought pure class to our program. We were finally getting a coach who understood the game and literally played the game. You wanted to emulate her because you respected her so much. Marian was the perfect fit for Kansas."

— **Cynthia Kelley,** a senior at Kansas in 1973-74, when Marian Washington began her first of 31 seasons as women's basketball coach

"Being an accomplished athlete of her stature carried great weight. Her contribution wasn't just as a basketball coach or as an athletic director. It was the combination of all three. Being a nationally recognized athlete, a woman of color, someone who was really strong, made her a role model, the stuff that history is made of."

— **Donna Lopiano,** former CEO of the Women's Sports Foundation and Past President of the Association for Intercollegiate Athletics for Women

"Marian Washington was not deterred by huge barriers to progress for women and particularly women of color. She was determined to use her considerable skills and talent to change the environment and create opportunities for female athletes at KU and around the country."

— **Kathleen Sebelius,** 44th governor of Kansas and 21st U.S. Secretary of Health and Human Services

"When Coach walked into the room, it was monumental to me. I did not know until after my playing days how instrumental she was for so many of the things I took for granted. I was blessed to have an opportunity to play for her and see her every day."

— **Tamecka Dixon,** All-American, Big Eight Player of the Year, 1996; Big 12 Player of the Year, 1997; and three-time WNBA All-Star

"We had letterhead at Kansas that read, 'We Strive for Excellence.' That's Marian Washington. She strived for excellence."

— **Kathy Meek,** Marian Washington's first assistant basketball coach, 1976-80

"As I think about Coach Washington, terms that are commonly used are trailblazer, pioneer, incredible leader and mentor of many. All are appropriate and very accurate, but as I've gotten to know her even better, a word that keeps coming to my mind that I think really describes her is fighter. I think about the courage that it had to take in her time to fight the necessary battles that were unpopular to fight, and it's that courage that I tremendously respect and admire."

— **Brandon Schneider,** Kansas women's basketball coach

Dedicated to my family with love.

Love is patient, love is kind. It does not envy, it does not boast, it is not proud. It is not rude. It is not self-seeking. It is not easily angered. It keeps no record of wrongs. Love does not delight in evil but rejoices with the truth.

1 Corinthians 13:4-8

— MEW

To Harry and Ben, who remind me of life's infinite possibilities.

— VLF

Foreword

by Kathleen Sebelius

During any period, Marian Washington would be seen as a force of nature: someone who persisted despite enormous obstacles and challenges. Even though it is impossible to do "reverse time travel" to set the stage for her remarkable career, the reader must return to the 1960s to fully appreciate Coach Washington's accomplishments.

Marian Washington played basketball at West Chester State College (now University) before Title IX, the 1972 amendment to the Education Act that created opportunities for talented young women to earn scholarships to play college sports. A remarkably talented player, Washington led her college team to the first-ever National Women's Championship in 1969.

Her basketball skills, first at the college level and then with national teams, attracted the attention of the University of Kansas, and in 1973 KU hired Marian Washington to coach basketball. She was a Black woman coaching at a Division I school in an era when women, and particularly women of color, did not get hired for coaching jobs at top universities. It was a smart hire for KU, launching Washington's three-decades-long career there — her remarkable journey to change women's basketball at Kansas and throughout the country.

When I came to Kansas in early 1975, I got to watch a talented Black woman lead her team — a very rare sight. I loved sports and had played basketball throughout high school and college, which was very unusual in the late '60s. Before Title IX it was only at all-women's schools, like the ones I attended, where girls could play sports throughout high school and college. I didn't have the athletic skills of Marian Washington, but I knew enough to greatly admire her talents.

Although Title IX was the law of the land when Coach Washington arrived in Kansas, few schools followed the letter — or the spirit — of the rules. Many people, mostly males, resented the law and women's sports, falsely subscribing to the notion that "girls" were "taking scholarships away" from male student-athletes. While scholarships might have begrudgingly been made available, there was no "separate but equal" treatment for college women.

At KU, Coach Washington had to fight for staff, for trainers, for adequate facilities and for proper food for her team. She had no decent locker rooms or travel budgets, yet her teams won more than 60 percent of the games she coached.

In addition to her basketball job at KU, Washington served for five years as the first director of women's athletics and started the track and field program for women, for which she served as the first coach. Her induction in 2004 to KU's Athletics Hall of Fame was well-deserved.

Coach Washington's efforts were not confined to campus. Both as a player and coach, Marian Washington was influential nationally and internationally. She played for the U.S. national team and was the first Black woman to coach a U.S. team in international play. She was the first African American to serve on an Olympic women's coaching staff, serving as an assistant coach for the American women's 1996 gold-medal team.

Marian Washington's peer Black coaches recognized her remarkable career by naming her the Black Coaches Association Coach of the Year in 1992 and 1996, by electing her as its first female president and by presenting her a lifetime achievement award.

The awards and honors are significant for any coach in any sport at any time. But for a Black woman who started playing pre-Title IX, when women's college sports were essentially non-existent, her achievements are almost unimaginable. Marian Washington was not deterred by huge barriers to progress for women and particularly women of color. She was determined to use her considerable skills and talent to change the environment and create opportunities for female athletes at KU and around the country.

Women who come to Kansas to play basketball will now enjoy the Marian E. Washington Women's Basketball Suite as part of the beautifully updated locker room facilities. This tribute is for a coach who had to block spaces in the public restrooms during games to huddle with her teams.

Coach Washington coached and mentored one Hall-of-Fame player, Lynette Woodard, and several of her players went from KU to play professionally.

I was so proud to watch Coach Washington blaze a new path and create the momentum for a first-class program for talented KU female student-athletes. In 2020, KU created the Marian Washington Trailblazer Series, which annually recognizes the achievements of prominent African Americans and their impact on Kansas athletics. Each year during Black History Month, current and future student-athletes have the opportunity to learn about the remarkable tenure of Coach Washington, who created opportunities for their success.

I attended a tribute dinner for Coach Washington when the Trailblazer Series was announced. Her former players came from all over the country to honor their remarkable coach, and the love and respect they showed for her role in shaping their lives was powerful. Hopefully, they, and those who follow them to KU, will continue to be inspired by her leadership, her commitment to excellence and her career spent in helping the next generation live up to its potential.

Marian Washington is truly a force of nature.

— **Kathleen Sebelius,** 44th governor of Kansas and 21st U.S. Secretary of Health and Human Services

Chapter I

Suite

To *myself,*

I'm 18 years old, and I'm writing this letter on Nov. 11, 1964. I'm home sitting in the big chair by the window. Now I realize I've written these words so large I don't have much more room, so I hope and pray all troubles will soon be over and I'll get to go to college.

I **wrote that** in cursive on the back of my senior high school picture. I realized immediately after starting on a slant and writing so large, I wasn't going to have room to say everything I needed to say.

There has always been a lot to me and my story, too much to fit onto the back of a 3x5 yearbook photo. Back when I penned those words, the hopes and dreams inside of me weren't focused on anything specific beyond wanting something else, something entirely different from how I was living.

My family wasn't just poor. Living in rural West Chester, Pennsylvania, my mother; my father; me the eldest followed by my brother, Butchie; and my sisters Isabel, Janet and Cathy were dirt poor. My sister Josephine should have been after me but she died as a baby.

We lived in a bus, and it was not an RV you think of today. At one time, I'm sure, paying customers rode on it. But it was our home, one without a bathroom or a refrigerator. We four girls shared one sagging mattress.

It was hard to sleep much. I didn't. Nonetheless, I dreamed. Always big. That's something that didn't change no matter how old I got. I was just a little girl when Mom would leave me in the back seat of the car while she rushed inside for a few groceries. I'd roll down the window and start singing whatever song came into my head whenever anyone walked past. I really thought I could sing. My voice was pretty good, though it sounded even better at home in front of the box fan, which gave it a quiver.

Ol' Man River

I knew all the words to that one. In old movies, you'd see Black people sing that song, and I imitated them in my best deep voice.

That ol' man river
he don't say nothin'
But he must say somethin'
(Then the vibrato ...)
Cause he just keeps roooollllin'
He keeps roooollllin' along ...

Maybe someone will discover me! Was I thinking Hollywood? Not really. I just wanted someone to hear how talented I thought I was. Maybe I could get rich. I fantasized again and again what I would do if I made a bunch of money. Mom would be first. I'd get her whatever she wanted. I could buy a big house so we'd have a nice place to live.

Sometimes I imagined being a nurse. If I were a nurse, I could help heal people. Or maybe I could be an artist. I liked to draw, especially with charcoal pencils. I used to find these advertisements in beat-up magazines that had you draw a face or an animal just like the one on the page. You were supposed to mail it in so they could judge if you had talent. If they selected you, they gave you money. I would try to draw a face exactly as I saw it, but I never had the chance to mail any of them in. Back in the 1950s, Disney characters were a big deal. I read in a book from the school library how to make the circles to draw Mickey Mouse's face and ears. I would get so frustrated if I couldn't get them precise.

Whatever I did I wanted it to be near perfect. I liked to be the best at everything, and nothing quite matched the feeling I got from competing. Most of the time it was me versus my brother: who could mow grass faster or who could drive to the stop sign at the end of Bolmar Street before the other. If I didn't win, I had to listen to my brother teasing me, but I knew the next time I would hit the gas pedal quicker when I heard "go!"

I fell in love with sports watching the Olympics on our tiny black-and-white television. It was like Christmas when they were on. I preferred the summer Olympics and couldn't take my eyes off Wilma Rudolph, the Black gazelle. In front of the TV, I tried helping the discus throwers heave their tosses and I moved with the long jumpers, picturing myself powering that last step to a winning leap. I hated when the Olympics ended because I knew it would be four long years until they came around again.

As I grew older and noticeably stronger than girls around me, I thought maybe I could be an Olympian someday. Any time I competed, I no longer felt like the shy, quiet, little Black girl who lived on Bolmar Street. I was just me, a winner. My first little trophy sits proudly on my bookshelf with some of the plastic gold cover peeling off.

I gained confidence from something inside of me, a *fierce* determination not to let my past hold me back. I didn't want to be judged by my circumstances. When people said hurtful things, I didn't want them to know how sad they made me feel.

I didn't want to be judged because I got pregnant at 13.

I didn't want to be judged by the color of my skin. I remember hearing Martin Luther King's speech about his dream for his four children one day living in a nation where they were not judged by the color of their skin but by the content of their character. That was the kind of world I wanted to live in. A world where we all cared and took care of each other.

People made a lot of assumptions about you if you grew up Black in the 1950s. They also made a lot of assumptions when you were poor. I knew I wanted something different, something more, but I couldn't figure out exactly what it was or how to get it.

I would ask God to show me the way. Mom always said to trust in God, and I did. When the pieces came together, they didn't make sense at first. I mean, Kansas? My feet have always been too big to fit into a pair of ruby slippers, but somehow I landed in Lawrence, Kansas, 1,148 miles from where I was born, and it became home for 40 years.

I don't like cold weather or snow, so St. Augustine, Florida, is where I now live most of the year. But a piece of my heart and a part of me will always be in Kansas. I make the 19-hour drive there every summer and stay in the same comfortable house that I bought in 1984. I love the people of Lawrence. Whether I'm walking my sassy Chihuahua, Bella, or stopping in Dillons or HyVee for a quick grocery run, I don't get very far before someone stops to say an extended hello. I don't always know them, but they know me. They might start talking basketball or expect a hug. I love giving hugs, and I'm told I give some of the best. Let's just say I didn't get the same reception in 1973 when a tall Black woman with a big afro drew some stares.

I gave my youth to the University of Kansas. I absorbed so much in my 32 years there, from dislike and negativity to sexual harassment and racism. I can still feel the darts thrown at me, some because of my color, others because I was doing the job someone else wanted to do, some who likely thought enough pushback would send me packing.

I used to wonder why God didn't move me somewhere else. I sure asked him about it enough times. Now I know I was exactly where I needed to be.

I was probably in Allen Fieldhouse almost every day for a little more than three decades. When I walked away in 2004, I knew I wasn't going to coach again. I thought I might be back as part of KU administration in some way. But that didn't happen.

It ended up being nearly 15 years before I would see the inside of the Fieldhouse again.

I was in my 70s and when I returned, it was for another fight, this one about correcting history.

That took some doing, but a new administration at KU was receptive. Then I received another invitation in October 2021. I experienced something I had never felt in all my time there.

Appreciation.

To my surprise, the Marian E. Washington Women's Basketball Suite was unveiled in front of my eyes. The first time I saw those capital letters spelling out my name, it was surreal. I found myself just amazed. It was so hard to believe this was done for me.

Travis Goff, KU's athletic director, and Brandon Schneider, the women's basketball coach, spoke from a podium right there in front of the newly named suite.

Brandon referred to me as a trailblazer, pioneer, leader and mentor, but the term he said that best described me was fighter. He said I had the courage that it took to fight the necessary battles that were unpopular at the time.

Being honest, I don't like the word fight and I don't like the idea of fighting. But this fight was about standing your ground and pushing back when you have to. It was about giving female athletes what they deserved.

In my heart, my parents have been with me every step of the way. Their work ethic was clearly a part of my DNA. I speak to them softly all the time. "Hi Mom. I know you and Dad are looking down. I hope I made you proud."

I have to believe I did a few things right in a life journey that took me to places I never imagined. So many experiences. So many relationships.

Standing here in Allen Fieldhouse beside a suite with my name on it, the memories flood back. I can see that high school senior writing out a message to herself hoping her troubles were over. If she only knew what was in store for her.

How did all this happen? Well, Darling, sit back.

I've got a lot to tell you.

Chapter II

Bib Overalls and Hats

I credit my father for being a girl dad ahead of his time. His confidence in me instilled a belief that women could succeed in this world at whatever they put their mind to.

In the morning, I would wake up to see Dad, who was always up early, walking toward the house, coming in from the fields. Dad dressed the same every day — extra-large bib overalls covered his slender frame from his chest to the tops of his shoes. Even on a hot day, he wore long-sleeve cotton shirts, leaving only his hands and face exposed to the sun. When his chest wasn't covered, you saw his honey-colored brown skin, golden almost, a contrast to his darker hands and face from the hot sun.

Dad always seemed to be in a hurry, his overalls moving around his body as he walked, with his hat pulled low over his face. For a long time, I wore a jacket in the summer to keep the hot sun off my skin just as my father did. It just seemed cooler that way.

Everybody knew Goldie Washington in West Chester. Even the mayor. Goldie, officially Joseph Goldie Washington, was never called Joseph or even Joe. Everyone called him Goldie, but to me he was Dad or Pop and sometimes Daddy. I don't remember him ever calling me Marian, let alone Marian Elizabeth.

I was Sister, the eldest. Butchie, my only brother, was three years younger, with beautiful almond-shaped eyes and an avid curiosity. Janet, so pretty in her braids, had a mind of her own. Isabel was a sweet, round-faced, chubby little girl who would go along with most anything we would say. The baby, Cathy, seven years younger than me, reminded me of singer Melissa Manchester. I always felt so protective of Cathy.

Ya, Sister! At the sound of Dad's voice, I knew he wanted me to stop what I was doing right that minute and come start or finish some task for him. When Dad asked me or any of my siblings to do something, he wanted it done right then, no dawdling. I was raised to say "Yes, sir," "No, sir," "Yes, ma'am" and "No, ma'am." "Please" and "thank you" were very big, too.

Ya, Sister! He called again, and I prayed to myself, "Please don't ask me to go get eggs from the chicken coop." Boy, I hated sticking my hands up under the chickens or on top of their nests. My mind would get the best of me, and I imagined all kinds of crawling things in those nests that I'd rather not touch. I never liked feathers and for some reason, I was especially afraid of fur. But if that's what Dad needed, I'd have to go and do it. I was never in a hurry to get to those eggs. In fact, I'd walk as slowly as I could, meandering to the hens. I would gather the eggs, carefully place them in my bucket and walk down the yard to give them to Mom. These were brown eggs, and boy, when she cooked them, fried or scrambled, they were really good.

Dad was a workaholic before that word was even invented. He just seemed to need to be doing something all the time. He kept our whole family pretty busy, too. He only ever worked for one person and that was himself. Pretty remarkable for an African American man born in 1890.

Pop found a way to live his entire life without ever being owned. He'd rattle off our names like a roll call in search of an extra hand.

Ya, Sister!

Ya, Izzeeeeee!

Ya, Jaaaanet!

Ya, Catheeee!

Ya Butchieeeee!

Someway, somehow, Dad would finally call the name of the one of us he wanted.

I doubt Dad spent much time in a classroom beyond a few years in grade school. He probably grew up helping his mother and father work in the fields so the family could survive. I never really saw Dad sit down and read a newspaper, and he could barely scribble his name. But that man sure could count! Dad knew how to make money, how to stretch money and how to save money. As far as he was concerned, he didn't need a bank. He'd hide his money in a lock box or would put loose bills in a tin can and bury it on some part of the property where we lived – 311 Bolmar Street.

I never met Mary Turner and William Washington, Dad's parents. I always wondered what they looked like. Did my father look like either of them? Were they nice? I wondered if my grandparents had been enslaved. Dad was born in Charles County, Maryland, today an affluent Black suburb that touts its heritage as the most powerful underground railroad destination in the country. Charles County is a little more than an hour away from Washington, D.C., and roughly 76 miles from Baltimore.

I so wish I had a chance to ask Dad about his parents and grandparents, and what his childhood was like. I thank God he wasn't alive to live in shackles, but it's possible his parents and grandparents endured some of the worst of that horrific chapter of our nation's history.

Dad wasn't one to spark conversation about the past, any kind of politics or even the Civil Rights movement. Truth be told, Dad really was an oddity in his family. He's the only one who strayed far from home, with a curiosity and determination guiding him. Those were traits, I'd say in retrospect, that he passed to me. When I was a little girl, if you had told me I'd build a life in Kansas, I'm not sure when I would have stopped laughing. Where was Kansas? That might as well have been the moon if you grew up in a mostly Black neighborhood in rural Pennsylvania in the 1950s.

Before Dad moved to West Chester, he lived in Culpeper, Virginia, about 70 miles southwest of Washington. I only know that because when Pop was in his 60s, he needed a record of his birth. I was happy to drive to Culpeper with Dad and my stepsister Sister Bernice to go to the Catholic church where Dad was baptized. Sister Bernice had contacted the priest there in advance because Dad thought they had a record showing when he was born. I was skeptical about finding information because I didn't know how records were kept in the church. But it turned out that after walking into the small Catholic church it only took a few minutes of thumbing through the ledger before we found Dad's name.

Joseph Goldie Washington, born April 25, 1890.

It was so exciting to see those words officially written out. Dad was relieved, knowing he had the documentation to get the government help he needed. And I was surprised, too. I thought all these years his first name was Goldie, not Joseph.

I don't know how or when Dad got to West Chester, the county seat of Chester County, about 35 miles west of Philadelphia. West Chester today ranks among the *100 Best Places to Live in America*, according to the real estate website Livability. Decades ago it wasn't such the lively destination it is today with million-dollar homes and condos. The West Chester I remember was quaint with narrow streets, shops, restaurants, clothing stores large and small, a pharmacy and a post office. Many of the small businesses were owned by Black residents and frequented by white people.

West Chester had benches that faced each other on both sides of the street. When I walked uptown, I always saw lots of older Black men and women sitting around and talking. The men would rest and smoke cigars, their canes beside them. If they didn't know who I was, they'd start questioning me to find out about my father and mother. As soon as one of them would piece it together, I'd hear, "That's Goldie's daughter!"

Like I said, it seemed like everyone knew Dad.

Dad had a way with people. He had a business in West Chester, though it never had a name, let alone an address or business card. People who hired him trusted him to do exactly what he said he would do, and that could be almost anything. Mowing lawns. Moving people in and out of their houses. Cleaning schools before the start of the year. Bundling newspapers to sell. Cutting up cars and taking old parts, metal and copper to the salvage yard to have it weighed and get paid for it.

Pop started his own waste-removal route, two of them, in fact, before it was fashionable. He'd pick up trash and garbage from residential houses and restaurants. Garbage was the wet stuff. Trash was paper products. Nobody used garbage disposals in the 1950s, so the cans designated for garbage overflowed with leftover food, vegetable peelings and spoiled meat. Dad often used some of the garbage to feed the three or four pigs we had.

I thought Dad was handsome. He had a faint mustache, big hands and long fingers. He wore gloves when he was cutting up cars or working with wood. His scuffed-up knuckles still reflected the physical toll of his labor. I liked to watch Dad shave. He would use a basin of water, soap and a razor or straight blade. There was a funny puppet show on TV called "Kukla, Fran and Ollie." Ollie only had hair around the bottom part of his head from sideburn to sideburn. That's how Dad's hair grew. He was bald on top with hair that went all around the bottom of his head. He wore a floppy Fedora everywhere he went that reminded me of a cowboy hat.

Dad knew how things worked — he was a mechanical engineer minus the degree — and he could make almost anything. There was no way he could have afforded a professional power saw, so he built his own, using a car, a rear axle and a wide conveyor belt. He used the saw to cut wood into whatever size he needed to heat our potbelly stove or for whatever project was next. Believe me, there was always a next.

Dad owned land, enough to build at least three of the houses on our street. I can't tell you how rare that was for a Black man where we lived. Most people rented. Owed money. Paid a man once a month. Once I got older and began making my own money, I instinctively knew that owning land was important. I had a real estate agent and his wife, good friends, who kept an eye out for property for me to buy. I bought my first house, a rancher, with a fireplace and no basement, in Lawrence in 1979 for $42,000.

I grew up knowing we weren't Dad's first family. He was 51 years old when he married my mother on July 7, 1941. Dad and his first wife had eight children together before she died. My older siblings weren't a part of my day-to-day life except for Dad's son Lester, who lived two doors down from us. By the time I was born, my stepsisters and stepbrothers were grown with their own families. They lived in Washington, D.C., and Philadelphia. Now and then they would visit. When they did, I was so shy I would hide until I heard them call my name. I would come out from wherever I was hiding so they could hug me and tell me how big I was getting.

At least a couple of times a year we'd drive down to see Dad's family in D.C. Those trips down sleepy Route 1 to the southeastern part of the city were special. We stopped once along the way — Dad determined where before we set out — to pick up beer or liquor. Dad always knew where he could get it the cheapest, and then we'd continue on. I remember seeing the Capitol building on our way to a section of the city where everybody was Black.

We'd usually go to Sister Bernice's rowhouse first. When you entered her home, you saw stairs that went to the second floor, where the bedrooms and a bathroom were. Downstairs, on the left, was a small, dark sitting room with furniture covered in plastic. I never found anything in her house comfortable to sit on.

Farther down the hall was Sister Bernice's kitchen and then the backyard where we'd barbecue and cook crabs.

We'd go on to see Dad's brother, Uncle Willie, and his sister Catherine. We called her Sister Catherine even though she was actually my aunt. Sister Catherine was a petite, proper woman who was pretty old-fashioned. She wore long dresses and would never think of using foul language. She did not let a man cross her threshold on certain days of the week. Uncle Willie and Sister Catherine were staunch Catholics. The entire family on Dad's side were strict Catholics. I even had a stepsister, Sister Vinetta, who was a nun. Dad never practiced Catholicism. I never even saw Dad set foot in a church except for that day in Culpeper — none of us attended church regularly because we worked on Sundays.

Still, Sister Catherine and Uncle Willie got such a kick out of Dad. When he would walk into their homes, he brought his energy and something else. His orneriness. Dad was *so* ornery.

He liked to tease them about their strict ways. They thought him to be wild. But everything they said was in fun, never mean-spirited.

Dad even joked with the neighbors.

I am not your daddy! he'd say, waving off this one neighbor, who admittedly resembled Dad. I don't know how he and so many others found out so quickly that Dad was in town, but word had a way of spreading back then. We would often visit with friends of Sister Bernice's and some cousins. Everybody enjoyed themselves, laughing, telling jokes and sharing stories of past times.

Even though Dad would drink some beer and sherry wine while we were there, I never saw him drunk. He liked those Pabst Blue Ribbon 7-ounce ponies. While the grownups sat around catching up on life, Butchie, Janet, Izzy, Cathy and I played with the cousins. Hide and Seek was big with us along with tag, cards and Truth or Consequences. Spin the Bottle was fun. Sometimes we walked to the store that was a half block up from Sister Bernice's house. It was cool to be in a place where we were close enough to actually walk to a neighborhood store. I liked to get Sugar Daddys, that sticky caramel candy, and peppermint Doublemint chewing gum. Or Tastykakes, ice cream and bubblegum. Sometimes, we sat on the steps of Sister Bernice's house blowing bubbles with those little plastic wands.

Sister Bernice's laugh was hearty like Dad's, only hers had a higher pitch. She wasn't nearly as proper as Sister Catherine. I was fascinated by her gold tooth in front. It seemed like a lot of Black people had one gold tooth back then.

We also visited Sister Kitty, Bernice's younger sister. Her husband was a professional chef, so we ate well. He made the best fried chicken. Sister Kitty was very sweet and easy to be around. Her home wasn't as formal as Sister Bernice's. We could play easily there, and it was even OK to jump up and down on her couch. She had lots of kids, my cousins, who were close to my age. We'd sit around her big dining room table and play card games like Old Maid. We really had a good time together.

All of Dad's older children had a certain spirit about them, an energy and a zest for life. They were all good people. Most of Dad's older sons served in the military. All of them had families and good jobs. However, they were different from Dad. Their lives seemed more relaxed than ours. They certainly did not work around the clock like he did.

I remember seeing Uncle Willie once in a three-piece suit. I never saw my father wear a three-piece suit. At home, Dad rarely took off his long johns or one of his bib overalls. He usually wore work boots, but when we traveled, he dressed in a nice shirt, trousers and good shoes.

As I got older, Dad let me drive him to Washington. I loved driving – still do! – and I like to drive fast, so I looked forward to those trips, just the two of us, windows rolled down the whole time. I never got any speeding tickets on those trips. Let's just say I was lucky. We weren't in the car long before Dad dozed off. My goal was to get him to where we were going before he woke up. I even turned the radio off because I didn't want anything to disturb him before we got there. When we were close to the city, finding my way to Sister Bernice's was somewhat of a challenge, but I knew my landmarks — the Capitol, Constitution Avenue — because we sure didn't have GPS. I didn't want to ask Dad where to go because that would mean waking him up.

Once I found Sister Bernice's house, I looked for a parking spot on the street. I had to parallel park, making sure not to be too far away from the curb. Once I turned the car off, I shook Dad, gently calling his name.

"We're here!" I'd say. Dad shook his head with that big smile of his. When he started laughing, I knew he was pleased. That meant the world to me.

Anytime we were able to take a trip, it was a break from work for all of us because once we were older, a lot was expected of us. I never saw anyone work as hard as my father unless it was my mother. Dad didn't rest much, so we never bothered him when he did. He easily fell sound asleep in our straight-back wooden chairs, his arms falling limp. He didn't snore, but we knew he was in a deep sleep. Of course, the moment he woke, he'd go right back to work.

It was important to my father to do every job the right way and cut no corners. That meant *we* cut no corners. I could never pack newspapers like Dad – so perfectly tied in a bundle so tight you'd have thought he was wrapping a gift. If I was too sloppy, he made me start over again. These bundles had to be loaded on a truck, packed just so, to get as many of them as possible to the paper mill. After a while, I got tired of starting over so I made sure to do things right the first time.

Dad let Mom do most of the cooking, and often he didn't eat dinner with us. He was usually still out in the fields doing something. We all loved seafood. Sometimes he'd bring home a bushel of crabs and make them his own special way. Friends of his would show up when he was cooking them. Pop took an empty barrel and put a metal screen on top of it. He burned wood at the bottom of the barrel and put the large pot of crabs on top of it. You could smell those crabs cooking everywhere. He'd season them just right with vinegar, salt and pepper. I don't know what else he used, but by the time they turned that red color, you didn't have to worry about anything other than eating.

Dad's sweet tooth was for peanut brittle, and sometimes when I went to the market with him he bought a hard roll of bread and a hunk of cheese. We headed to the car and before driving away, he sliced a piece of cheese and handed me some bread. The crust was hard, but the inside was nice and soft. That combination was just wonderful.

Sometimes on a Saturday morning, Dad took all of us to Kennett Square, another borough in Chester County, for an auction and a flea market. The auctioneer talked so fast I never knew what he was saying, but Dad was able to keep up and raise his hand whenever he saw something to bid on. In the meantime, we kids ran to the different stands that sold arts and crafts and toys that didn't cost as much as they did in the stores. I made friends with this young Black girl whose parents were vendors. She was really sweet and always talked about Johnny Mathis, the romantic crooner with the velvet voice. She acted as if Johnny Mathis was the best singer of all time. She wanted to marry him!

Every time I went to the market and saw her, she brought him up.

Butchie and my sisters usually went looking for popcorn or ice cream. Chocolate, vanilla and strawberry — cookies and cream didn't exist then. Meanwhile, I hunted for comic books, ones I could buy for 5 or 10 cents. I saved every one of those books in a trunk I claimed at home. I don't know that kids today have any idea how popular the comics were in the 1950s. That's when the archetype of the superhero became popular. My favorites were Mighty Mouse, who was always trying to save the day, Casper the Friendly Ghost and Little Richie Rich, who took care of his friends with the money he had. Little Dot was buddies with Richie Rich, and I really liked her. She was a heavy-set young girl who was stronger than everyone.

Just like Little Dot, I felt strong. Dad never made me feel like I couldn't do anything because I was female. You're talking about a man born in 1890 who had no restrictions in his mind about what women could and could not do. You'd have to think that was a good thing, even if I didn't always feel that way, lifting heavy cans over my head into his dump truck on a 90-degree day with flies buzzing about and the nasty smell of garbage in the air. Pop was a man ahead of his time. My father came from, shall we say, the old school. There was no way Sister Catherine would have approved of the way he worked us or my running all over the place playing sports later on. But Dad, in his way, had an understanding, an appreciation for what women could accomplish.

Pop went to only one of my athletic events. He was in the stands in D.C. when my college team was trying to make the national AAU tournament but lost in the qualifying round. I was so upset that I left without immediately going over to him. I waited until I calmed down. Then I went back into the gym and found him sitting, waiting on me to return. I could tell he enjoyed watching our team — watching me. He looked up at me and just shook his head.

"You're something, Girl!"

Every time I won a medal of any kind, I showed it to my father, and he would just smile.

As Goldie Washington's daughter, I knew I could achieve. I knew I was capable. I didn't need to hear it from my father. He instilled it in me by what he trusted me to do. The more I think about it today, the more I applaud how ingenious my father was in how he lived his life, what he was willing to do, the extent to which he would work, his effort and relentless determination to survive. He taught us how to work. He taught me not to stop until a job was done.

While Dad usually wore only that one hat, the truth is he wore many hats, something that helped us adjust to all the different challenges we faced as adults. We went from his trash route to mowing somebody's lawn to helping him move furniture out of a house to the next task. I didn't realize it then, but watching my father's work ethic shaped my own.

"Way to work," I often said to my Lady Jayhawks after a basketball practice where their effort chasing a loose ball or pulling down a contested rebound reflected their determination. Dad taught me the only way to work was to give 100 percent effort 100 percent of the time.

I credit my father for being a girl dad ahead of his time. His confidence in me instilled a belief that women could succeed in this world at whatever they put their minds to.

Pop worked until he couldn't anymore. He began to sell pieces of his land but didn't get nearly enough for it. When it was all sold, he ended up in a tiny ground-floor apartment. By then, Dad was starting to get sick. He didn't have his routes anymore. He wasn't out in a yard cutting up cars. He couldn't do any of that hard labor anymore. You could see he was aging. I didn't know how sick he was getting.

When I heard Dad had been diagnosed with prostate cancer,

I didn't know what that was. Treatments in 1971 weren't very advanced for that type of cancer.

By then, I only saw Dad a few times a year because my life was full, teaching junior high school in Kansas City, as a member of Team USA for basketball and playing on an AAU team in Raytown, Missouri. I made a special trip home in spring 1971 to visit Dad right before leaving with Team USA for the World Championships in São Paulo, Brazil.

I was not prepared. Dad was in the hospital, his back to me, sitting in a wheelchair. A nurse told me that was my father. You don't forget that moment. Seeing your larger-than-life father suddenly looking so small, so fragile, so frail, and needing a stranger to confirm to you that the shadow of the man you grew up with is indeed your dad. He was slumped forward, his head turned to the side, resting on his shoulder. My heart was in my throat before I ever saw his face. The loose hospital gown revealed just how much weight Dad had lost. His skin, which I used to think felt like silk, no longer looked healthy.

I walked over and looked into his eyes. He tried to talk to me, but he was in too much pain and full of drugs. I told him where I was going, and I'd like to think he heard me.

It was hard not to cry and harder to talk. Usually, Dad did most of the talking when we were together. He barely spoke. You could tell he was suffering. I told him I loved him. I wanted him to know I was going to Brazil to play basketball.

"I'll be back, Dad."

His eyes met mine. I know he heard me. But he said nothing. I hated leaving. I walked to the door and turned around for another look, saying a prayer as I made my way to the elevator.

Dad was able to leave the hospital. He went to one of my sisters' houses where Mom and my sisters took care of him. I had planned to see him as soon as I returned from Brazil, but I never saw my father again.

Pop died May 28, 1971.

My coach in Brazil broke the news to me after she got a call from my family. She immediately took me and my teammates to the Christ the Redeemer statue in Rio de Janeiro. If you've never seen the statue up close, you can't imagine its impact. We were in a van driving up the mountainside to get to it. I remember looking to the left and suddenly seeing this outstretched arm and hand reaching through the tall trees. I caught my breath. It was surreal to see part of this statue, an arm and hand before me. I wasn't prepared. I knew I was about to see something magnificent when we reached the top of the mountain. We parked, and I walked toward the statue. It was overwhelming.

The statue of Christ is so enormous, so tall. Clouds blurred the features on his face. When they passed, his face became clear with an exactness. In my heart and soul, I felt the spirit of Christ, and I knew my father was with him. As I stood crying, I called to God, "Please wrap your arms around my father. Hold him tight and take his pain away." Then I said, "Oh Dad. I love you so much."

I flew home for Dad's funeral. I couldn't look at him in the casket. I just stared at nothing and sat in total disbelief thinking Dad was gone. When we were called up to see him one final time, I didn't want to look at Dad. I didn't want to remember him so lifeless. But I reached down, touched his chest and placed one of my track and field gold medals in his breast pocket.

I feel fortunate to have had a father who believed in me. Dad not only allowed me to dream, he encouraged it. Later, when I was coaching at Kansas, I learned just how important it is to have fathers supporting their daughters in athletics.

Growing up, it was important to me to make Pop proud. I believe I did.

Chapter III

Earth's Angel

I saw Mom stand up for what was right. I saw her embrace and love all kinds of people. I'd like to think that's who I am.

"**Love you,** Mom."

"Love you, too, Dear."

"Love you."

"Love you, Darling."

"I love you."

"I love you."

Mom and I spent as much time hanging up from a call as we did talking on the phone.

The truth is I never wanted to say goodbye to my mother. I loved her dearly.

Marian Jane Lomax was the daughter of Walter and Bessie Lomax, born in Marshallton, Pennsylvania, in 1918, two years before women earned the right to vote. Walter, my grandfather, was a church deacon. I never had the opportunity to meet him. He died before I was born.

I have wonderful memories of my grandmother, Bessie, who had an identical twin we called Aunt Emma. Grandmum gave me my first and only birthday party during my childhood years. Grandmum made sure I had balloons, hats and a birthday cake with candles to blow out. Not a lot of kids came, but to be honest, there weren't a lot of kids in the neighborhood. I had my brother and sisters and my little "boyfriend" Washy, who lived next door with Mother Lawrence — I never knew his real relationship with that family. Washy was about my age, and I often sat and talked to him through the fence.

If we ever went to an amusement park, it was Coney Island in Brooklyn, New York. Grandmum took me, even though I wasn't a fan of roller coasters or any ride that swung you up high. She enjoyed all the rides. There was a parachute ride, the newest feature at Coney Island, that cranked you way up and then dropped you quickly. There was no way I would get on a ride like that. I was afraid of heights. "It will be fine. Come and sit next to me," Grandmum said.

I shook my head and said, "Please, no. I don't want to." I could feel my heart pounding in my chest. I stood watching Grandmum waving as she was pulled to the top and suddenly she parachuted down. Wow! I didn't know how she could do it, but she did. I was more excited about riding on those fake rocking horses. Grandmum made sure she had lots of nickels to put in the meter so I could ride again and again.

Grandmum gave my brother and me experiences we never had before. I remember once taking a ride on a ship that seemed really big to us. We were sitting on the upper deck outside on chairs and Butchie was pointing at another boat and got so excited that he kicked his shoe off into the water. Grandmum had to carry him off the boat and all the way to her car.

Grandmum worked as a housekeeper for families. Mom went to see her sometimes and brought us along, but we didn't go in. Grandmum met us at the back door, holding the screen door open. She would smile and say hello to us while talking to Mom. Grandmum often handed Mom five miniature envelopes, our names written on each. There were pennies inside, and Mom gave them to us right there. We were so excited and thanked her. Grandmum looked at us and said, "Now don't forget to put your money in the bank."

Back in those days, in grade school they encouraged you to save in a bank and start a ledger to keep up with your account. I remember the first time Mom took me to First National Bank in uptown West Chester to start my savings account. I never forgot that feeling of being in a bank and what was possible there. I didn't get very far saving my pennies until later in life.

I remember we lost Grandmum when I was 8. Mom was 36 when Grandmum died of a heart attack. I remember hearing Mom cry so hard, and Dad putting his arms around her to comfort her. I know Dad loved Grandmum, too. When it was time for her funeral, I didn't want to see her in the casket, so I asked not to go. Mom seemed to understand, so she let me stay home.

It was hard to see Grandmum's Elks Lodge uniform that Mom left hanging on a hook in her bedroom for a long time. Grandmum wore that uniform marching with the West Chester unit of the Elks in the parades that were so fun back then. I'd be mesmerized watching Grandmum snap her head to the right and then to the left, her arms moving in unison with the rest of the Elks. They looked so sharp! Parades were really big when I was growing up. Marching bands came from Philadelphia, Chester and New Jersey. You'd see drill teams and girls twirling batons. Crowds of people would cheer and wave. It was exciting to stand and watch. The parades moved through the town and down Market Street, where Pop set up a food stand selling hotdogs and sodas, another opportunity to make money. I remember helping mom fix sandwiches, grabbing drinks for customers and collecting dollar bills and coins that went into a metal box.

After Grandmum died, a lot of times when we would ride in the car, I could almost see her in the tree branches that seemed to outline the shape of her head and her face. It was my imagination, of course, but it was something I felt. Maybe it was her spirit that stayed with me for a while.

Grandmum was calm and soft-spoken. My mother was the *complete* opposite. Mom was fiery, feisty and didn't allow anybody to push her around. Mom wasn't afraid to stand up for herself or fight for the underdog. If you disrespected her, she'd call you out in a heartbeat. If you were wrong, she'd let you know.

She was a beautiful woman, with almond-shaped eyes and thick hair that felt even silkier as she aged when it became a wonderful salt and pepper color. Mom certainly wasn't fat, but she wasn't skinny, either. She and I talked only once about her being an athlete growing up. She told me she was a good jumper; maybe that's where my leaping ability came from. She kept herself tidy and rarely wore makeup when I was young. Her complexion was void of any pimples. Mom blessed all of her children with beautiful skin. She was a modest dresser who wore low heels the times she and Dad did go out.

I remember one of my sisters telling me a story about our mother. Apparently, Mom bought a brand new blouse to wear to a nightclub. She was just sitting, socializing, when she started getting grief from another woman who would not leave her alone for some reason. Maybe the woman had too much to drink. Mom got tired of it, and she took off that new blouse and set it aside so as not to get it torn. Mom went outside with the woman where she made sure she wouldn't be bothered again. I'm not kidding!

Like Dad, Mom took pride in getting the small things right when she worked. She overlooked nothing when finishing a job. My mother could iron like no one else. She would fill a basin with water and stick her hands in it. As she pulled her hands out, she flicked her wet fingers over the clothes, making them damp, not wet. Mom rolled up whatever she was ironing into a tight ball. When it was time, she pressed the clothes, and they would stiffen. If Mom had freshly ironed a shirt, it looked as if it had been starched. A professional dry cleaner would be envious.

Mom would be so tired at night. All I wanted to do was help her. One way I knew I could make a difference was by trying to keep everything in the house neat. I was a stickler for having everything clean, but my brother and sisters were always playing. By the time Mom got home from working all day, it looked like I hadn't done a thing.

Mom was a spiritual person. Maybe that came from my grandfather being so active in the church. She almost always wore a cross around her neck and loved to sing spirituals. I remember hearing her sing "Just A Closer Walk With Thee" while she hung clothes on the line or stirred dinner on the stove.

I am weak but Thou art strong;
Jesus, keep me from all wrong;
I'll be satisfied as long
As I walk, let me walk close to Thee.

My youngest sister, Cathy, recalls Mom singing to her when she was little.

And He walks with me, and he talks with me,
And He tells me I am his own;
And the joy we share as we tarry there,
None other has ever known.

Mom told us all the time that she loved us, and "God loves you, too." We didn't go to church, but we grew up knowing God existed and understanding God was in our lives and loved us. We said our prayers at night starting with "Now I lay me down to sleep. I pray the Lord my soul to keep."

Mom would kiss us on the lips and hug us tightly. Dad was the disciplinarian. Mom was not about spanking her kids, and she'd often rescue us from Dad. If he pulled a switch off a tree, she would go bonkers. She didn't want Dad hitting us. If I hadn't gotten the eggs from the chickens as quickly as Dad wanted or forgot to bring the wood in, he would get so angry. He wouldn't hit me, but I always thought his tone was worse than any spanking. Mom wouldn't be happy about his harsh words, but it was better than a spanking.

Once before Christmas I saved up enough to get Mom an artificial plant from the flea market in Kennett Square. I thought that thing with its big wide green leaves was beautiful, and I was so happy that I was able to buy it and keep it hidden from Mom until Christmas. When she saw it, you'd have thought I'd given her diamonds and pearls.

Oh, Honey, I love this! she beamed.

Mom sure could fuss at Dad. If he had been outside with the pigs, Mom made him take off his overalls before coming in. *"You're bringing the outside in,"* she'd snap.

But most of the time, Dad would come in after a long day in the heat and make a beeline to whatever Mom was cooking for dinner. Maybe it was liver and onions or a pot of soup. Dad just could not help himself. He liked to add some seasonings to whatever was on the stove and that set her off.

"Go clean up!" she ordered when he would dip a spoon in for a taste. *"Get away from that food. Goldie! Wash your hands!"*

They would use foul language sometimes, but it didn't mean anything — until it did.

I don't think Mom knew how hard life would be when she married Dad. Mom told me later all she wanted was to be an old man's darling. Those thoughts were soon forgotten. Work was all my mother knew, doing everything Dad did plus laundering other people's clothes. I don't imagine this was the life she anticipated when, at 23, Mom married a man 28 years her senior. Sometimes it became too much for her. When things got really tough, she left home for a few days at a time without telling anyone where she was going. When she came back, she'd tap on the back window to wake me up and have me open the door so she could get in.

Dad would be so angry she left, and they'd go at it. Sometimes more than words were thrown around.

Mom was really strong, so when she got angry, sparks flew. Once she grabbed a small cupboard full of dishes and threw it on top of Dad. Mom could also be jealous. I remember seeing her up the yard near our barn. I stood in the doorway with Grandmum, and we heard Mom yelling and fussing. She had Dad on his back and was sitting on top of him. Grandmum held me and tried to quiet my fears. She knew her daughter. She waited until Mom calmed down. Later, I found out Mom thought Dad was flirting with our neighbor, and no, it wasn't Mother Lawrence!

Another time when Mom was riled up, my siblings and I locked Dad in the shed right outside our front door to protect him. Mom picked up cinder blocks and threw them at the door. I only ever saw Dad hit Mom once, when he slapped her across the face after one of the times she left us for a few days.

I was a nervous wreck every time they fought. It seemed I was always in the middle of the commotion trying to make sure no one got hurt. And when I say in the middle, I mean that literally. I'd be standing in between my parents, one hand on Mom's chest and the other hand on Dad's. I could feel their hearts racing as an argument between them became an all-out war.

Mom left Dad when I was 12. She took Izzy, Janet, Cathy and me to live with her while Butchie stayed with Dad. Mom needed her own space, even though that came with its own set of challenges.

The five of us moved to an open one-room house just a few minutes up the street from Dad. Everything was more of a struggle then. Trying to keep a roof over our heads. Making rent. We'd go without lights for long stretches. Any utility could go off at any time. During the winter, when our heat was shut off, it was so cold in our house you could see your breath. We piled clothes on top of us to keep warm on those nights. Mom worried all the time about everything and so did I.

When we went without electricity, we cooked with Sterno cans, the kind you use today to keep food warm in a chafing dish. The cans sat under a metal frame so we could heat soup or water or food on it. When we wanted to straighten our hair, we put the metal comb on the frame until it got hot enough to use.

We had something to eat every day, but it wasn't much. Dad came by from time to time and tried to help Mom. Most of the time it was meat, fresh ham or one of the chickens he had. Sometimes Mom heated cans of Campbell's chicken noodle soup mixed with Campbell's vegetable soup. We liked that combination, especially if we had some Saltine crackers to break up in it. Mom was always sending us to the store to buy a quarter pound of cheese and a quarter pound of bologna. That's all we could afford. I ate bologna and cheese sandwiches all through my teens into my 20s. I stood in line to get the cheese and butter and dried milk the Red Cross handed out. I always thought the butter had the best taste. I ate a peanut butter and jelly sandwich for dinner. Mom could make spaghetti go a long way or her goulash dish with hamburger, elbow macaroni, onions and peppers. We loved those pasta dishes. I still enjoy homemade spaghetti and meatballs and especially Cathy's goulash.

I began working at a grocery store owned by a Jewish couple. I made home deliveries. I don't know whose car I drove because we didn't have one. I'm sure it belonged to Harry, the owner. Every penny I earned went to Mom.

Mom worked cleaning houses and motel rooms. One time she did laundry in the basement of a nursing home; in fact, she got me a job there. I started as a dishwasher and later helped the cook in the kitchen. He taught me how to core a head of lettuce and to chop vegetables without losing fingers.

When I got on my feet in Kansas, I sent Mom money. She was living in a senior citizen apartment building by then. I found out Mom was sharing the money with others she thought needed it more. So I arranged to pay her rent directly. That way I always knew she had a place to live.

West Chester summers were humid, and none of the apartments had air conditioners. I can't tell you how many fans I purchased for Mom. But they didn't help, so I finally bought her a window AC unit and put it in myself. It got so cold in her small apartment that she had to open the door to let the cool air out. Neighbors would stop in to cool off.

I flew Mom in and out of Kansas all the time. Mom enjoyed flying. She went with my teams to places she had never been — California, Hawaii, Chicago, Texas and Mexico. When she went home, she told her friends all about her trips.

Mom knew no strangers at any point in her life, even from 30,000 feet and above. As she got older, I tried to book her a direct flight into Kansas City and back to Philadelphia, but one time I couldn't, and she was stuck in Chicago when her connecting flight to Philadelphia got canceled. I just about died. Here she was by herself in an airport having to figure out what to do. The phone rang and I heard her voice, so upbeat.

"Hi, Honey. Don't worry. We're having a good time."

We? I thought. Then I heard a second woman's voice.

"Don't worry. We've got your mom! She's OK!"

Mom had made friends that fast with the family next to her on the flight. Now they were taking care of her. God, was I relieved.

At Kansas, we had the same bus driver for almost all of our trips to games and to the airport. Bob Milner and his wife, JoAnn, took great care of me, my team and Mom. I remember going to Kansas City for the Big Eight Tournament. There's a lot of down time between practices and games. One evening, the Milners took Mom to a casino. She had a great time playing the 25-cent slot machines. Do you know they had to get on the public address system and call my mother when they were ready to go home?

When Mom heard her name, she met them at the door,

grinning from ear to ear, her hand in a pocket jingling with quarters. Bob loved to tell that story.

My players have their own stories to share. She was a friend and sometimes a grandmother to them. They could cuddle up and lay their heads on her shoulder and just talk.

Evette Ott, who played for me from 1984 though 1987, adored Mom and shared this recollection.

> *She was the coolest. Her voice and how she spoke was so laid back and so cool. You'd walk in and say, "Hey, Mom!" And she answered you with, "Hey, Sweeeetie! How ya doing, Sweeetie." She was so warm and welcoming, and she gave the best hugs. She wasn't bashful, either. If we said something ornery, she'd get ornery right back.*
>
> *If we were watching TV and we saw somebody cute, maybe Denzel Washington, we might say, "He's a fine thing." She would chime in, "He suuuure is, Honey!"*

It meant a lot to me how much Mom loved my players and how they loved her back.

Living my life a plane ride away from Mom was tough. I uprooted in 1969 when I got a weekend-only job in D.C., the start of the distance from West Chester and me that would grow by the minute. When I got the invitation to play basketball for Team USA, the coach lived in Missouri and I eventually moved there to join her AAU team.

"Oh, my God, how can I leave Mom and my family?" I wondered. I was scared, but I knew I had to go. I really wanted to continue to compete and possibly become an Olympian. It was so difficult to say goodbye to Mom. We both cried, I squeezed her tight, and I looked back, always trying to remember her face and her touch.

"Love you, Mom."

"I love you, Honey."

I'd walk a few steps and turn around.

"I love you."

"Love you, too, Darling."

We would do that until one of us was out of sight.

I boarded every plane with tears in my eyes.

I never returned to Pennsylvania to live, though I made every effort to go there at least once a year and when I was recruiting on the East Coast. Mom still lived in that same efficiency apartment, and I would sleep right in her bed with her. I liked to plan a surprise visit. I wouldn't tell her when I was coming. Sometimes we would be talking on the phone as we normally did every day. She'd think I was in Kansas. Only I'd be right at her doorstep. She'd hear a knock and tell me to hold on. There I stood. Mom would tear up and call my name, "Oh, Sister!" We'd hug and even dance. Mom liked to do the two-step. Then I would move on to surprise the rest of the family, but Mom always came first.

Sometimes she visited me in Kansas for as long as a month before she wanted to go home. I finally got Mom to live with me in Lawrence. I had asked for years until she finally said yes. I was so happy. I can see her now, trying to do whatever she could to help me. She loved folding clothes, so while she sat in her favorite rocking chair, I would put a basket of clean laundry at her feet. She sat rocking and folding things neatly for me.

We had some wonderful years there together until her blood pressure got extremely high and she struggled to walk. Mom was diagnosed with congestive heart failure, which was the beginning of her decline. I arranged for a physical therapist to come to the house and do some exercises with her. Mom was not the best patient, and the therapist, who loved Mom dearly, knew she was only going to do what she wanted to do.

By then, Mom did not want to be alone. Eventually I got someone to help with her, and we brought in a hospital bed. But just like Dad, Mom could be ornery. She would find a way to get out of that bed and look for her walker. I could hear her pacing up and down the hallway. I'd see her peeking into my bedroom, checking on me. I used a baby monitor even though she was right next door to my bedroom. I wanted to hear her if she needed me. We often laugh about the time I thought Mom was sleeping. Then I heard her voice over the monitor softly calling out, "Trouble ... trouble ... trouble!" I ran to her bedroom to find Mom sliding off the bed onto the floor. There she was lying between the nightstand and her bed, looking up at me, smiling. I fixed her. I raised the sidebars up every night after that.

Those were exhausting days for me that extended into the nights. Mom wanted to watch what she wanted to watch on TV — "The Golden Girls," "Sanford & Son," "Good Times" and westerns starring John Wayne, the Lone Ranger or Hopalong Cassidy. When she would nod off, or so I thought, the moment I would switch to something else, I would hear her voice.

"I am not asleep. Do not change that channel, Marian." Oh, I forgot to say, once Mom got to Kansas, she started calling me by my proper name sometimes.

As time passed, Mom started getting her days mixed up with her nights. I was Sister again. She slept all day and was wide awake at night. I came home after a full day of work and practice or late after a home game and was exhausted. She would lie in bed and call me — softly at first.

"Sister."

I wanted to sleep so badly, so I didn't always go running.

"Sister," this time a little louder.

I pretended not to hear.

Then she'd scream it. "Sister!"

I'd figure out what she needed, get her a glass of water and then go back to bed. I'm telling you it couldn't have been much more than five minutes later when I would hear her voice: "Sister."

It became too much for me, so Mom returned to West Chester to live with Cathy. I arranged for my sister to take time off from her job to watch over Mom until the end of basketball season. Mom didn't like being in the dark or alone there any more than at my house. Cathy would sleep on the couch that was just five steps from Mom's bed. But if Mom couldn't see you, it wasn't good enough.

I hated to do it, but I knew Mom needed to go into a nursing home. I flew her back to Kansas, and she went straight there. I knew if I brought her back to my house, I'd never do it. I went to see her throughout the week and so would some of my players and assistant coaches, along with close friends of mine.

Even though Mom had a lot of visitors, it was me she wanted to see. I knew inside how much she wanted me to stay. I remember telling her when I was going recruiting that I was coming back in three to four days.

"That's like you being away for a year to me," she said.

During the spring of 2005, I was surprised to get a call from Butchie's son, Little Butchie. He was engaged and wanted me to stand in for his father and walk him down the aisle. It wasn't convenient but it was clear how important this was to him. I agreed to go.

Before the flight to Philadelphia, I went to see Mom right around lunchtime. Her wheelchair was parked in front of the reception desk. As the elevator doors opened, my eyes met hers. I kissed her right dead on the mouth; we always did that.

"I'm going to Pennsylvania! Little Butchie is getting married." I quietly said.

But Mom was in another world. It was as if she was watching a movie in front of her. She wasn't a part of what was going on. She seemed out of it. I couldn't figure out why. I wheeled her into the lunch room, but she just sat there. I tried to feed her. She wasn't really there. I wanted her to hear what I was saying so I spoke right into her ear.

"Mom, I'll be right back. I'll be back." Then I said it again. "I'll be back."

I asked her to repeat it to make sure she heard me. I think she tried. A friend later told me that Mom was already gone, not part of this world anymore. She had moved to the next.

I walked away looking back at my mother sitting there in that wheelchair. "I'll be right back."

I got to the wedding and walked my nephew down the aisle. I hadn't been at the reception long when I got a call from Renate, one of my dear friends at Kansas. She was one of the emergency contacts I had listed for Mom.

"Your mom passed," she said softly.

I dropped the phone and walked straight to the parking lot, speaking to no one even though all of my sisters were celebrating Little Butchie's wedding. All I could do was scream. I screamed at the top of my lungs again and again and again. I screamed so long and so loud until I couldn't anymore, until nothing more came out.

"You didn't wait for me. You *didn't* wait for me," I screamed through tears.

Marian Jane Washington was 87 when she died on May 14, 2005.

All that ran through me was that the moment Mom needed me, I wasn't there. I wanted her to wait for me. I told Mom to wait for me and she didn't.

If I had been there at the end, I don't know if I could have said goodbye. God removed me just as he did with my father. I know both of my parents are resting in His arms and at peace now.

As much as you love your mother when you have her, you appreciate her in a whole other light when you don't. Even to this day, when I think about my mother, I recognize many of the things she had to overcome. You only get one mother in your life. Mine was the very best.

Chapter IV

By My Side

I didn't have a lot of close friends growing up. I had Butchie. He was right there for me, and we would fulfill all our fantasies together. We were cowboys and Indians, with make-believe horses. I always had someone to play with because of him.

B**utchie couldn't** beat me at anything. Not if I could help it.

My brother and I found a way to compete no matter what we were doing, especially while we were working.

We'd ride on the back of Dad's trash truck, and before it came to a stop, I was already looking for the heaviest barrel to dump. Only I had to outrun Butchie to get to it. Dad drove slowly enough that Butchie and I could straddle the sides of his pickup truck without him knowing it. We pretended we were riding horses while Dad drove from one house to the next. We didn't think about how dangerous it might have been.

Dad would have all of us in the garden picking tomatoes, onions, cabbage and whatever else was ready. We'd be outside playing, and he'd shout, "Go pick some string beans."

Butchie and I would hurry to fill our buckets so we could get back to our game. I was definitely going to fill my bucket to the top before he did. One Thanksgiving, we even tried to outeat each other. It was not something we talked about before dinner.

We just looked into each other's eyes and knew the race was on.

"This is good! This is really good, Mom. Can I have some more?" How many times did we say that? By the time we were finished, we went to bed with the worst stomachaches!

My baby brother was my best friend when we were young. He and Cathy were my biggest cheerleaders when I grew up. Mom named him David, but like most everyone else in our family, he had a nickname. Everybody called him Butchie. Today we call his son, my nephew, Little Butchie.

Butchie shared my mother's almond-shaped eyes and long lashes, my grandmother's straight nose, and like most of us, his smooth, chocolate skin showed no blemishes. He was slender with a small waist. I had some height on him with my long legs and arms. Unlike him, I had lots of hair that Mom kept in plats, usually three — one in the front and two in the back.

One of my earliest memories of Butchie was us riding in the back seat of Mom's car, coming home from the store. It was a nice day, he was just a toddler, and we were almost home when her two-tone blue Mercury crossed over some railroad tracks. All of a sudden Butchie decided to open the back door of the car. It flung open and with the help of the wind, he flew out! Mom brought the car to a screeching halt. She was hysterical, crying and praying to God that he was OK. She ran to my brother, scooped him up off the ground, put him back in the car and drove us all home. Butchie was skinned up pretty good. Mom was a nervous wreck and so protective of him that she set him in a baby carriage, covering it with netting so the flies and other bugs would not touch his injuries. I was in shock. I couldn't believe he would do something like that. But that was Butchie.

I didn't know it then, but that was the beginning of the two of us sharing adventures behind the wheels of cars. I would always tease him, telling him the only thing he ever beat me at was driving at an earlier age. I began driving at something like 9 years old, and by the time Butchie was 6 or 7, he was already driving all over the back fields where we lived. We would make our own dirt paths because Pop had so much stuff lying around, especially cars that he cut up.

Butchie was so small and short that he had to sit on a pillow to see over the steering wheel. He would end up sliding forward as he stretched to reach the brake and the accelerator. He knew how to shift all four gears — the three going forward and one in reverse. But one day Butchie was trying to back up Dad's pickup truck and his foot missed the brake. He ended up getting too close to one of Dad's buildings. He got one of the back wheels caught on the front frame of the building. Butchie just about pulled the whole thing down!

"Dad is going to get you," I snickered.

But mostly, Butchie and I were united, on the same team in the thick of whatever we were doing together. A lot of the time, that included getting into trouble with Dad.

"Do not leave the yard," Dad would warn Butchie and me.

Then he'd repeat, "Do *not* leave the yard."

Next door Mr. Lawrence had a strawberry patch. All we had to do was climb the fence to be in the middle of it. The fence had wire hooks that would catch our clothes if we weren't careful, but Butchie and I knew how to get over it without getting snagged — on a hook at least.

Dad backed out of the driveway, and as soon as his truck was out of sight, we hopped over the fence, landing on our bellies. We stayed low so Mr. Lawrence wouldn't see us as we feasted on those delicious strawberries. Suddenly, we heard Dad pull back into the driveway. It seemed as though he was only gone for a few minutes. While we were able to scramble and get back over that fence in time, he knew what we had done. He began to scold us and went looking for a switch off a tree. Butchie tried to run to the house to hide, but Dad met him at the front door. Poor

Butchie was just a little too slow, and Pop caught him with the switch. I managed to hide, but I sure got a howling at.

The summers were scorchers, and we didn't have air conditioning. Dad built a little pool in our backyard. It couldn't have been more than three feet deep. He dug out a fairly good-sized hole, finished it with concrete and painted it blue. Then he took a hose and filled it up. We would jump in and try to swim, though all we were doing was crawling. It helped us cool down on those hot summer days.

I was always thinking of things to do that I thought were funny. One day, I decided to zip up my brother in a plastic garment bag and put him into the pool. I wondered if he could float. I can still see him now trying to get out of that bag while it was in the water. He wasn't doing very well, squirming and upset, and my sisters began screaming. Mom and Dad came running to see what was going on. They snatched the bag out of the water and unzipped him. In the meantime, I prepared myself to get yelled at for putting him in such danger.

"Ornery!" That's what I kept hearing from Mom and Dad. "You're just ornery!"

Butchie had a one-horned billy goat that he adored. He got it in his mind that the goat was going to pull him in costume during West Chester's Halloween parade, a big deal when I was young. The goat cooperated, only that thing smelled so bad anyone nearby could hardly stand it. That didn't discourage Butchie. He stayed in the parade until it ended.

Butchie and I both loved to drive — *fast*. Often we took two cars out on our street drag racing. Bolmar Street was relatively quiet, and many times you could speed up and down it without seeing another car. We would race side by side trying to outdo one another.

They made the Hydra-matic shift for cars just before they made the automatic shift. Dad let me drive Mom's Hydra-matic

1950ish Dick Tracy-style car. I was racing Butchie in it and I knew waiting for it to shift would slow me down, so I kept the car in first gear as long as I could until it automatically shifted. By then, I was ahead.

Our fun behind the wheel didn't end when I went to college. One night we were on Wayne Street, where we definitely should not have been speeding. Wayne Street was much busier than Bolmar Street. Somehow we got into that competitive way of ours and another race was on. Butchie got the jump on me. We had to cross over a busy intersection before Wayne Street came to a dead end. I know Butchie thought I would slow down because of possible oncoming cars, but I took the chance looking left and right and gunned it. My heart was beating pretty fast when I stopped, and he was behind me. I knew it was dangerous and I never did it again, but I couldn't let him win. I get so tickled because he had yet to beat me doing anything in a car. Ever.

As little kids, we played a lot of cowboys and bad guys or cowboys and Indians. One of the chicken coops was our main play area. It had an A frame, so the roof came to a peak. We could fantasize while hiding behind barriers of some kind. Butchie and I would be a team against whoever we imagined was against us.

Our play guns would be pulled, and I'd shout, "Butchie, cover me!" I'd crawl to the top of the roof to peek over to the other side.

Sometimes I'd tell him, "I'm hit!" and slide back closer to him. I really loved my toy guns and holsters, especially the one that opened like a real pistol.

When Mom and Dad separated, it was hard on all of us. I was sad my brother was not coming with us to live, but Butchie wanted to stay with Dad. As I look back, I realize Dad, who was in his early 60s by then, needed somebody with him.

Butchie never liked school much. He couldn't sit still that long. He'd rather be in the yard, doing all the things Pop did or tinkering with cars. He loved cars, and that's something he was much better at than I was. As a teenager, he could take an engine apart and put it back together.

The only time I ever saw him participate in athletics was at a gymnastics event when he was in junior high school. I never knew he even liked gymnastics until I had a chance to see him do an iron cross. A teacher helped him reach some rings, and as he hung suspended, he stretched his arms out to his side and held that position for what seemed like several minutes. People started to applaud, and I thought, "Wow! He's really strong!" Butchie never got a chance to explore sports the way I did. Even though he never set foot in a weight room, his upper body strength was tremendous. He grew to have a big chest, and his arms and shoulders were well developed. As a grown man, he maintained his chiseled body without an ounce of fat on it.

Just like Dad, Butchie embraced the idea of women playing sports, and he loved being a bat boy for one of my softball teams. In fact, he could tell us more about how we did in the game than I could. He was really proud of me, and that meant a lot. He often bragged, "No one is a better athlete than my sister!"

Butchie dropped out of school without finishing tenth grade. Dad told him if he wasn't going to go to school he had to enlist in the service. That wasn't something Butchie wanted to do. My father's older sons all served in the Army, and I think Dad thought this was the best thing for my brother. Because Butchie was so young, Dad had to sign for him to go.

I worried the whole time Butchie served in Vietnam, wondering how he would stay safe. I have a letter he wrote me, something that I treasure today because he had never written to me before. The envelope contained a picture of him and his buddies, soldiers in his unit standing together in front of their tent. *"I love you,"* he wrote. It was the first time he ever said those words to me.

Butchie became a machine gunner and flew in helicopters to pick up casualties. He told me a story about trying to carry the body of a soldier when his hand slid right into the man's chest cavity. I know that really affected him. Even though he received ribbons for his incredible courage, my brother never talked about them. I never knew he even had them until much later in life.

Butchie didn't reenlist after his time was up. By then, it was pretty clear that he suffered from Post-Traumatic Stress Disorder. Like so many of our veterans, he had trouble with noises like fireworks. He felt uncomfortable in big crowds.

Butchie hadn't been back in West Chester long when, while walking down Market Street alongside a friend, he got shot. The shots were directed at his friend, but Butchie got caught in the crossfire. He took four bullets, yet ended up getting to his house, his friend still with him. The shots continued through my brother's front door. The shooter left before the police arrived.

I was scared to death when I heard the news, and all of us rushed to the hospital as fast as we could.

The doctor wasn't happy with Butchie. "We've got to get your son to rest," he told Mom. "He will not rest."

When we walked into Butchie's room, he looked up and smiled. He began to reassure us that he was fine and to prove it, he dropped down to the floor and started doing push-ups. Right there on the bare floor of the hospital room. He included a couple of one-handed push-ups.

"Look, Mom. I'm OK!" he insisted.

Now, Mom and Dad always told us to keep moving when we weren't feeling well. We were encouraged to move around when we had colds, especially when we were congested. But moving around right after being shot was not something even they would have advised. We understood what Butchie was feeling, but sometimes it makes more sense to do what the doctor says!

Butchie was released from the hospital with a bullet in his chest that the doctors were unable to remove. He never complained about it, and he worked as hard as always. Butchie married his high school sweetheart, used his G.I. Bill benefits and eventually bought his own piece of land in West Chester. He had enough land to park cars that needed fixing, and he had a garage where he could work on them at night. Even though he never got a high school diploma, he worked for himself, just like Dad. Butchie called his business Washington, Inc.

The trouble was that my brother didn't always get paid properly for all the work he did for people. He had a kind heart, and he tried to help anyone who asked. They would tell him over and over again, "I'll pay you next week, Butchie." But next week never came. He worked around the clock just like Dad. When I would visit, I worried about how tired he looked. Yet he seemed to have a need to keep going.

Butchie hosted family gatherings during the holidays at his house. It was always special when he did that. We were older then, and each of us had children. We would meet up at his house, where he grilled hamburgers and hotdogs and others brought side dishes and desserts. He set up picnic tables with games for the children. He loved playing horseshoes and was pretty good at it. I tried to get back to those gatherings as often as I could, but it was hard for me to find the time once I started working at Kansas.

When I did get home, I liked to surprise everybody with a gift of some kind. Kansas was one of the earliest women's athletic programs to have a contract with Nike. We got allotments of gear, and I could buy things at a discount. One year, I gave everybody a sports watch. My brother just shook his head and laughed. Butchie had a great laugh. He had *my* laugh.

Just like Dad, he'd say, *"You're something, Girl."*

I finally got Butchie to visit me in Kansas. The timing was great because it was just before one of the women's Big Eight championships in Kansas City.

As soon as Butchie arrived at my home, he was thinking about cars. I had a 1989 Saab 900 convertible at the time — red with a soft black top. It's still parked in my garage today. He drove that car all over Lawrence. The first place he went was an auto shop to see what was in stock there. I was so happy he was relaxed and enjoying himself.

I remember taking him to JC Penney, and I bought him a bunch of clothes. Butchie looked good in everything he put on. He was still really slim with a great physique. He was so proud modeling everything for me. We ended up leaving with polo shirts, slacks and shoes. I wanted him to feel really good about himself when he met my team and the fans. I remember when he took me aside while we were in the store and said, "No one has ever taken the time to do this for me, Sister. Thank you!"

Butchie rode on the bus with me and the team on our way to Kansas City. I introduced him to as many people as I could, even some media. I was so happy for him. He was so handsome and carried himself well. He had a quiet way about him, but he was serious and thoughtful, watching our games intently while sitting behind our bench.

We talked about his moving to Kansas. "If you come out here, you can live with me," I told him. "I will help you set up your business, your auto shop. I know people in this community will just love you, Butchie."

My brother said he was going to get his affairs in order, and he planned to come back. When I waved goodbye to him as he boarded the plane, I had a feeling he wouldn't be able to get away from West Chester. It's tough leaving home. It was for me. I prayed he could do it.

When I answered the phone on Oct. 22, 2004, Cathy was crying. "Sister, we just lost our brother," she said. I held the phone, stunned by the words. I started shaking, asking her what happened. Butchie had a massive heart attack and died. It didn't seem possible. He had always been so strong. He didn't smoke or drink.

We never told Mom that Butchie passed. She was failing by then. For months, she would ask to talk to him, and then all of a sudden she stopped asking. We thought that somehow she knew her only son was gone.

It saddens me to think that maybe I could have done more for him. Maybe I could have flown and picked him up and brought him back to Kansas with me. Butchie did so much for so many and got so little in return.

I was determined to give him the best funeral I could afford. White horses pulled a carriage with his casket that was draped in an American flag. The coachmen and the team of horses rode slowly through West Chester on their way to the graveyard. His friends helped direct traffic so the carriage could move without stopping. I saw people on the sidewalk stop and watch. Some saluted. The Army sent soldiers who gave him a seven-gun salute for his service to our country.

I stared at it all in disbelief. I had focused so much on making sure he was buried with the utmost respect that it wasn't until later that it hit me. I cried and cried. Butchie was gone.

I didn't have a lot of close friends growing up. I had Butchie. He was right there for me, and we would fulfill all our fantasies together. I always had someone to play with because of him. My sisters were pretty little, but Butchie was only three years younger than me.

I felt lonely without him. During those years I had my brother by my side, I never felt lonely. Suddenly, at the age of 54, Butchie was gone. My little brother was gone.

Chapter V

The Bus

We lived with what we had and didn't think about what we didn't.

I **didn't grow** up in an apartment, much less a house. I grew up in a bus. I haven't said that aloud to many people over the years, and when I do, it's easy to understand why they might look shocked and confused.

You lived in a bus?

I lived in a bus for the first 12 years of my life.

Being a kid, I didn't take the time to think much about where I was living. As I grew older, it didn't take long for me to recognize that this was something different from anyone in the neighborhood or around town. But it was my life, so it was what it was. I don't remember fantasizing about moving. My dreams were about making the Olympics or getting rich.

All I knew was that Dad turned an old bus into a home. I think it was an old Short Line bus, but for reference, imagine a Greyhound bus with the seats removed. The side of the bus where passengers would enter faced the street. Dad added to our home by building an addition that he fixed to the entire length of the bus on the other side. It gave us a little more space for a potbelly stove, a bedroom for him and Mom, a couch, a small table and chairs, and a wood-burning stove that Mom cooked meals on. A door led in and out of this added space. The walls were covered with plaster boards.

Our sitting room was actually a small section in the back of the bus. As you moved toward the front, there was room for a bed where all four of us girls slept. Dad removed the driver's seat so he could put in an icebox. To the right of that, where passengers would have entered, he made a tiny storage area.

Two chairs were placed around the table and one chair was put in front of a window near the potbelly stove. The stove burned both wood and coal. The gray L-shaped chimney that led outside would sometimes get so hot it would turn slightly red. It didn't bother Dad because he liked it hot in the house. I could barely stand it. Even though Dad wore layers of clothes, he seemed to stay cold.

We never had an oven, but the cooks at one of the restaurants where Dad took care of their trash and waste baked a turkey for us every Thanksgiving. Dad brought the turkey home and Mom would cook a couple of sides. Thanksgiving was one of the few times all of us ate dinner together. We didn't have a table big enough for everyone to sit around, so we'd find a chair or a place on the floor and put our plates on our laps. No one really talked because we were busy eating. Turkey wings were my favorite, and Mom always saved me one. She wouldn't eat until everyone had what they needed.

I believed in Santa Claus for a long time when I was a kid and wondered how he got through that narrow stove pipe with the awkward shape. I thought he must have to come through the window since we had no fireplace. Like most kids, I tried to stay awake all night.

Mom put up a small tree in the sitting room, where we opened gifts. Every year for Christmas I asked for a nurse's kit. My siblings were my guinea pigs. I'd take their temperatures, listen to their hearts and give them some "medicine." The "pills" that came with the kit were candy. Some kits were better than others, but they all had a thermometer and stethoscope.

Eventually we got a small black-and-white TV. "Howdy Doody," was one of my favorite programs and I loved watching "Winky Dink and You" on Saturday mornings. Winky Dink was a cartoon boy with a large star on his head. For 50 cents you could buy a kit with a panel of green vinyl to stick on the front of your TV set during the show. It stuck because of the static electricity. Winky Dink would tell you to draw a house, and you could watch him enter the house. If Winky Dink hid behind a tree, he would show you where to draw the tree. Then you'd see Winky Dink go behind the tree, hiding from maybe a dangerous wolf.

The whole family tuned in for "Amos 'n' Andy," the first television show to feature an all-Black cast. Looking back, I realize they were gifted actors who didn't have many opportunities for other kinds of roles, but they were very funny. I was disappointed when they took the show off the air even though I understood why. CBS caved in to pressure from the NAACP and others who thought the show reinforced stereotypes of Blacks as inferior.

Janet, Izzy, Cathy and I shared a double mattress. Going to bed at night often meant waking up a few hours later to a wet sheet, a situation Mom would address in the morning. On a hot night, the pee smelled particularly bad, and while Mom could launder the bottom sheet, the smell never really went away. Oh, those darn bed bugs. In the morning, the evidence would be up and down our arms and chests. The bites would itch, and we had to be careful scratching for fear of scarring.

One night, a rat bit Cathy while she was sleeping. She was so scared. She said she was *never* going back to bed. Dad put out a trap that caught the rat. The next morning, he had the trap with the rat in his hand and motioned Cathy to come outside with him. Dad was carrying his shotgun and right in front of her, he shot it.

"That rat will never hurt you again," Dad told Cathy.

As gross as that might seem, it sure helped Cathy get over her fear.

The icebox had no electricity. It just contained blocks of ice to keep things cool. We used to drive to a building that stored blocks of ice. We'd buy it, place it in the icebox and put our food around it.

We ate what we grew in the garden — everything was fresh, right out of the ground. The tomatoes were the best. In our back fields, Dad planted a larger garden where he pushed a plow before he got a tractor to break up the ground. We would all follow behind him and lay down seeds. It was strictly a cornfield. We never sold our vegetables, but Mom would give away some if a neighbor needed food.

We had fresh eggs from the chickens we raised. Dad would slaughter a pig when we needed meat for the winter. Without a refrigerator, we had to cure the meat. Dad took it to a place where they cured it; then he would bring it back and hang it in the shed for months.

Chickens ran free in our yard. When Mom wanted to cook a chicken, we would help her chase one down. She would grab the chicken by the neck, spin it and with a snap, the chicken's neck broke. Then she would take an ax and cut its head off. Next, she immersed the rest of the chicken in a bucket of hot water, which helped remove the feathers. I couldn't watch any of it.

We kept other animals — rabbits and ducks and a family dog named Trixie, a terrier that never came inside. Cathy always wanted to pet the ducks. When one of the mama ducks had babies, Cathy started petting them until the mother duck jumped on her back and started pecking her on the head. Cathy started screaming and running. Her arms flailed trying to get the duck off her back.

Dad went to help and hollered, "I told you to leave her ducklings alone!"

That was the last time Cathy played with the baby ducks.

The first time I saw a really nice carpet on a living room floor was in a Brownie leader's house. I remember walking on it and thinking how thick and soft it felt under my feet. I imagined how nice it would be to have that where I lived.

Pop piled so much against what would have been the actual door to the bus so you couldn't enter or exit. One night, I tried to pry it open. It was after one of the rare times when I went to the movies with a few others. We saw "The Blob." It was so scary, the story of this giant jelly-like alien terrorizing a town. As I walked home, I imagined that the blob was on its way to get me. That night, I had some kind of nightmare, and I felt the urge to get outside. I tried to open that door by stepping over all the boxes and clothes, but I couldn't reach the handle. I had to go back to bed and try to sleep.

One of the things I liked to do was find my favorite coloring book and bring it into the sitting room. Using a dark crayon, I outlined each object on a page, whether it was an animal or a house or a ball, in a special way. I shaded in what I had traced using the side of the same color crayon. I tried to get Janet to do it my way, but she didn't quite get it. I thought being exact was the only way to color. I'm not so sure I made coloring fun for her.

"Sister was always trying to get me to color *her* way," she says, and we laugh about it to this day.

If you wonder where the bathroom was, it wasn't. We had an outhouse that I hated. Even though Dad tried to keep it clean, it still smelled bad. I mean, it was an outhouse. I always wore shoes because in the summer berries dropped from our tree right along the path to the outhouse. I didn't like stepping on berries, and I would often sweep them in a pile and use a shovel to pick them up. In the winter, we wore rubber boots for trips to the bathroom.

Mom pulled out a small basin to give us a bath every day. Sometimes Dad would bring a big tin bathtub into the house that he filled with water. We didn't always have running water, but we could fill up buckets of water using the pump down the street. Mom and Dad loved spring water. About four or five miles outside of West Chester was a place alongside the road with a rock embankment and natural spring water running all day and night. Mom and Dad filled empty jugs there to bring home.

If Dad found something along his trash route that he thought we could use, he kept it. We'd get clothes that way, and Mom shopped for us at the Salvation Army. Once a year, each of us got one pair of school shoes and one pair of sneakers. If you wore out your shoes before the year was up, too bad. I remember many a time having a hole in the sole of my shoes. In the winter, I put rubber boots over my shoes, but they didn't keep my feet warm. If need be, Dad stuffed newspaper in our shoes to help keep our feet warm or to cover a hole.

As hard as life could be, my sisters and I, and especially Butchie and me, found a way to entertain ourselves. It was nice when Mom wasn't so serious all the time. She was lighthearted with us. Sometimes when we sat on the floor in a semicircle in front of the TV, Mom would quietly sneak up to scare us. Then she grabbed us while we were screaming and we would all laugh together.

We had a great time when Grandmum's boyfriend, nicknamed Sugarfoot, came over. We waited until he fell asleep. While he slept, I put lipstick on him and got my siblings to help me dress him up with makeup and a head rag. We were so eager for him to wake up, giggling every time we looked at him. When Sugarfoot awoke, he couldn't believe how he looked.

Goldie! Look at what these kids have done!

Dad was never angry. He busted out laughing, too, shaking his head.

You kids!

I remember one time when Mom and her cousin Mamie decided they were going to Chester to get finger waves like Josephine Baker. Mom had such beautiful hair, and her finger wave was so pretty. But Mamie came back with a scarf on her head. Her boyfriend was there, hoping to see how she looked. She didn't want to take off the scarf. When she finally did, Mamie was completely bald because she hadn't told the hairdresser that she had recently dyed her hair. The dye and the lye didn't mix well. She was devastated and embarrassed. It took everything not to laugh. It did grow back, though.

Sometimes at night when Dad was cooking crabs, his friend Vince Martin would play the steel guitar right outside the bus by the mulberry tree. The crabs would be fresh. He bought a bushel of them, usually in Chester or Philadelphia. My sisters would squeal because Dad always picked up a live crab and let it wander all over the place.

Vince taught me how to make music by moving my hands back and forth over my knees and chest. Sometimes I'd slap so hard I'd beat up my knees, but soon I learned the right way to create rhythm. Dad would be clapping and patting his foot, having the best ol' time. Mom loved country music and singing along with the spirituals Vince would play.

Our neighbors on Bolmar Street joined us, including the Lawrences and the white family next to them. It felt like one community. When I think about it, we were very isolated from uptown West Chester and a faster way of life.

As I got older, I grew self-conscious about people learning that I lived in a bus. I wanted to be a Brownie, and after the first meeting, one of the leaders drove me home. She asked me where to pull in and I pointed to Mother Lawrence's driveway, not my own. I was uncomfortable having her drive up to the bus, but I felt worse when I saw Mom waiting.

"Why did that lady drop you off at Mother Lawrence's?" she asked.

I don't know how I answered, but it didn't matter. I instantly realized I had hurt her feelings. She probably knew why I did it.

I was ashamed to have this white woman see where I lived, even though Mother Lawrence's house wasn't all that great. But it was a house, not a bus.

My friends at school never came over. None of my siblings had friends over, either. I never talked about where I lived, even when I got to Kansas. Over the years I probably could count on one hand the people I've told about living in a bus. I didn't want anyone to judge my life, and if it couldn't be understood in all its ups and downs, I didn't want to talk about it at all.

We lived with what we had and didn't think about what we didn't. I grew up seeing other people with more. I watched and tried to learn how they succeeded. It wasn't about being envious. I just wanted to learn how people reached the heights they did so maybe I could do the same.

As I've gotten older, I realize just how strong Mom and Dad were. They faced so many challenges over the years. Mom did hard labor most of her adult life. She never wavered in her faith and in her belief that good things would happen for us.

I don't know if Dad prayed a lot, or some, or at all. Dad was a self-made man. He started his own business. He owned all this land that he farmed and provided for us without owing anybody, which was unusual at the time for a Black man. I never asked him how he did it or how he got it done. He just did and people respected him, even though he was an old guy wearing bib overalls living in a bus with his wife and five children.

Chapter VI

Off to a Flying Start

Athletics helped my sense of self-worth. Being poor didn't matter. Your color didn't matter. If you had that chance at the starting line with everyone else, you had the opportunity to be successful. Now that didn't mean you were always first because I wasn't always first. It was really about having opportunities. That's all most of us ask for.

I **lifted overflowing** garbage barrels above my shoulders to dump them into Dad's trash truck. I made my way to the chicken coop with containers filled with grain, carrying those along with buckets filled so high with water that they splashed my pant legs. Each was as heavy as I could make it — anything to cut down the number of trips back and forth until the job was done. I moved lumber and bales of hay and carried parts of vehicles – car wheels or one end of a transmission — getting them where Dad needed them to go.

Doing physical labor as part of my regular chores was yet another way I became stronger as Dad's daughter. I didn't need a weight room. Dad was a taskmaster, and Butchie an incentive. My arms, my legs and my mind were challenged every day, and eventually the trash cans began to feel lighter.

My upper body strength was on par with a grown woman when I was still a young girl. I started practicing the shot put in high school. My gym teacher, Miss McKenna, a tall, thick, young woman, was outside throwing one day. I joined her just for fun and managed to throw farther than she did. I was hoping to see Miss McKenna at the next practice, but I never saw her toss a shot put again.

As much as Butchie fueled my competitive instinct, I discovered it was especially rewarding to compete against someone I didn't know. And I discovered something about myself early on. Something that would not change no matter how many birthdays I had.

I hated losing. I wanted to win.

Most of my role models besides my mother were Olympians, women I watched on TV while I dreamed of being one. I never grew tired of seeing Wilma Rudolph, who set world records in the 100, 200 and 4x100 relay at the 1960 Olympics in Rome. That relay was amazing. I sat in front of the television cheering for Team USA. By the time Wilma got the baton, we were behind by a good bit. I was mesmerized watching her run down the leader, her long legs eating up the track. It was thrilling when she passed everyone to win the gold medal for Team USA.

I watched those performances imagining the joy and exhilaration of winning at the highest level. One of my favorite movies from the last 15 years is "Secretariat" — the story of how this incredible athlete, this magnificent horse, won with sheer determination after being so far behind in the Kentucky Derby in 1973. If you know the history, Secretariat had an abscess in his mouth when he finished third in his race before the Derby, a fact that made his come-from-behind performance more inspiring.

I felt a special joy watching anyone, even a horse, overcome challenges. Wilma Rudolph was crippled as a child, yet she became one of the greatest sprinters of all time. Achieving in athletics helped my sense of self-worth. Being poor didn't matter.

Color didn't matter. If you had that chance at the starting line with everyone else, you had the opportunity to be successful. Now that didn't mean I was always first because I wasn't. It was about having opportunities. That's all most of us ask for.

I went to the library looking for a book on my role models, but the only one I found about a Black female athlete was a children's book about tennis player Althea Gibson: *I Always Wanted to Be Somebody*. Althea was the first Black athlete, male or female, to win a major tennis championship. She won five Grand Slam singles titles, though she was denied membership to the All-England Club after winning Wimbledon because she was Black. Joining the LPGA Tour in 1964, she was often forced to dress in the car because the whites-only hotels would not let her inside.

I was eager to learn how she became so accomplished. I took my time and read her story over and over again. Althea hit a tennis ball against her garage door at night. She was by herself. She did not have it easy, but she found a way to develop the skills she needed to be successful. If Althea could find a way, so could I.

My introduction to athletics was nothing remarkable. It dates back to recess at West Goshen Elementary School when teachers got involved for play days. I got excited when I realized the teachers wanted us to race each other. They would line us up two or three at a time, and as long as you won, you got back in line to wait for your next turn. Sometimes it was difficult to win because older students raced against us. We even ran in the snow. I'd slip and slide to the finish line.

The Presidential Fitness Test was part of physical education classes in public schools when I was in high school. Girls had to do sit-ups, a shuttle run, the arm hang, a standing broad jump, the 50-yard dash, a softball throw for distance and the 600 — a lap and a half around the track. I had the top broad jump score in school, but the distance run was stressful for me. I about hyperventilated trying to make a certain time and struggled before finishing the first lap.

The older I grew, the less I liked running. Whenever I started to run, I had a hard time breathing. My throat seemed to close, but I would push through until I got a second wind. I could usually reach a point where I wasn't laboring as much and be OK the rest of the way. I think some of my problems were because I grew up with coal. Dad burned coal and wood to heat our home. Sometimes smoke would fill the place, and we'd have to go outside. I'm sure inhaling the smoke and byproducts from the coal affected my breathing.

After finishing all the tests, I did well enough to earn the Presidential Fitness Award whenever it was offered.

I played basketball, but it was by no means my primary sport until college. My strongest memory of the game before then happened in seventh grade. My gym teacher, Mrs. Finney, wanted us to shoot free throws like Wilt Chamberlin, who was a fan favorite then, having grown up in Philly. As great as he was, he was not a good free-throw shooter. At the time, he shot free throws underhanded.

In one of my seventh-grade games, I got fouled and my teacher wanted me to shoot a two-hand underhand free throw like Wilt. I had practiced Wilt's free throw over and over, but it felt awkward. So, I shot a one-hand free throw, cradling the basketball from my chest, up toward the basket. I missed it.

Mrs. Finney pulled me out of the game. She was angry I didn't shoot the way she wanted and proceeded to tell me, *"You couldn't make a basket if you stood on a 10-foot ladder."*

Her words stung. As you can see, I never forgot them. Later, when I had success on the court, I silently wished she could see me now.

I can't say I realized it at the time, but her harsh way influenced how I would later speak to my own players as a coach. You have to be careful with your words and how they affect young minds. I think encouragement is the best way to get the most out of someone. I've always said if you want to correct someone, start with something positive. They'll hear you and be more receptive to what you're trying to teach them.

I had fun competing in a lot of sports, including softball and field hockey. I was a standout softball player who played center field and often pitched. I didn't like playing in the infield because I didn't think my throws between the bases were as good as my teammates'. I liked covering the outfield, watching someone hit a long fly ball left or right of me and having the determination to run it down. There's nothing better than trying to keep someone from hitting a home run.

At first I played with a community center team in West Chester. Butchie was our manager and took a lot of pride in that. He not only enjoyed being around the game, he appreciated that women were playing good softball. It wasn't something he said out loud. Like Dad, you could tell he respected what females were capable of.

During high school, I was invited to play for an AAU team in Ardmore, Pennsylvania. That was pretty competitive. They always wanted me to pitch because my stride was so long. Sometimes it felt like I was halfway to the batter! Two of my newer friends from high school, Brenda and Shirley, played on that team. Brenda was really low to the ground, but she sure could swing a bat. Shirley could run down the long balls. We played the outfield together.

If there was a female athlete I admired in West Chester, it was Hester Dorsey. I had always heard she was a great softball player. One day she came to me and asked if I would play on her AAU team, The Amazons, in Philadelphia under the lights. They were short a player and she wanted me to fill in. I couldn't believe it.

The Amazons were older women, and softball in Philadelphia

was big at the time. Hester was a catcher, a stately woman, strong with a distinct, husky voice. I was almost 5-9; she was probably 5-11 or 6-foot but she looked 6-2 or 6-3. She carried herself tall with confidence.

"You look just like me," she told me.

When I looked in the mirror, I did favor her a little. I had a round face and our complexions were similar. We both had athletic builds.

I started out pitching my fastball in that game. That would be my only time pitching. I don't remember if they were hitting off me, but they moved me to center. I got on base, and it was neat to hear Hester cheer for me. When I batted, I swung for the fences. I was just a kid and she watched out for me, helping to settle my nerves. I played with Hester one other time. Each time there were fans in the stands, supporting the Amazons.

I picked up field hockey because in high school an "Athlete of the Year" award was given to the male and female who accumulated the most sports points. If you didn't make the team but served as a manager, you still received points. When I went out for field hockey, I struggled to control the ball while running with my hockey stick. I decided I was too late a bloomer for that sport and was ready to give it up when one of my gym teachers suggested I play goalie. I had no idea how to do that. Somehow, someone paid for me to go to a weeklong camp to learn with some of the best field hockey players in the state.

Mom drove me to the camp outside of West Chester and dropped me off. It was at a place that looked like a country club, with a white fence all around the property. The grass was so green, and there was so much land. The coach for the goalies was well-known in the sport. She immediately started drilling us. There were probably 10 goalies from other schools, but toward the end of camp, she spent extra time with me. I soon found I could move my feet quickly, and even though I was wearing pads over my knees, I could stop a lot of shots with my feet or with the field hockey stick. I was the only Black player there.

I left that camp feeling pretty confident. When I went out for my high school team my junior year, I made varsity. At the end of the season, field hockey players all gathered at West Chester High School before the all-state team was named. Every player had to compete in her respective position. That meant I had to compete against all the other goalies in the Ches-Mont League. My sister Isabel was there cheering me on. I was nervous, but my adrenalin overflowed. Each goalie had to stop a number of players shooting from a certain distance. I remember stopping more than half the shots with my stick and many more with my feet. When the competition ended, the coaches got together to name the all-state field hockey team. I was the only goalie selected.

I thought I had enough points to win the Female Athlete of the Year Award. Everybody thought John Green, who was also Black, had enough points to win the Male Athlete of the Year Award. Neither of us won. I saw John in tears during graduation practice. The Female Athlete Award went to Miss McKenna's sister. It was a bigger deal than I realized because the NAACP visited the school and met with the principal about the decision, which didn't change.

When you're young, every milestone matters. You get torn down so often with mean things people say to you and about you. I was made to feel less than, at times because of color and lack of means. So my deeds had to mean something. I thought achieving would counter the negative words I so often heard. I looked forward to being named the best athlete because I worked hard for it. Not getting it was crushing.

One of my strengths has been the ability to find a way to move forward. I continued to invest in track and field, where I enjoyed success in the field events and loved winning medals, especially the gold ones.

West Chester High School didn't have a girls track team. Most high schools didn't in the early 1960s. One student at the school who was pretty popular, Kathy Facciolli, was a star hurdler who would later be named an All-American. Her father, James, a no-nonsense coach, taught at my high school and coached the West Chester Athletic Club that I joined. His wife made the uniforms — red blouses with white shorts.

Mr. Facciolli realized I was not one of his top sprinters, so he directed me to the field events. My events became throwing the shot and discus. I could throw by using sheer force and determination, even though nobody showed me much beyond the basics — how to start, the slide, the follow-through. I soon became a shot putter and discus thrower. I tried to throw the javelin a couple of times but didn't like it. Maybe because I just didn't know how to throw it.

West Chester was a tiny track club, but what we lacked in numbers, we made up for in work ethic and a fire that lifted us to impressive heights. A *Philadelphia Inquirer* article from Sept. 22, 1963, headlined "Off to a Flying Start," celebrated the club winning the Middle Atlantic AAU title in just its second year of competition and defending the title the following season. It refers to a summer meet when West Chester finished third, bested only by teams from New York and Chicago. There were only four of us — Kathy in high jump and hurdles, Lois Dawson in the 100- and 200-meter dashes, Beverly Pritchett in the 400 and me in the shot put and discus.

The article notes the widely held belief at that time that "except for an occasional Wilma Rudolph, U.S. girls are unwilling to make the sacrifices necessary for success in international track and field competition. There are 20 girls in West Chester, Chester County, who dispute this view."

Girls and women were always underestimated when it came to being athletes, wanting to compete and how hard they would train. I was fortunate to train under Mr. Facciolli, a father excited to coach girls in track and field who pushed us to be successful.

Yet I knew I could improve. If I had better technique, I would be stronger at the discus. I wanted to get better but didn't know how. Years later in a college biodynamics class, I was able to see my movement throwing the shot by having someone film me. They broke down the tape so I could see everything I was doing. I could see how I was moving across the ring and where I was losing momentum and power. I would have been a sponge for that type of information as a teenager.

I set records for West Chester and later the Delaware Track & Field Club in both shot and discus. A May 6, 1966, article in the *Delaware News Journal* refers to my throw of 42 feet, 3½ inches in the shot at a Middle Atlantic Association AAU meet as the top indoor mark in the nation. I don't know how long I held that mark, but it belonged to me for a while.

When I'd compete in meets in Wilmington, Delaware, a few of my friends would ride the 20 or so miles from West Chester with me. Most of those meets were weekend evenings when it was cooler. Afterward, we'd stop at Jimmy John's Pipin' Hot Sandwiches, the place with the electric trains, for the best hotdogs I ever tasted.

Without a true field events coach, I had to be creative in finding ways to perfect my movement. Credit Dad for passing along some of his handiness. I wrapped a small apparatus around the handle of a door at home. It was a cylinder that had a rope through it. I could dial it in one direction to add resistance. I tied my discus on the end of the rope. Pulling that rope all the way through with my hand on the discus helped me work on my follow-through.

My nerves often got the best of me. Sometimes I'd tighten up right before it was time to compete and that affected my throws. It cost me a lot of distance.

I was in high school when I was invited to compete in Madison Square Garden for what was one in a series of American-Russian track and field meets. Those of us representing the United States were on a bus, and when we got there, we were ushered to a room in a building next to the Garden. The room was full of medical personnel. I was told to open my mouth, and a medical technician took a stick and scraped the inside of my jaw. They sealed the sample in a container and we returned to the bus. That was the beginning of gender testing. Afterward, we were able to go into the Garden.

What a thrill! The track initially was full of hurdles. Sprinters warmed up in the infield. Fans were waving American flags. The whole building vibrated with energy. I was in awe to experience an event like this. USA vs. Russia. It was just amazing to be part of something that big.

I was inside the Garden warming up in the biggest indoor arena I had ever been in. I tossed the shot and my ball rolled. As I walked to pick it up, I heard this agitated voice:

"Move out! Move out!"

I turned around to see this giant Russian woman throw the shot as far as mine had rolled. That was something of a reality check. I stared at her. She was so broad. Her hair was pulled into a tight bun. She didn't crack a smile.

I thought right then and there — I'll never be able to get that big. That was my introduction to Tamara Press, who was a three-time gold medalist in the Olympics. Many believed her to be a man. She retired when sex verification became mandatory, though she insisted all along she was female.

After that experience, the discus became my focus. I was better at it than the shot because of my quickness. I remember being at a big meet, a qualifying meet of some kind, and I saw this strange older woman who looked like a detective. She wore a big trench coat, the collar way up. Her hair was white — maybe it was a blond wig on her head. Her lips were painted fire-engine red.

After warming up, I sat down on an embankment and she started talking to me. She was Stella Walsh, renowned for being the fastest woman in the world, known for setting world records and recording false starts at a time when runners weren't disqualified for them. She won gold in the 100 meters for Poland in the 1932 Olympics and was so versatile that she was dubbed the "female Jim Thorpe." Years later, records showed she had male parts, but I didn't know any of that when she struck up a conversation with me.

As I sat watching another woman warm up on discus, Stella said, "She is *my* player." She started filling my head with how great a thrower the woman I would be competing against was. She went on and on. I watched her throw as Stella kept feeding me stuff. By the time I got into the ring, I was no good. Done before I started. I don't know where I placed, but I was done. When I sat in the stands later, other athletes began saying the same thing. Stella Walsh was messing with all of us young throwers to pump up the athletes she coached.

Although she looked really old to me, I watched her compete that day in what was called a special event — "the great Stella Walsh versus today's great sprinters." At that time, Stella Walsh looked like she could be 90 years old. She hand-picked who she ran against, including one field event athlete, an older former athlete and one young runner. I watched her false start over and over. She'd step out of the blocks early, and then jog around and take her time. She did that three times! She was psyching out her competitors. Finally, she stayed in the block, and at the sound of the gun, sprinted down the track, her white mane blowing in the wind. She won! I was flabbergasted, unsure of what I was seeing. I wish I could have watched it over again, but we didn't have phones in our hands to record things back then.

I returned to New York another time, with my English teacher and her husband as my chaperones, and was at an outdoor meet when I got the chance to see Al Oerter, the four-time Olympic discus champion, throw.

After the meet, my chaperones went up to him and talked to him about their young thrower — me.

I met him and we talked for a few minutes, and he surprised me by saying, "If you can find a way to stay up here for a week, I'd be more than happy to work with you."

My chaperones found me a place to stay. I knew I had to do this. Coaching in field events for women was practically nonexistent back then. I couldn't believe Al Oerter wanted to work with me.

Al met me at an outdoor track every day after work and threw with me. I was nervous, but he was there faithfully. I would try to mimic his body movements, but I didn't totally understand how to use my hips and legs to get more power into my throw. I appreciated what he was giving me, but I needed more time. I was still in high school.

In the end, he told me I had potential but I needed a coach. I would love to have had someone with experience work one-on-one with me. I definitely felt positive reinforcement after working out with Al. At the end of the week, he mentioned something else.

"If you ever get to Kansas, look up my college coach, Bill Easton."

Easton was the track and cross country coach at the University of Kansas, where in his 18 years there, his teams won 39 conference championships.

I listened and told Al thank you. "*Where the heck is Kansas?*" I thought.

Chapter VII

Baby Girl

When one door closes, another door opens. God makes a way where there doesn't seem to be one.

W**hile I'm** writing my life story now, part of the process in doing so reminds me that in the early years of my life I was a closed book. I am a shy person, uncomfortable with revealing too much about myself. In many ways, I lived a double life as a teenager. Nobody outside of my close family and a few neighbors knew what my life looked like when I turned out the lights at night.

That was intentional. I didn't want anyone judging me for my limitations. I didn't want anyone to have that opportunity. I could relate to Butchie needing to do pushups on the floor after that surgery to remove bullets from his chest. He didn't want to surrender control. Like my brother, I didn't want to let circumstances define who I was. I wanted to be the one in charge of my life and my future.

But when you're a little girl, you're not in charge.

I was molested again and again when I was young. No one knew. I didn't know what to call what was happening to me. I didn't want to remember those times with men old enough to be my grandfather doing sickening things to me. I was scared. I was embarrassed. I was confused. I can't be certain when it all started. I didn't want to remember but I couldn't forget.

My earliest memory of it is being lifted high on one of the boxes in Dad's shed with my legs dangling. I wasn't even in the first grade. I remember this man touching his private parts and mumbling something to me. I thank God he did not penetrate me. I thank God none of them penetrated me. They would rub their penises against me or have me touch them.

Who were these men? Remember, Dad was up in age. Many of his friends were older than him. They would stop by and drink a bottle of beer or swallow a shot of sherry. Some of the men were looking for work and wanted to find out if Dad had something for them to do. I would be in the shed getting something for Dad, only to turn around and suddenly a man would be standing there. None of the men ever spent long touching me because they knew Pop would come looking for me.

I didn't know how to tell Mom or Dad what they did. I couldn't find the words. So I stayed silent. Instinctively, I knew if Mom or Dad found out about it, they would have shot the men dead.

As I got older, I made sure to stay out of reach of any of the men who wanted to grope me. As an adult, it was difficult for me to trust men. I had to take time to be sure they meant well. Unfortunately, that wasn't the end of having to protect myself against uninvited advances.

At 14 years old, my world changed. I became a mother.

Mom moved us closer to the center of town, and my new schoolmates at West Chester Junior High School exposed me to a faster life. I soon realized I had been i0solated living on Bolmar Street. West Chester Junior High and West Chester High were in the same building, so as a seventh-grader I was going to school with juniors and seniors. I didn't realize how much Dad tried to protect us until I started going to a school where I saw a different world. I was told I was "country." Too country. I didn't smoke. Or curse.

The new crowd I met teased me about how I talked and how I dressed, about not having any real experience with cigarettes and alcohol or with boys. During my first two years in junior high, I was proud I had made the honor roll a few times. Then the new kids I met made fun of me for being so conscientious about schoolwork. They thought I was too serious, that I raised my hand too much. Many of the kids who made fun of me were Black, and they'd say, "Oh, she thinks she's so smart." I stopped participating in the classroom as much.

One boy remarked that my butt was so high it was sitting on my back, so he came up with "Swayback" as my nickname and it stuck. I didn't like that name for a long time; I finally got comfortable with it when they dropped the "back" and started calling me "Sway." Today many friends still refer to me as Sway.

I never felt like I fit in. When I look back, I realize I was being bullied. Somehow, I ended up falling in with a group of older girls. We all lived close to one another. There were sisters named Dodi and Carolyn, who were the leaders, along with Janie and Earlene. They had the idea of starting a singing group. It took a while to settle on a name, but we all agreed on the Delvatones. I always thought I could sing, going back to when I was that little girl Mom left in the car while she shopped for groceries.

We found some songs and worked on our harmony. Janie was a baritone. I was an alto. Our harmonies did not always blend well. She would get angry and tell me I was out of tune, but it was definitely Janie who was off-key! I can laugh about it now, but back then it was serious. Most of our backup sound was doo-wop. Our footwork was the basic shuffle. One of the songs I liked was "A Million to One," and that was the one song I thought I should have led on. But no, Dodi sang lead. We sang at community center contests all wearing the same outfit, a white blouse with a round collar and a plaid kilt skirt. Thank goodness I was still working at the grocery store because each of us had to buy our own. We looked sharp.

We always finished second in the contests behind Barbara Watkins, who later became a dear friend of mine and went on to sing in nightclubs in Philadelphia.

There was something about Janie. I wanted to be better friends, but she always seemed angry. One day, Janie tried to get me to smoke at the back side of the school. She knew where to go to light up a cigarette at school. I never wanted to smoke. Thinking about it made me sick to my stomach. But when you're new somewhere, you don't want to stand out. I didn't want to be different. I wanted to fit in. Janie and I were outside the school one day when she lit a cigarette.

"Take a puff!" she urged, handing it to me.

It was in my hands before I knew it. Wouldn't you know that I drew on it and inhaled the smoke at the exact moment a teacher walked out of the school building? Janie turned around and ran away. There I am, standing with a lighted cigarette. Then the teacher did something I'll never forget. He turned his back and said, "I don't know what you have in your hand, but I suggest you throw it away."

I did just that. That teacher never told on me. I was so grateful. I never wanted to be in trouble, and I never wanted the school to tell Mom and Dad.

One day, out of the blue, Janie asked me to go on a double date to a drive-in movie with her and her new boyfriend. I couldn't believe she was asking *me* to do something with *her*. I thought she was actually being nice to me. I thought about letting Mom know what I was doing and where I was going, but she was working late and I knew when she got home she would have to look after my little sisters, so I just went.

Janie's boyfriend, Ike, was a man, enlisted in the Army, and so was his brother, Ira, my date. They both served in Vietnam. Janie was a senior in high school and I was 13, although I was tall for my age and most certainly looked older.

The whole thing made me uncomfortable from the beginning. I had no confidence in that setting and was trying to be someone I was not. I fought off Ira's advances in the back seat. Up front, it became pretty clear that Janie was really involved with her boyfriend. At some point, I realized she was having sex with him while I was in the back seat with Ira. I'm screaming inside, "Oh, my God!" It was absolutely a shock.

Then Janie asked me to go with her on another double date to a house party outside of West Chester. She needed someone to hang around with Ira again while she was with Ike. Was it peer pressure I felt? I had never been to a house party.

I agreed, not knowing how to say no. We went to the party, which was packed, and I was really out of my element. I didn't know anyone except Janie, Ike and Ira. A bunch of kids were slow dancing to loud music. I didn't drink but once again I felt pressured, pushed into drinking beer. It didn't take much to get me high.

The four of us were on our way home, but we ended up in a park. The others had vanished and I was left alone with Ira. His hands were on me again, Only this time it was with more aggression. I was telling him no and pushing him away, but I wasn't in control. I knew Ira was going much further than the first time. I felt a burning sensation and then pain inside. My head was spinning. I felt intoxicated. I remember Ira saying something about how he was unable to have babies. I found water nearby, in a pond I think, and tried to get rid of whatever was in my body once it was over. I wanted to clean myself up. That was the end of it, I thought.

I didn't go out with Janie or Ira again. He came by the house constantly letting me know he really liked me. Mom met him, but she certainly didn't know what had happened. I didn't want to see him. I was never going out with him again.

Then I missed my period. The next month I missed it again. I finally felt I had to say something to my mother, and we went to see a doctor. I was sitting beside my mother when the doctor looked at her and said, "She's three months pregnant." I think Mom had suspected that even though we never talked about what happened that night with Ira.

I began to cry. Mom put her arms around me and held me. When we got home, I remember Mom rocking me in her lap. I know she was angry, but I felt her sadness. She let me know over and over again that she loved me.

"It's going to be OK," she whispered.

I told her the baby's father was Ira, but I didn't disclose any details. The next time he came by, Mom got up in his face in the backyard. She jumped all over him. She was cursing and threatening him. He stopped coming by for a long time.

Then everything got worse.

I was sitting in a classroom one day when my teacher heard a tap on the door. She went to talk with the person, and then I heard my name being called. The teacher motioned for me to take my books and leave the room.

I didn't know what was going on. I knew I hadn't done anything wrong, but I was very nervous. Once I was outside the classroom walking down the hall, I was told, "I understand you're pregnant. You cannot stay in school."

There were only a few months left in the school year, but they wouldn't let me finish ninth grade because I was pregnant. I don't know how they found out. Crushing doesn't begin to describe how I felt walking out of the school by myself.

I walked home to let Mom know, and that was really hard. I hated being out of school. I hated that everyone else was in school and I wasn't. I hated that people knew I was pregnant.

I don't think Dad knew any of what was happening to me — no longer being in school and certainly not about being pregnant. Whenever I would go to see him, I wore a long-sleeve white men's shirt over my jeans. By wearing my shirt out, I didn't think he noticed. I could button up my jeans almost to the top even when I was eight months along because I carried my baby high. I can't tell you how Dad found out I was pregnant, but when he did, he didn't come looking for me. He took a shotgun and went hunting for Ira.

I saw Dad the day he went to meet Ira, who was coming from uptown. They met in front of a bar. I was on my way to see Dad. I was about half a block away when I saw them standing in the street, facing each other. I stopped and stood still so they didn't see me.

I could see everything. I could also hear everything.

Dad was yelling at him and had the shotgun pointed right in his face. Ira looked scared. Then I heard him say these words to my father.

"Do you think I was the only one?"

Do you think I was the only one?

I never forgot those words. Ever. My father no longer knew what my life was like, but Ira knew he was lying and said that to protect himself. Ira knew I was a virgin.

At 14 years old, I made a decision right then and there that defined how I lived the rest of my life. I vowed that I would never ask anybody for anything. I would never, ever ask Ira for anything. I would find a way to protect myself, to protect the "little Marian" within me. I turned on my heels and walked away. My childhood was over. I would find a way to make it.

Mom and Dad never made me feel it was my fault. All they told me was that they loved me. There was never a doubt that I was going to keep the baby and raise it.

I was having bad pains at home every so often. Then they started coming more frequently. My mother told me what was happening, and it was time to go to the hospital.

Grandmum's twin, Aunt Emma, worked at the hospital. She found me and sat with me, trying to help me through the labor pains. Mom held my hand. I had to have my water broken and a catheter put in. That was excruciating. When they finally took me to deliver, they gave me gas, but I was still aware of them working on me. I could feel a tearing, pecking sensation.

"You're cutting me," I screamed.

Then they knocked me out.

Six-and-a-half-pound Marian Josephine Washington was born in Memorial Hospital on June 13, 1961. I wanted to name her after my mother, my father and my sister we lost, Josephine, as well as myself. It was the perfect name that touched four lives.

Josie was a beautiful baby. She had thick eyebrows, large eyes and a head full of curly hair.

I wanted to breastfeed at least for one day so someday I could tell her I did. The nurses let me do that. Then they wrapped my breasts tight against my chest until my milk dried up. It was painful and took more than a few days. I knew I wanted to go back to school, and the idea of pumping breast milk wasn't something anybody talked about back then.

Everybody was crazy about Josie from the start. I can see my mother now with Josie in a baby carriage pushing it through the alley. My father just loved her, too. Ira started to come around to see her. He adored Josie, and she ended up being his only child. I let my mom deal with Ira. I was determined because of what he said to my father that I would never have any kind of emotional contact with him. Even though he showed a lot of love for Josie and showed that he cared about me after she was born, I was so hurt inside and so ashamed. I wanted to tell my father that Ira was not telling the truth, but I didn't know how to bring it up.

Josie was a really good baby. She knew me as Mommy. I would sing and play the piano for her. I made up my own songs and wrote my own music at 15. I loved holding her. There was never a question in my mind that she would be with me going forward — wherever I was. It wouldn't be easy; I knew that. But I knew wherever I went in life, Josie would go, too.

By the fall, another junior high school was built — Stetson Junior High, and I would go there for one year. For a long time, I never mentioned to anyone I had a child — not then and not later either.

As difficult a time as that was for me, I grew more determined than ever that I would find a way to make it in this world. Everything happens for a reason. When one door closes, another door opens. God makes a way where there doesn't seem to be one. Had I not gotten pregnant, I wouldn't have needed to repeat the ninth grade. I am so very lucky that I did.

That's where I met someone who would change my life forever.

Chapter VIII

Stiff Upper Back

At no time in my life did I hesitate to speak up if I felt something was wrong. I didn't know that I would become an advocate for change, let alone a pioneer.

Ruth Redding graduated Phi Beta Kappa from Hunter College, completed degrees at the Philadelphia School of Osteopathy at Temple University and was a Fulbright Scholar at the London School of Economics.

When I went to Stetson to repeat ninth grade after Josie was born, I met Mrs. Redding, the only Black teacher I ever had.

She was beautiful and she was brilliant. Mrs. Redding went on to teach in the West Chester Area School District for 38 years, and whenever she spoke up about anything, the school board listened.

Everybody listened. Everybody watched when she walked into a room. I had never met anyone like her.

After a few days in her math class, Mrs. Redding pulled me aside. She asked me what I thought about what I was learning.

"It's pretty easy," I admitted.

Most Black students at Stetson were placed in vocational classes to prepare for a trade or blue-collar job. Without my asking, Mrs. Redding made sure I was placed in her algebra class. Maybe she saw my seriousness. Maybe she knew about my having a child so young, although she didn't hear it from me. As soon as

I got back to school, I was pulled into an office and told not to talk about the things I'd experienced. Translation: Don't tell the other girls you've had sex and have a child. I had no intention of talking about it anyway, but it was yet another reminder that I was different and judged as tarnished in some way.

Once Mrs. Redding pulled me aside, there was no question she knew I could achieve at the highest level if given the chance. At the end of the school year, she helped me fill out my schedule for my tenth-grade year. She placed me in all college-preparatory classes.

After my first day at West Chester High, she called my house to talk to me, wanting to know how my classes went. That seemed so incredible. A teacher calling *me* at home! When I told her I had been placed in vocational classes again — typing, sewing, home economics, those types of things — she didn't say much.

At school the next day, I was immediately called to the principal's office. I was nervous because I didn't know what it was about. "Sit down," he told me, while he scooted his chair from behind his desk to face me. Then he asked me if I thought I could do college prep work. I quietly answered, "Yes."

The principal moved his chair back behind his desk, and after he looked down at some papers, he looked at me and said, "I'm afraid all those classes are full. You will not be able to get into those classes this year."

Shortly after I got home from school, Mrs. Redding called. She wanted to know how it went in school. I told her what happened. She was quiet at first and then said, "Don't worry. I will take care of it."

The very next morning, I was called to the guidance counselor's office. She handed me my new class schedule — all college prep classes. I stayed in those types of classes until I graduated in 1965.

Before meeting Mrs. Redding, I had become accustomed to trying to achieve on my own. As an athlete, I taught myself how to play all the sports I excelled in later. I was usually by myself shooting the basketball or throwing the discus and shot, trying to get better. No one in my neighborhood who looked like me talked about college.

Once Mrs. Redding became part of my life, I wanted to do well for her as much as for myself. She took me under her wing. She found tutors when I needed them. She gave me words of encouragement when I was struggling. As I look back, I realize that Mrs. Redding and probably all the other teachers in the school district knew I had a child. Many years later, Mrs. Redding told me that right after I was dismissed from school for being pregnant, a new program started for young, expecting girls. They no longer had to leave school because they were pregnant. They could continue their education.

While I hated having to repeat a year, if I hadn't, I would not have met someone who saw that I was more than a kid with athletic talents. I rarely talked about my athletic achievements with Mrs. Redding. It was always about my education. It wasn't until I started working at Kansas as an administrator and coach that I realized Mrs. Redding was following my career. When I got the chance to go home to West Chester I would visit her apartment, where she pulled out newspaper clippings about me and my teams. A couple of times she mailed me articles on young talent in the Philly area. She would address letters to "Dr. Marian Washington" after I was awarded an honorary doctorate from West Chester University in May 1998.

Through Mrs. Redding I found inspiration. I could once again start believing that I was capable. That hadn't happened in school before. I was capable of going to college and earning a degree. Wow!

When you are young, so many things affect you. I can remember sitting at my desk in grade school, where I might have been the only Black child in the classroom. There were hardly any Black kids in all of West Goshen Elementary School. My history teacher told us to open our books and turn to a certain page. When I looked at what was on the page, my mind froze. It was difficult to look up at the teacher. Pictures of Africans were in the book. One man had a plate in his mouth and another had a bone through his nose. I can't remember what was being taught. I found myself unsure and a little embarrassed. Is that how white people saw us? Not once did I learn about the African kings and queens. Not once did I hear about how smart and creative Africans are. I left class not sure of who I was or where I was from.

Everybody in my class saw those pictures, and I thought, "This is not right." Those were the only pictures representing Black people, and I knew when everybody in my class looked at them, they related them to me. That's when I realized my people, Black people, are treated differently.

But here was Mrs. Redding, who presented a powerful, positive image of Black America. She wore traditional African dresses with pride. She kept her hair natural, as did her three young daughters. That was important in retrospect because back in the 1960s, Black people struggled within their own race. If your hair was straight and your skin was lighter, that was considered more "acceptable" in society. We had racism within our own race. A lot of that changed when James Brown sang, "Say it Loud - I'm Black and I'm Proud!" This became my mantra. There were t-shirts and stickers on cars that Black is beautiful!

I didn't think about color or prejudice as a little girl. I watched the way Mom and Dad treated people and heard how they talked about others. They didn't have a prejudiced bone in their bodies. We lived in a small community of white families, Black families and Puerto Rican families, and all of us got along well.

I believe I was in first grade hiding under a bed or maybe a couch in someone else's house when I heard fighting between a husband and wife. I can't remember who they were, but their language scared me. They cursed at each other. The words were horrible. They were words I didn't say, words I had never heard.

I heard the man shout, "You Black bitch," and something about his wife being a Black whore. That was the first time I thought about my color and how it made me different.

As I grew older, walking to junior high school along Gay Street, carloads of white boys yelled slurs out of the windows as they rode by. They didn't have the courage to stop.

*Nig**r.*

Your mama's a bitch.

*Nig**r.*

I heard those ugly words smack in my face. In the beginning, I didn't say anything. Eventually, I got tired and started shouting back, "So is your mother!"

I developed a stiff upper back, and I kept walking. I kept walking because I had places to go.

Sometimes when I was by myself, I wrote down how I felt. But I never got far in the story. I made a promise to myself: I wasn't going to let anyone see me cry if I could help it. I never told my parents about any of it. Once again, I didn't know how. I didn't know what to say. I realized there was nothing they could do, and they had so many other things to worry about.

Injustice of any kind to anyone has always bothered me. In elementary school I remember a smart, shy white girl named Tina who was being bullied during recess by a boy. I don't know what got into me because he was much bigger than me, but I ran down to where he was on the playground, hit him in the stomach and ran away. Recess was over and my class was lining up to go inside. But the line moved slowly. The bully caught up with me and punched me in the arm. It hurt, but I wasn't going to let him know that. I don't think Tina ever thanked me, but it didn't matter. At least the bully knew what he did was wrong.

I had an awareness of the Civil Rights movement and the disparities in the way society treated Black and white people.

Black people weren't considered for the better jobs. Black students who didn't have a Mrs. Redding in their lives often dropped out of high school. College wasn't talked about and certainly not encouraged.

In 1963, I was sitting in a high school classroom when news broke that John F. Kennedy had been shot and killed. They let school out early, and in a daze I wanted to find Mom. She was working quite a way from school. I found myself walking until I got there. Mom loved our President Kennedy. She sat me down in the house where she was taking care of an elderly lady. We turned on the TV and watched an account of the assassination over and over again. It was awful.

Kennedy had given Black people some hope in the way he wanted to govern this country. And we lost that. Five years later, I had the same sick feeling when Martin Luther King Jr. was assassinated. I was just stunned. I couldn't believe it. I felt my heart was bleeding. I had listened to his speeches, especially "I Have a Dream," over and over again. He meant so much to Black people and to everyone who wanted to make this world a better place. The day he died, I was glued to the television, watching every broadcast I could about what happened with tears in my eyes.

Two months later when Robert Kennedy was shot and killed it seemed as if the world was falling off a cliff.

My foray into social activism began thanks to a very dear friend of mine, Mary Jo Hetzel, a brilliant woman and transformative voice in urban education. Mary Jo was the founding director of the Boston Campus of Springfield College School of Human Services, which primarily served low-income adult students of color.

Mary Jo and I were athletic opponents in high school. She was white with reddish blond hair and a solid frame. Her family was wonderful to me, so open-minded without a hint of prejudice. She can recall our time on the same basketball court. I remember us as field hockey foes. We also were on opposing teams in fast-pitch softball. We didn't speak to one another, but we competed like mad against each other.

I'm going to share Mary Jo's precise words here because she was willing to write down her recollections of the early days of our friendship.

Mary Jo called me Sway and still does. Marian sounds too formal to her. Her senior year she was the female Athlete of the Year at Westtown, a Quaker boarding school in West Chester. If you remember, I thought I had won the same award at my high school, only it went to my gym teacher's sister.

In Mary Jo's words:

> *Sway was the most fabulous athlete I had ever, ever come across, male or female. I didn't know her name in high school. But I knew she was the one I had to stop because if I didn't, West Chester would win. She was also pegged on me. I was crazy about basketball, and from a very early age I had a real thing about racial and social injustice. From childhood, it was clear to me Black people were being treated poorly. I would grab the sleeves of adults around me, people my family knew, and say, "Why isn't somebody doing something about this?"*
>
> *My last week at Westtown was finals week and we had some rigid rules. You were not permitted to have the light on in your room past 10 p.m., particularly during finals week because they were worried everyone would pull an all-nighter. If you had a light on past 10 the week of finals, you would not graduate. You had to make it up in the following term. That's how seriously they took it.*
>
> *So, early in the day at Westtown, we had a celebration of awards in a huge auditorium. There was an award for Most Valuable Athlete, and I won it. It was the*

last week of school. I had been at loggerheads with the headmaster for years because while I was winning, I was also pushing social and racial justice and anti-Vietnam war stuff. He hated me. The athletic award was a huge trophy, and the entire place went nuts when I won. All these students were screaming and hollering, which was odd because I didn't have any dates in high school or many friends! I was as happy as a human being can be.

That night I went to an adult Civil Rights group meeting, which I had been doing for months. I'd sit quietly among the adults and was being tutored about every single issue of racial injustice. Somebody got up and said that very day at the high school in West Chester, Marian Washington, the greatest athlete of all time at that school, was denied the greatest athlete award there because of fucking color. I realized that was the girl I was constantly competing against.

I went from being on top of the world to being so sad. I felt like it was unjust. It was so bitterly ridiculous. It was so awful to deny someone their due. It's worse than stealing from someone or punching them. It's taking away who you are as a person.

I felt horrible. Horrible. I knew she was 10 times, 100 times the athlete I was. Here I was, being held up and honored in my school, and she got nothing. I went back to my room, and it was late, lights out. I had my flashlight and went under the covers, and I wrote a letter to Marian. I told her, "Everybody who knows you knows you are the greatest athlete they ever met. No one can take that away from you. You are much greater than all the rest of us. We all

> *know that. We love you. We honor you. This is a total miscarriage of justice." Everything I felt was heartfelt and strong.*
>
> *I gave the letter to one of the leaders of the Civil Rights group and they gave it to her. A day or two later I got a letter back from her, thanking me for acknowledging what she was going through. That started our friendship.*

Mary Jo and I became great friends. We met and would walk arm and arm, me Black and her white, back when people, especially women, didn't do that.

Mary Jo shared one more story that also touches me, something I didn't know about until I started the process of writing my life story. I'm again sharing her words about one of the times she spent the night at my house.

> *We would wake up in the morning, and I was hungry. Finally, after some hours, I'd say, "Do you want to get something to eat?"*
>
> *Sway would say, "OK." And we would go down the street and she'd buy a bag of potato chips. It would be 11:30 in the morning. I was starving. Her breakfast was a bag of chips at lunchtime. Sometimes she only got a meal a day. I learned from Sway what it was really like to be poor.*

Mary Jo reaffirmed what Mom and Dad had taught me. Don't judge people by the color of their skin. Mary Jo fought against discrimination that didn't affect her. She took me to my first Civil Rights meeting, where I heard Bayard Rustin speak. He was a key adviser to Martin Luther King, the deputy director of the March on Washington and also a graduate of West Chester High School well before my time.

I remember all of us standing in front of this real estate agent's home for a protest. Back then there was discrimination in housing. Black people had a difficult time renting a nice place. Too many people didn't want a Black person buying a home in their neighborhood. We joined hands and sang "We Shall Overcome." That was the first time I had gotten involved in that way.

At that point in my life, the goals I had were athletic ones and to get a college degree. But I've always been a fighter. I always felt strongly about doing right. At no time in my life did I hesitate to speak up if I felt something was wrong. I didn't know that I would become an advocate for change, let alone a pioneer.

As things happened along my journey and I knew I could find a way to make a difference, I went about doing it as best I could. Sometimes I would get knocked down because I was outnumbered, especially if there were a lot of men who wanted their agendas addressed first.

I knew that to change the way things are, to make an impact, takes hard work and determination. That was part of what Mrs. Redding instilled in me.

As a college coach, when I would go to the homes of parents to recruit, I couldn't boast about the facilities at Kansas compared with many other programs, but I proudly talked about Kansas being an excellent academic institution. I was able to sell myself, to make a commitment to parents that as long as their daughters wanted an education, I was going to make that happen. That was more important than anything else.

Mrs. Redding didn't just send me off to high school. She followed up with me when I was there. When she realized how hard I was working to make extra money, she had me work for her, ironing and babysitting. She provided me with tutoring when I needed it. She was a counselor to me as well as a friend.

I was that person to my student-athletes, doing what I could to help them adjust and become successful in their journey. If you played at Kansas or on any of the international teams I would go on to coach, you were always my player. I was always your coach.

Likewise, no matter how old I got, I was still a student to Mrs. Redding, until she died in 2005. She was always my teacher, always Mrs. Redding – never Ruth – to me. I'll never forget her or the indelible mark she left on my life.

Chapter IX

A Collegiate First

I had a natural instinct for the ball and got a thrill hitting the boards, pulling down a rebound. I was never intimidated by someone else's size. You had to be a heck of a lot taller than me to outrebound me if we were going after the same missed shot.

My **pregame** meal was a bologna and cheese sandwich I carried in a brown bag from home. We wore gold tunics with purple numbers that looked like a one-piece short dress with bloomers underneath. Just about everyone carried a white jacket to travel to away games. I had to borrow one because I never had my own. I wore No. 5, but the important number on March 22, 1969, was 1.

My team, West Chester State College, won the first women's national basketball championship, a 16-team invitational sponsored by the Commission on Intercollegiate Athletics for Women (CIAW). After Western Carolina scored the first basket, we led the rest of the way to win 56-39. We played in front of a crowd of 2,000 in our home gym, Hollinger Field House, where fans filled an entire side of bleachers.

The CIAW became the Association for Intercollegiate Athletics for Women (AIAW), the precursor to women being recognized by the NCAA. Yes, women's basketball *did* exist before women's sports were part of the NCAA, even though the record books say otherwise.

It's a forgotten history. We often talk about standing on the shoulders of those before us, yet overlook how or when things started and who earned the right to be recognized for what they've achieved. I have stood on a soapbox throughout my career trying to recognize those who came before. I give a lot of credit to the Amateur Athletic Union (AAU). Many of the players and coaches today are unaware of the significant role the AAU played in the growth of the sport. The AAU sent women's teams abroad to play, and prepared a United States women's team to compete in the Olympics in 1972. If it weren't for the AAU sponsoring a women's division in basketball, we would not be where we are today.

I saw opportunity through basketball in college that I didn't see in high school. As much as I loved track and field, basketball became my focus as a collegian.

Those were different times for sure. West Chester played Iowa in the national semifinals, and we thought it was weird to see women wearing shorts instead of tunics. It might be hard to believe today, but seeing women playing in shorts was a topic we chatted about as a team. Not that tunics were convenient. When I was on the free-throw line, preparing to rebound a missed shot, I tried to push some of the tunic between my legs so that extra material didn't get in the way of my stance. That seemed to work well for me, as funny as it might sound today.

West Chester played the rover game: two forwards on the offensive end, two guards on the defensive end and two rovers. None of the players, except one of the rovers, could cross midcourt. I was a forward. Back then they thought women didn't have the stamina to play the full-court game, and I knew that was ridiculous. Men assumed that because physically we didn't have the same strength as they did, we didn't have endurance of any kind.

We were brash, bold, confident and unstoppable.

Coming out of the locker room the day of the championship, we walked down some steps onto the indoor track in the corner of where we would enter the court. I led us in a singsong chant: "Zoom, zoom," and then three times fast, "Zoom, zoom, zoom!" My teammates shouted, "We are a mighty, mighty team!" We were ready to go!

No TV cameras recorded anything, but news of our national championship victory made Page 77 of *The Philadelphia Inquirer*, where we got seven paragraphs the next day under the headline, "West Chester Wins Title in Girls' Tourney." The term *women's basketball* didn't exist. There was just *basketball* – what men played. The media referred to AAU and college women's basketball as *girls basketball.*

All of us wanted to stay on the court after the game. So many parents and children were there to cheer us on, including Mom, Josie and one of my sisters. Officials presented trophies and announced an all-tournament team, which I was disappointed not to make. Everybody celebrated with sandwiches and drinks. Iowa Wesleyan, led by Betty Grundberg, who once scored 50 points in a game, beat Iowa in the consolation game.

Winning a national championship represented a culmination not only for me, but for coach Carol Eckman, an assistant professor of health and physical education at West Chester. She had the foresight to organize a national tournament with the top college players, a movement no one but she was driving at the time. Carol was a pioneer in the game. The Women's Basketball Coaches Association presents the Carol Eckman Integrity in Coaching Award annually at the Final Four — an accolade I was honored to win in 1991. They call Coach Eckman "the Mother of National Collegiate Championships," and in 1999 she was rightly inducted with the inaugural class into the Women's Basketball Hall of Fame. Yet very few know Carol's name today. If the NCAA handed out a Carol Eckman Award after the national championship game, it would help our young fans and athletes appreciate her vision and better understand her impact on the history of the sport. We know who Naismith was. We know who Vince Lombardi was. How many know the name Carol Eckman?

Carol was a tall, slim, attractive woman with long arms. She wore glasses and had a quiet way about her, soft-spoken even. She was a ball of nerves; her hands always seemed to be trembling. She smoked quite a bit but never in front of us.

When she became the coach at West Chester my junior year, AAU Senior Nationals was the highest level of competition available to women. These were teams that played 30 or 40 games together a year, and unlike college, there was no cap on how many years a woman could play. Throughout the 1950s, a small private school in the Texas panhandle town of Plainview dominated nationally. The Wayland Baptist Flying Queens won 131 straight games from 1953 to 1957 and four national championships, and believe it or not, offered 13 full scholarships and air travel to road games. By the 1960s, Nashville Business College, distinguished by its satin jerseys with stars, would dominate, winning its first of 10 AAU national championships, including eight straight, beginning in 1962. Their most decorated star, Nera White, earned AAU All-American honors 15 consecutive times and was inducted into the Naismith Memorial Basketball Hall of Fame in 1992.

Carol thought West Chester could compete with those teams and reach AAU Senior Nationals – until we lost a regional qualifying game in Washington, D.C. We played our opponent, an older and more experienced team, close, but they were better. It was heartbreaking at the time. That was the first and only time my father attended one of my games. I couldn't even speak. I was too upset. I walked outside to calm down before going back to find him. He was still sitting, waiting for me with a big smile on his face. He enjoyed watching our team and especially seeing me play for the first time. As much as I wanted to win, it was really special that he was there.

I can't remember many of the details of that night, but I cherish those moments with Dad.

When Carol and the rest of us left the gymnasium to drive back to West Chester, we discovered our vehicles had been vandalized. Some of our windows were smashed and our car doors were broken into. It was such a mess. I remember Carol being more upset than we were. We went through all of our gear and clothing to see what was missing. We were lucky only a few things were gone. On the way back, Carol decided, "Enough is enough. We're not going to do this anymore."

Carol planned to organize a national championship just for college women the next season. She had support within the physical education department but not throughout the university. A few of my teammates and I were interviewed for a *Philadelphia Inquirer* story looking back at that 1969 game, and we talked about the athletic department locking the administration doors during the tournament. Because of that, calls to report scores to the newspaper had to be made from pay phones on campus.

We were determined we were going to help Carol realize her dream completely. She was not only going to sponsor the first national collegiate tournament for women. We were going to win it for her.

West Chester won all of its regular-season games for a second straight season, playing close games only with Ursinus and Southern Connecticut State. Only four of our 10 opponents during that 1969 season reached 40 points. We dominated in the tournament, and Carol made sure the top teams were there. This was a national championship after all! We beat Northeastern by 46 in our first game, Lynchburg by 25 in our second and Iowa by 40 on the way to the final.

We were inducted as a team into the West Chester Hall of Fame in 2012.

West Chester advanced to the finals the next three years, though we didn't win it again. In 1972, the first year of AIAW play, they lost to Cathy Rush's Immaculata team, the Mighty Macs.

I think about Carol and her vision for college basketball. I think about my teammates and the commitment we made to each other, our university and our coach. It's a largely forgotten history. West Chester State, which is West Chester University today, deserves better. My teammates and Carol deserve to be remembered as the first national champions in the sport.

West Chester wasn't my first college. I spent three semesters at Cheyney State before transferring.

I have one funny memory about my time at Cheyney: My father had fixed me up this 1950-ish Ford to drive back and forth. Once you got off our main Highway 202 and turned toward Cheyney State, it was two-lane back roads. At the end of my freshman year, I was racing to get to school on time for my last final when I heard this terrible noise that got louder and louder. All of a sudden, my transmission fell to the ground. Cars were behind me, so I had to slowly coast to the side of the road. When I got out of the car I was in disbelief, seeing my transmission hanging by a wire, most of it lying on the road. I became frantic because I was already late and I really did not want to miss this last exam. I started pacing, trying to figure out what to do next, thinking that if I tried to walk the rest of the way I would not make it. But God is always on time. A car came by with some students, and they gave me a lift to campus. As soon as I got a chance, I called Dad and told him about the car. He found it and towed it away.

I played a year for Cheyney under Phoen Terrell, a beautiful middle-aged Black professor who coached basketball. Cheyney had one team of walk-ons as opposed to West Chester, which supported four women's basketball teams. Cheyney played against West Chester when I was there, but we didn't face its best team.

One day I went to Mrs. Terrell's office to talk to her about wanting to compete at the highest level possible. She supported my transferring to West Chester State. Many top female athletes in the state who wanted a degree in health and physical education or general education knew of West Chester's reputation for outstanding academics in addition to its strong athletic program for women. Physical education was going to be my major. I have to laugh at myself because as a child I wanted to grow up to be a nurse. That idea was completely gone! My interest changed to teaching.

One more historical note about Cheyney: Had I been born 13 years later, I'm guessing I would have stayed there for all four years. In 1982, a coach named C. Vivian Stringer took Cheyney to the NCAA Women's Final Four, a first and only for a Historically Black College or University (HBCU).

At West Chester, I tried out for the first team with confidence. Rarely was I going to be the leading scorer, but at 5-foot-9 I could play forward or post. I could defend any position. Defense came easy for me. I loved to rebound, and had great leaping ability. When you're young, you feel like you're flying. I had a natural instinct for the ball and got a thrill hitting the offensive boards, pulling down a rebound. I was never intimidated by someone else's size. You had to be a heck of a lot taller than me to outrebound me if we were going after the same missed shot.

I remember Carol introducing me to everyone. She was going to let the team decide whether they wanted to add me. After running a few drills with them, the captain went over to Carol and said, "She's on."

My college basketball experience would be hard for anyone playing now to visualize.

I felt as if I had one life on campus and another off it. Today, college teams say they're a family. It wasn't like that when I played. There was no pregame meal. Sometimes I had something to eat on the way, but a lot of times I didn't eat anything. When we went to an opponent's gym to play, we rode a yellow school bus. We never spent the night anywhere. I never spent any time after practice or games with my teammates. We were close in the locker room and on the court but no one knew my life. I don't recall any of my teammates even knowing that I had a daughter.

Josie came to games when Mom could bring her. She would clap, but I didn't want her being too loud or running around. I knew where she sat in the stands, and I could give her the eye when I needed her to sit down. Then she stopped what she was doing to be the wonderful girl I knew she was.

I always held a job while I was in college. I'd usually go to work from 11 in the evening until 7 in the morning. I remember trying to get a job at Lasko, the fan-production company that had a manufacturing plant in West Chester. I wanted to work there because it was decent money, and I could walk there. They told me I was too educated.

Even though I wasn't one for needles, I walked to the blood bank to earn extra money. I would give blood, and if they mishandled it, they had to pay me extra because I was AB positive, a very rare and valuable blood type. That was always a good day.

I did anything I could to try to help Mom and support Josie. I had a job making life-saving vests of rubber that reminded me of the inner tube in a bicycle wheel. The vest fit over your head. I had to seal the edges around it with glue and smooth out any bubbles. If it had bubbles, it wasn't airtight. We submerged all the ones we finished in water. If there were any bubbles you had to take that vest back, break through the seam and start again. My God, that was such hard work! I had to start over with most of them. As you can imagine, I didn't stay in that job long!

I had another job at a plastics company that manufactured cups of all sizes. You had to examine the cups when they came out of a machine. If they were burnt, you discarded them. They came out so fast, it was hard to keep up. Remember "I Love Lucy" and the chocolates speeding onto the conveyor belt? That was me and the cups!

But that wasn't the worst part. I packed those cups in boxes that would be sent out. I always thought my legs were strong, but I admired my female coworkers. Many were in their 50s and 60s, and they could stand and bend over, reaching and packing cups all day. I remember thinking they had to have incredible endurance, a type of stamina I was not used to. I was an athlete, and I was the one struggling.

I got off work in time to get cleaned up and spend a little time with Josie. Then I headed out for class and practice or games if we had them. When I got back home, I saw Josie some more before it was time for her to go to bed and for me to go to work again. I slept very little. I always had trouble sleeping and still do. I tend to think I am going to miss something.

At one point, everything became too much. Managing my grades, finances, work, home life, sports and taking care of Josie was exhausting. I was hungry after games and went home to very little to eat. I had never talked with Carol about any of it, but one day I got enough nerve to confide in her. I was struggling to keep my grades up and I was often tired in practice. I could tell Carol was nervous, not knowing what I wanted to talk to her about. "You don't know what I'm having to do after I leave school," I finally said. I shared some of my challenges and mentioned Josie. She was definitely surprised, to say the least, especially when I said that most nights I worked an eight-hour shift that began at 11 p.m. Carol listened, but it was a lot for her to take in, and she could not offer much in response. I didn't need a problem solver, but I could have used encouragement. I don't know that Carol was equipped to deal with a player in my situation.

As a coach I found myself almost to a fault being available to my players and permitting them to talk to me about their challenges off the court. I had players scarred from things that happened when they were younger. I had kids who were homesick. Some dealt with family issues, and others struggled with academics. Only a few professors during my early days of coaching provided tutoring. I listened and tried to help as many as I could.

After my first year at West Chester, I realized I needed to get into an environment that would be more conducive to focusing on my classwork. I met some girls who lived in an apartment complex straight behind Mom's house. They needed a fourth roommate to share the rent. Being so close to home, I could easily get back to Josie, by then a bubbling 5-year-old who loved to ride her bicycle. Mom and my sisters helped keep her busy. I could only afford to live there for a year. Then I had to move back in with Mom.

I should have graduated in 1969, but Carol thought, since I transferred from Cheyney mid-semester, I could get an extra year to play. Unfortunately, the ruling came down after the fall semester that my collegiate playing days were over. That meant I lost the chance to graduate that fall. I was upset with Carol and hurt about how it happened. I thought she should have known for sure about that extra year before telling me to avoid taking classes I needed to graduate. It was one more thing to deal with. I could have been finished and on my way to something else.

Carol and I ended up meeting years later when she was recognized at the Women's Final Four. Time had softened that wound. After not seeing each other for some time, we had lunch together. She apologized for what happened, and that meant a lot.

By then I could say, "All is forgiven, let's move forward." I'm so glad we had the conversation. Carol died of cancer in 1985 at just 47 years old. She was one remarkable woman, an overlooked pioneer.

I didn't know it at the time, but a selection committee visited Hollinger Field House to watch us beat Western Carolina in that 1969 CIAW championship game.

I couldn't have guessed I was about to receive an invitation to try out for another team, one far better than the national champion West Chester Rams.

Chapter X

Olympic Dream

It was never in my DNA to give up. I wanted to be that person who persevered despite the obstacles, an example for my coaches and teammates and later my players and peers, to instill in them strength and determination to push forward past whatever adversity they were facing.

I **rarely treated** myself to new shoes, a luxury after growing up using newspapers to fill the holes in my annual pair of sneakers from Mom and Dad. But being invited to try out for a United States National Team seemed like a good reason to splurge.

The letter I received shortly after West Chester won the national championship was the kind of mail you dream about. Plans were in place for women's basketball to make its debut in the 1972 Olympics in Munich, Germany. I was one of 34 women invited to Ouachita Baptist University in Arkadelphia, Arkansas, in August 1969 to compete for 12 coveted spots on Team USA.

Wow! I had a chance to make a U.S. National Team. Oh, my God.

Once I got the invitation for the 10-day tryout, not making the all-tournament team after the national championship didn't hurt as much. This was bigger. So much bigger.

At the end of my college semester that spring, I was still working at the plastics company and needed to finish a handful of classes toward my bachelor's degree the next year. As much as I could, I would still donate blood — anything I could do to bring in money for Mom and Josie. Day-to-day life was a struggle. Mom still needed help with everything. Josie was growing up and needed more. There was never enough money for the essentials.

I didn't know it during the championship game, but the director of a Catholic community center, Doris Adams, brought some of her inner city kids from Washington, D.C., to watch us play. She thought all of us were good role models for the young girls. After the game, Doris talked to me and a few of my teammates about working at her center during the summer. I got an offer to coach basketball. My first coaching job!

Doris allowed me to stay in a room in her home for the days I worked in D.C., and I returned to West Chester on the weekends. I was excited to teach young children and enjoyed showing them basketball skills and relating those lessons to life. Some of the kids remembered seeing me play in the game, which was nice. Here I was working alongside experienced professionals, living in a place where I didn't have to worry about rent, utilities and food. I thought, "Look at me! It's happening. Things are changing. I'm experiencing the kind of life I want to have."

Josie didn't like it when I left, but I told her, "Mommy's going to go to make some money for us, and I'll be back." She stayed with Mom, and my sisters helped out a lot.

When I got the letter inviting me to the Olympic Trials, everyone from the center was encouraging, especially Doris. She was an older woman who served in the military before becoming director of the center. Doris became a good friend who helped me make the 1,000-mile drive to the Olympic tryouts in her light blue Thunderbird. Off we went, the farthest I had ever been away from home.

The Midwest seemed so flat. With the windows down to catch the breeze, I looked around and saw rows and rows of corn and wheat that looked like art. The farmers seemed to plant everything in an orderly fashion to create perfect rows of crops. The cornfields were massive compared with the tiny plot Mom and Dad planted when I was young. I was amazed at what farming on a larger scale looked like, and I was shocked one family could own so much land.

The ride was long, and at times I'd rest my head on my forearm when I wasn't driving. I closed my eyes and imagined tryouts. I visualized again and again making the team. As uneasy as it was, going into new surroundings and meeting new people, at least I knew two of the other players invited, Pat Ferguson and Sue Benfield from my college team.

Before going to Arkadelphia, we made a stop in Iowa for five days of a pre-training camp for all players who needed an introduction to the five-player game, the standard for international competition. Although the federal Office of Civil Rights wanted to ban six-player basketball as early as 1958, most states didn't adopt the five-player game until 1971. Girls in Oklahoma played with six players as late as 1995.

The international game was full-court and far more physical than anything we played in this country.

For five days in Iowa, we played five on five. In international competition, the markings on the floors are different. The lanes were wider on the baseline than they were at the foul line. I enjoyed this new contact sport much more than the rover game. Because girls and women were considered so much weaker than boys and men, the rules of our women's game in the U.S. favored limiting contact. Touch somebody and the whistle blew. (And yes, depending on the officiating crew, there is still too much of that today.) I found very quickly that international rules suited me better. I could be more aggressive, and I loved that.

Making the transition from offense to defense was so much fun in the faster, full-court game. The problem was those shoes.

My new Adidas basketball shoes, three stripes against a white background, were size 10. During those early years that was the largest size sold for women. But my actual size was 10½, so most of my shoes were too small. They never had my size anywhere; even in magazines I never saw shoes larger than a 10. I remember the first time I saw half sizes years later in Macy's in Kansas City. How wonderful, I thought. It took a long time for the big shoe manufacturers to make 11s for women. While I have no problem finding what I wear today, 11½, or wearing 9½ men's basketball shoes, back then it was a different world. It never occurred to me to look in the men's department for bigger shoes.

Because most of my shoes were too small, I could barely walk around in the ones I wore every day let alone run in them. When I wore loafers, I could stretch them a bit. But that didn't do the trick with my Adidas 10s. I could feel my toes pushing against the nose of the shoes. Adidas basketball shoes had hard rubber at the top. My feet hurt badly, with my big toes getting the worst of it.

After a few days at the camp, all I could do was pray that by the time I got to the gym, I would be able to adjust to the pain. I reached a point where the pain was so great I actually got lost in it. By then, my big toenails were turning blue and I knew I was going to eventually lose them. But I didn't complain. I didn't want anyone to know about it. This was my chance — the biggest of my young lifetime.

I couldn't have known that my world was about to change after meeting a woman named Alberta Lee Cox.

Bert, as we called her, was well ahead of her time. She was a five-time AAU All-American and on the U.S. women's basketball team that won the 1957 World Championships in Brazil. She became the first head coach for the USA Women's National team in 1965 and took that team to the Pan American Games in 1967.

Bert's father, Leroy, sponsored the Raytown Piperettes, a consistently highly ranked AAU women's basketball team that she coached for eight years out of Raytown, Missouri. Leroy Cox was also the mayor of Raytown and owned a pipe stringing company, which explains how the Piperettes got their name.

Meeting Bert in 1969 started our friendship that spanned 45 years.

Bert had a larger-than-life presence. She was strong and confident, demanding yet compassionate. She carried herself well, took a lot of pride in her dress and kept her hair immaculate. She walked as easily in four-inch heels as she did in sneakers.

Bert ran the 10 days of tryouts in Arkansas. The word that comes to mind: grueling. For three hours in the morning and three in the afternoon, all of us went at it hard. One drill required 30 minutes of running around the court interrupted only by dropping to the floor to do 15 pushups. My feet were killing me at the end of practice, and our calves were so sore every afternoon that we walked up the stairs backward.

One player from Texas had finished only her freshman year of college at Wayland Baptist, and after the first day, she admitted she wanted to get cut so she could go home. But like the rest of us, the longer tryouts went, the more determined she became. Bert came by every so often and gave me a kind word. That helped a lot.

At the end of each session, the assistant coaches posted the names of those who should return the next day. I held my breath walking up to the bulletin board to see if my name was on the list. You could tell when somebody didn't make it: Tears would flow. When my teammates were cut, they left quickly. I never had the chance to say goodbye.

On the last day, Bert brought us all together for a meeting. Some of us were in chairs and others, including me, sat on the floor. I was in the back, near the corner of the room, when Bert opened the meeting by thanking all of us for working hard. She talked about how difficult this last cut was for her and the assistant coaches. She told us even if we did not make the team that year we should continue to work hard to improve our skills and come back to next year's tryouts.

"Here are the names of the 12 players on the 1969 United States National Team," Bert said.

You could hear a pin drop.

"Carol Bollinger. Colleen Bowser. Susan Britton. Myrna DeBerry."

With every name called, I instinctively counted.

"Lynn Gamble. Ellen Mosher. Margaret Propst. Pat Ramsey."

Five, six, seven, eight.

"Cherri Rapp. Judy Schneider. Mary Tope."

We were at No. 11 and I knew I wasn't going to make it. Tears were already high in my throat.

"Marian Washington."

Washington! Did she say Marian Washington? Bert had been going in alphabetical order, and I was the last name called. I was about to pass out. She said my name. I was a member of the 1969 U.S. National Team ... unbelievable! I sat with my eyes closed, shaking my head. It was wonderful. Nobody screamed or jumped up and down. We felt respect for those who didn't hear their names. But I was absolutely turning cartwheels inside.

I called home to let everyone know that I had made the team. That was rare for me. Long-distance calls were expensive. Back then no one walked around with a phone in their hand all day. I dialed from a pay phone using loose change. Almost always if I called home, it was to talk to Josie or to ask about my parents and siblings. I never wanted the focus of the conversation to be on me. But this moment was special enough to make an exception.

Everyone was happy for me, but it was hard for them to grasp what I had endured the last couple of weeks.

I was one of two Black women named to the team. The other, Colleen Bowser, was a smart, no-nonsense 20-year-old point guard who attended Drake University, where she received free tuition and books because she was sponsored by *Look Magazine*. The *Look Magazine* team had finished sixth at AAU nationals the year before. We were the first two African American women to integrate a U.S. women's basketball national team. Credit Bert for that.

The day after we learned we survived the cut, we left from the Dallas airport for a 10-day Latin American tour that started in Mexico City. We would play the national teams from Mexico, Panama and Colombia, and yes, I was still wearing the only pair of shoes I brought. Things felt like they were happening very quickly: new faces, new coaches and a new way to travel – by plane.

I was nervous about the trip and scared of flying. I had never flown before. How long would we be in the air?

When Bert realized I was afraid to fly, she came to my seat and pressed a quarter into the palm of my hand and told me it would keep me safe. I believed her! Later she gave me Dramamine. That pill got me so sleepy and dizzy I could barely walk down the steps off the plane. I held on to that quarter tightly on each subsequent flight, but I had to limit the Dramamine.

From the beginning, Bert made it clear that as members of the U.S. National Team, we had to take ourselves out of the equation. It was not Marian Washington anymore. It was *OOSA!* — that's USA. That concept was important to her, and she wanted us to understand how foreign countries would view us. She was very patriotic and instilled that in us. On the bus to games, we sang "My Country 'Tis of Thee," "America" and "He's Got the Whole World in His Hands." We didn't leave the bus until we repeated the Pledge of Allegiance. We gave small American flags to fans, and everywhere we went, we drew a crowd.

I got to know members of the National Team in a different way than I knew my teammates in college. We were together for almost two weeks nonstop. We ate our meals with each other and shopped for souvenirs together. Our rooms were next door to each other. The most fun I had was with my roommate, Ellen

Mosher, a legendary scorer in Iowa girls basketball who would later coach at UCLA and Minnesota.

Ellen and I clicked immediately, finding humor everywhere we went. Ellen would talk about her boyfriend and I would talk about the kind of guy I wanted in my life, and we would just laugh. Bert would have us join in when we were at dinners with a country's officials. Ellen and I were always game whenever Bert wanted us to do something. I remember playing the maracas, and I think Ellen sang.

Bert wanted us to pair up with a teammate whenever we went out in public. Most of the time, Ellen was by my side. Bert taught us how to barter with the vendors and told us never to pay full price for anything. The dollar was worth a lot at the time, and I'd save as much of our per-diem money as I could for expenses back home. It was fun shopping in Mexico City. Everything seemed so cheap at the markets. Bert warned us not to buy a lot at this first stop and certainly not to buy anything that would be difficult to travel with because we had more places to see.

I think it was later that afternoon that one of my teammates, Mary Tope, bought a golf bag, all leather and so beautiful. Bert was beside herself when she saw it. She had just instructed, "Do not spend all your money here." Luckily, another teammate's family had flown to see the games in Mexico City. They took the golf bag back to the U.S. for Mary. We laugh about that memory today.

In Mexico City, we played in the gym that had hosted the Olympic volleyball games in 1968. We won three of our four games there, including one by 33 points. As Bert would later say to the media, "We wooed the crowd, kissed the men, held the babies and have been pawed to death."

Fans weren't always kind to us in South America, and the facilities were often horrible.

One of the worst experiences was in Bogota, Colombia. We had to dress in a room reminiscent of an enclosed dugout. It had a dirt floor. To go to the bathroom, we had to take a corner and dig a hole to create a spot to urinate. There was no privacy. To make things worse, the game was outside and at night. We played on asphalt, which, you can imagine, is hard on your knees. It was cold in Bogota, 45 degrees at game time. Our summer is their winter.

There were no bleachers. People stood around the edge of the court to watch. The crowd seemed to be made up of mostly students. I was surprised to see so many cameras and media trying to stick microphones in our faces. There was a string of incandescent lights deliberately dimmed when we were on our end of the court, making it difficult to see the basket. People shouted, "Down with the U.S." and "Up with Cuba." When we were trying to leave, they circled us, but Bert stepped in and told us to stay calm. We got out of there safely, thank God!

Bert never seemed overwhelmed. She demonstrated control, whether we were trailing in a game or surrounded by protesters in South America. She was a fierce lady, laser-focused on the task at hand. She taught us to do what we had to do and move on with our heads high. We learned how to deal with different challenges like that. One of her key phrases to us was, "Adjust, Oosa." Anytime we ran into a snag or problem, she would say "Adjust," and we found a way to do just that.

Bert's reminder to adjust stayed with me beyond basketball. It was never in my DNA to give up. I wanted to be that person who persevered despite the obstacles, an example for my coaches and teammates, and later my players and peers, to instill in them strength and determination to push past whatever adversity they were facing.

During one of the more fun times, Bert had us put on demonstrations for the media. We had more height than most of the other countries. For one drill, she started us at the free-throw line, one at a time, and we had to run to touch the backboard. I don't know if she was trying to psych out our opponents or she was entertaining the reporters. Bert was keenly aware of my jumping ability. When it was my turn, she told me she knew I could touch the rim. I didn't think about it. I just ran and grabbed it. That was the first time I became aware that I was blessed with a unique leaping ability. I was so pumped that had there been a small ball, a softball or baseball, I might have dunked it!

Years later, when I was teaching at Kansas, some of the basketball guys in my skills class had heard how high I jumped, so they persuaded me to try to dunk. I had never dunked the big ball because even with my large hands, it was difficult to control. I don't know how clean a dunk it was but they said I did it. And they went crazy! I don't know, maybe I did, but for sure I was up there!

When the tour ended, we had won all but one game. Bert took us out to a dinner club, and I remember she wanted me to dance with the performers there. I was shy about almost everything, but somehow I ended up on the dance floor. The rest of the team left their tables and started dancing, too. We ended up having a great time.

After we got back to the United States, we went our separate ways. In the eight years of her life, I had never been apart from Josie for so long, and I was dying to see her. Mom took good care of her and read all of my postcards to her, some that Josie still has.

Hearing Josie talk now about her memory of my return touches me. She remembers walking home from school when she saw a car she didn't recognize slow down and pull alongside her. She kept her eyes fixed ahead as I always told her to do if a strange car approached. Now Josie insists it was a limousine, and I can tell you this: It might have been a larger car than she was used to seeing, but it was not a limo.

I pulled up alongside her and called her name. When she realized it was me, she ran to the car and hopped in. I picked her up and smothered her with kisses. Her face lit up when she saw the dolls I brought back for her from every country I visited.

Josie regards that as the start of our journey together, just me and her. From that point forward, Josie would live with me no matter where I went. By then, that meant Silver Spring, Maryland, as Doris had invited me to work full time back at the community center in Washington.

Mom was worried about the idea of me moving. She didn't want me to go, and she certainly didn't want me to take Josie. Mom was always concerned about my welfare, yet she was still struggling to pull dollars together for food and rent. A quarter-pound of bologna and a quarter-pound of cheese remained the staples. Mom was working, often as a caregiver, and we lived in a rowhouse on Wayne Street next door to a pastor who was also her landlord. Sometimes I would have to talk to him about giving her extra time until we could get rent money together. He was always generous, but his wife wasn't quite as gracious.

Leaving West Chester was in many ways bold. No one else in the family had done that. Butchie lived within a couple of miles and so did Dad. My sisters stayed with Mom.

We were a family that lingered over goodbyes. Pulling away, I looked back to see everybody waving and blowing kisses. I think I even drove around the corner and came back again to see everybody still standing there waving.

I was tied to West Chester, and not just because of my family. I had to finish up those few credits to graduate. As a physical education major, one of the major hurdles I had left was something I dreaded — passing an advanced swimming class.

I'm not sure I could have passed the class if I had taken it at West Chester State. Learning to swim and passing the beginner's course was one of my more difficult academic challenges. I somehow got through despite hovering near the edges of the pool most of the time. But to graduate, I needed to pass the advanced class. For someone who could barely stay above water for more than a few minutes, passing an advanced class didn't seem possible.

But guess what? I took Bert's advice. I adjusted. Instead of taking the class at West Chester, I enrolled at the University of Maryland. The advanced class there was like the beginner's class at West Chester. I still swam plastered to the side of the pool, but the instructor was sympathetic and extremely patient with me. There were no games or races that I might shy away from or be embarrassed because I was last to be picked. She worked with me one-on-one and made sure I made the grades.

Yet the agony wasn't over. The final exam was jumping off the high diving board and swimming to the side of the pool. I had to return to West Chester State and make that jump in front of an instructor there. For what reason, I don't know.

I was terrified, deathly afraid of heights, and when I got up on the board, I felt like I was standing on the Empire State Building looking down at the sidewalk. I saw my swimming instructor talking to another professor while waiting for me to jump. I prayed so hard asking God to help me. I so wanted to climb back down, but I could not fail this class. After what seemed an eternity, somehow, I willed myself to jump. My arms were flapping like the wings of a bird. I must tell you I don't remember my head ever going under the water. Somehow I made it to the side. I passed!

Living in Maryland, I wasn't able to play much basketball. Bert sent me a letter inviting me to move to Missouri and play for the Raytown Piperettes. She wanted me to transfer to the University of Missouri-Kansas City to finish my coursework. As upset as I was with not receiving that extra year of eligibility, I wanted my degree to be from West Chester State, and I didn't want to take the risk of losing credits in a transfer.

I told Bert I couldn't move then. But I respected her vision of wanting to strengthen Team USA's chances at the 1972 Olympics.

The foreign teams were like professional teams that played and practiced together year-round. They didn't do that in the United States, which gave women's teams two weeks — *two weeks!* — to prepare for international competition. Fourteen days and we were off to try to beat the best teams in the world — teams subsidized by their governments. We weren't set to have another international tour until the summer of 1970. If we were going to have a chance at qualifying for the Olympics, Bert knew she needed to have a nucleus of us play together for a year. She wanted the Piperettes to form the core of the Olympic team.

By then I found the strength to tell Bert I had a child. She was not upset by the news, and I always loved her for that. I never confided in Bert or Carol about living in a bus or how many times in life I went without electricity and food. I didn't want anyone to feel sorry for me or pity my family.

Instead of moving to Missouri, I flew to Raytown for certain games, usually on weekends. Bert sent me an airline ticket, I'd jump on a plane, play the game and then fly back home. Our sponsor was better than most other sponsors of AAU teams. Bert's father supported us. We were given a small per diem for away games, and I saved most of it. When we drove to an opponent's gym, Bert rented Cadillacs to drive there. Most of us had long legs, and she wanted us to be comfortable. Josie traveled with me to most away games on weekends.

As Piperettes, we dressed nicely. Bert wanted us all to have matching shoes and handbags, so she gifted us with purses and had us sew on the beads. Raytown played colleges and other AAU teams and was one of the top two teams in the nation.

In December 1969, Bert wrote me a letter asking me again to move to Missouri. I still have it. It starts:

Dear Marian,

We understand you have a daughter that is ready to make Raytown, Missouri her home. The Piperettes just wanted to first let that little (perhaps we should say young) girl's mother know that we have a place on our team for her any time she's ready to join us.

Bert listed the entire team underneath, urging me to *"Hurry on to see us!!"*

Moving even farther from my mother would be difficult, but I decided to accept Bert's offer. I was hungry to compete and I wanted a better life. This was an opportunity to play for the U.S. National coach more regularly. It got me a step closer to my Olympic dream. That was enough of a carrot for me to leave everything I knew behind.

Josie was 9 years old when we moved to Kansas City in 1970. We were on the Missouri side, about a 40-minute drive from Raytown.

I got my first teaching job at Martin Luther King Junior High School, where I would work during the day and practice and play in Raytown at night. I was one of two physical education teachers in an open gym trying to instruct something like 60 kids in each class. I learned in college that classes ideally are no larger than 30 students. What they called open-door classrooms were difficult to manage. You could walk by and see everybody. There were no doors. It was chaos.

I was a stickler for organization. I wanted the kids to learn discipline, but that was a challenge with this system. I first thought I wanted older students, but by the time I got to see what those older kids were up to, I was happy with my seventh-graders!

I tried to introduce the students to new experiences. I planned an All-School Olympic Day for them to experience various competitions. We gave ribbons to the winners of individual events. I tried to organize the teachers to help. No one else had done anything like this. Our principal let us have a half day, so this was a special opportunity. You know the saying, "Your eyes are bigger than your belly?" Well, that was a saying about food, but in my case, my thoughts surrounding this Olympic Day for these kids were bigger than what I was able to manage. In the end, everyone seemed to have fun, but I was exhausted.

After work, Josie and I headed to Raytown as usual. I was one of a few teachers on the Piperettes, which also included secretaries, a pharmacist and a chemist. One woman was a dentistry student Bert was supporting in college. Seven of us from the National Team played for the Piperettes.

Josie became the Piperettes' mascot, and was she ever cute! I had one white and one blue outfit for her. They were skirts with a sailor backdrop and a pipe wrench on them. She wore Adidas black and white shoes. (Hers fit well!) Bert just adored her. She'd sit with us on the bench or right behind it. All the players knew Josie and looked out for her. She'd get the ball for us and give us water cups during timeouts.

Some opposing teams wanted Josie to be their mascot. "Can we have her sit on our bench?" they'd ask. Bert told them no! Josie became a little celebrity, and kids in the stands wanted her to spend the night in their houses. She loved Bert and has happy memories of that time. Bert was also an accomplished equestrian, and she let Josie pet her horses. Josie also loved Bert's dog, Babe, named after Babe Didrikson.

During the summer of 1970, I set out on another South American tour with the National Team to Panama City; Lima, Peru; Santiago, Chile; and São Paulo, Brazil. Joye Ray, the first female basketball referee to travel with a United States team, joined us to be part of the officiating crew. Joye had been the Female Athlete of the Year at Weber College in 1951. She has never been recognized for being the first American woman to officiate on foreign soil.

I remember being part of a tight game in Santiago when Joye called a player for her fifth foul. The crowd wasn't happy and began throwing coins; pennies pelted our arms and legs. Bert told us to stay on the court, and we began picking up the money and handing it to children in the stands. I don't know what made us think of doing that, but it sure helped to calm the crowd. We even got some cheers. As soon as the game ended, we went straight to the bus. I remember the mob surrounding the bus shaking it. Finally, the bus driver made his way through all those people and drove us back to our hotel safely.

Our visit to Peru was only a few months after the Ancash earthquake, still considered the most catastrophic natural disaster in that country. It killed something like 70,000 people. The poverty there was unbelievable, people living out of cardboard boxes. Bert provided blankets that we carried, and whenever possible we presented them to the people there to demonstrate our concern for them. We soon got to our hotel and our room on the 11th floor. I looked out and thought I saw another building moving. People began talking and running. That's when I realized our building was moving. It was an aftershock.

Bert held tryouts for the National Team every year, and there was never a guarantee that just because you made it one year, you were still on the team the next. We spent all day in camp, three-a-days again, and then late in the afternoon or early evening we'd go into a room with a bulletin board. If you saw your name, you were good to return the next day. By the time Bert picked the team, we were only together a couple of days before we'd leave for the tour.

The FIBA (FIBA is the international governing body of basketball) World Championship for Women was the following year, in May 1971. That's when I left Dad at the hospital in West Chester, not knowing then that I would never see him again.

The team started in São Paulo, which felt like New York. I enjoyed the energy. I loved shopping there and still have some of the stones in a bag that I bought. I have coins from there, too. I always enjoyed having another country's currency.

I remember playing well in Brazil. The papers there wrote that I was averaging something like 16 rebounds per game until I hurt my ankle. Bert was upset to lose me for a while. She read the article aloud to me and the team. I was surprised that a sportswriter noticed a rebounder. Usually the high scorer snagged all the headlines.

The United States finished eighth in the World Championships with the Soviets winning. We were excited for our shot at the Olympics the next year.

It never came.

I'm not sure how soon it was after that when Bert asked the Piperettes who were on the National Team to come to her house. That wasn't unusual. We'd often go there with the notebooks she gave us that contained clippings about our highlights. She called us together, and we sat in chairs with some of us sprawled out on the floor.

Then Bert told us we weren't going to the Olympics.

Nobody said anything.

We were told the International Olympic Committee scheduled men's basketball as it normally did, but there was no room left for women's basketball on the schedule at the Games. She told us they forgot they were going to introduce women's basketball in 1972.

According to the book *Celebrating Women Coaches: A Biographical Dictionary* by Nena Rey Hawkes and John F. Seggar, the Olympic Committee had too many events to add women's basketball to its summer schedule.

We were not going to the Olympics.

Some of my teammates began crying. I was devastated.

I remember leaving Bert's house unable to see in front of me. My mind was going in so many different directions. This was crushing news for me, my teammates and Bert. I don't remember any newspaper article being written about it, no public outcry. Nor was there mention of it when the 1976 Olympic team was inducted into the Women's Basketball Hall of Fame in 2023. Bert isn't even in that Hall of Fame. That's a glaring omission, one her family and other supporters have tried to correct. Those pleas have fallen on deaf ears.

Bert coached 38 All-Americans. She was the first woman to coach a U.S. Olympic team sport and the first woman to coach a U.S. women's basketball team on foreign soil. Selecting Colleen and me was a milestone for African American female athletes.

While I respect everything the 1976 Olympic team accomplished, I am saddened that the 1972 team and Bert continue to be overlooked. We were forgotten then and again some 50 years later. What happened in 1972 to Bert and the 12 of us is almost never mentioned in any historical account. I believe the adage Keep the Past in our Present captures the importance of being aware of the historical contributions of pioneering women in basketball like Joye and Bert. Keep the Past in our Present. Why is that so hard?

I watched the 1972 Olympics from my Kansas City apartment with Josie at my side.

The dominant story was the tragedy when eight members of a Palestinian militant group climbed over a fence to storm the Olympic village before dawn. They broke into a building where the Israeli Olympic team was staying and killed the wrestling coach and a wrestler before capturing nine hostages. In a 20-hour span, 11 Israelis were killed along with a Munich policeman. Five of the terrorists also died.

I sat glued to every news report and saw the horror on the face of ABC sportscaster Jim McKay when he confirmed on live television, "They're all gone."

It was unbelievable and another sign of how fleeting life can be. We must treasure each and every day.

The Games continued even though many people thought they shouldn't. I spent a lot of time watching the track and field events. I saw Kansas alumnus Jim Ryun, fresh from running the third-fastest mile leading into the Games, trip and fall in the 1,500, ending his Olympic dream.

I still had mine, and my mind began spinning about another way to get to the Olympics.

And I can't say I knew it then, but maybe a seed was planted during a conversation with Ellen Mosher during one of our layovers in an airport. When you're young, you think you'll play forever. You never think a time will come when you can't get up and down the floor.

I think she said it first. "If I ever do retire, I'm going to coach."

"I'm going to coach, too," I said.

"I'll beat you," she insisted.

"No, you won't," I responded. "I'll beat you!"

We joked about that memory every time we met on court — 10 times altogether while she coached Minnesota. Kansas, by the way, won nine of those games!

Chapter XI

Final Shot

God blessed me with enough athletic talent to play several sports. I am so grateful. I realize that each athletic experience contributed to my journey in life.

I **wasn't what** Bill Easton was expecting when I walked into his office.

I was a kid in high school when Al Oerter told me to look up his college coach if I ever got to Kansas. After walking out of Bert's house devastated by the news that I wasn't going to the Olympics for basketball, I felt lost, blinded by my sadness, struggling to think of what was next. I needed to feel there was another next. Then it hit me. I lived in Missouri, a border state to Kansas. I remembered what Al told me all those years ago and who I should contact if I was ever in the area.

As much as I loved basketball, it seemed like a dead end in terms of my playing in an Olympic Games. Times were starting to change in women's basketball with the formation in 1971 of the Association for Intercollegiate Athletics for Women, an association for women run by women with 280 charter member schools. The new umbrella for women's collegiate athletics had more or less replaced the AAU, and it became clear that the 1976 Olympic team would be made up of collegians and amateurs. Bert's tenure was over as an Olympic coach. Billie Moore, the longtime UCLA coach, was the new National Team coach. The

AIAW was dismissive of the contributions the AAU had made in advancing women's athletics, and the NCAA in the 1980s would adopt a similar attitude to all that the AIAW accomplished.

But I still had track. I could still throw the discus.

I was too shy to call Coach Easton myself. He had coached 32 All-Americans and eight Olympians and world record holders, Al Oerter included, in three decades at Drake and Kansas. By the early 1970s, he had retired as a coach, but he continued to work in the Department of Health and Physical Education at Kansas.

I had a friend contact his office one morning while I listened in on the call. Coach Easton asked her questions, and she relayed them to me for the answers, which she repeated to him. He asked, "How tall is he?" and "How large are his feet?" She never mentioned I was female. By the time she got done describing me, he said, "Send him down to my office!"

Needless to say, he didn't expect a 5-9 woman to walk in the door, let alone a 5-9 Black woman. But after we talked for a while, he invited me outside so he could watch me throw the discus. He found a spot between two trees that was wide enough but not so much, which forced me to work on control.

I struggled with control for years. When I lived in Maryland, I worked with a coach who I thought could teach me techniques to make me a better thrower. Only he had me training in a way that left me barely able to walk when I was finished. His approach was going to extremes with every part of my form. He was a successful long jump coach, but I didn't think he knew much about the discus, and in the end, his style wasn't for me.

People gave me pointers over the years, but they were probably reading the same books I did. As knowledgeable as Coach Easton was, he wasn't a field events coach, but he knew more about the discus than anyone else I knew.

Coach Easton introduced me to the weight room at Kansas. I was the only female there. I was in pretty good shape, but I was self-conscious around all the male athletes. Coach Easton stayed with me and had me do things that required my full attention, so I forgot about the guys. We immediately started working on my core. I was doing inverted sit-ups, pull-ups, medicine-ball routines, weightlifting and more. It didn't take long for the guys to get used to my being in the weight room, and I learned to relax. This was my first experience with actual weight training. I enjoyed my workouts, and later, as a graduate assistant, I introduced a weight-training class for women.

Even though I was becoming more confident with my throws, I wasn't as loose as I needed to be before stepping into the ring and while going through my movements. Too often I tried to power through the discus. When I could relax and put some things together, I had some impressive throws. I held the Junior Olympic national record for a while.

One day I read about a hypnotist in Missouri who worked with athletes. I made an appointment to see him, hoping to learn to relax, especially in competition. After explaining how my anxiety affected me, he was eager to put me under.

I never felt hypnotized, not for a moment. The whole thing was a waste of time and money, but I didn't have the heart to tell this doctor it wasn't working. I kept responding to his directions. "Keep focus on my voice. You are getting sleepy." I closed my eyes waiting for something to happen, but it never did.

After we spent some weeks together, Coach Easton encouraged me to pursue my master's degree at Kansas. It was a big decision, but I thought it was a good opportunity and I could continue working with him. I applied to be a graduate assistant in the physical education department. When I got my appointment in 1972, I took a leave of absence from Martin Luther King Jr. High School. I continued to commute from Kansas City, often sharing transportation with an older Chinese student who lived near me and was also attending KU.

Graduate students with assistantships got their tuition paid but didn't make a lot of money after that. Like Dad, I knew how to stretch a dollar. I had been saving as much as I could from my salary as a teacher, so it helped when I got an additional stipend for assisting with the women's basketball team. I wasn't an assistant like coaches are today. I didn't break down film or scout opponents. I followed the direction of head coach Sharon Drysdale. When the head coaching job became available the following year, I was encouraged to apply. In 1973, my stipend increased when I became head coach. (How could I have had any idea I'd be in that role for years?)

Although there was no Olympics for women's basketball in 1972, I received an invitation to the Olympic Trials that year for track. The Trials were held in Maryland, where I finished fifth in the discus. As disappointed as I was, I had to keep reminding myself I had trained for less than two months. I was competing against athletes who trained year-round. Still, no American thrower at that time could contend with Olga Connolly, who was Czechoslovakia's only Olympic gold medalist in 1956 when she was Olga Fikotová. Her marriage to American hammer thrower Hal Connolly made her an American citizen and an Olympian for the United States. She even carried our flag in the 1972 opening ceremonies. The United States sent one thrower at that time, and it was Olga.

I was getting disillusioned. I heard over and over again that I had potential. Potential with no coach is not a formula for success. Maybe I needed to decide on one sport and then train as hard as I could. It was clear to me I needed to train like Olga if I were to make the discus my focus. I didn't have the luxury of doing that.

I thought my basketball-playing days were behind me after the disappointment of 1972, but I continued to get unexpected opportunities. I was invited to play for an AAU team in California, National General West. National General would fly me in and out of California to play for them just like Bert did when I played with the Piperettes. I depended on a few families in Lawrence to help me if I needed to leave Josie. I will always be grateful to the Mitchell family, who often watched Josie for me.

Ellen Mosher and I reunited as teammates again on the National General West basketball team. We ended up playing against Bert and Raytown in 1974. I was named an AAU All-American a second time. The first time was as a Piperette in 1972.

As exciting as that honor was, I recall being saddened to see a young player on the team crying in the hallway of the hotel where we were staying. She was upset she didn't make the All-America team. I sat with her and told her how talented she was. I didn't want this disappointment to discourage her because she had a bright future. Her name was Ann Meyers.

National General West asked me to move to California. They wanted to get me a job so I could play for them full time. Ellen got the same invitation and ended up moving there, but I just couldn't go that far away. The West Coast? No, I wasn't ready to do that.

A year later, the national chairman of AAU asked me to try out for a team coached by Wayland Baptist Coach Dean Weese. The 1975 National team was headed to the Soviet Union for an eight-game series. The invitation I received on April 22, 1975, noted that transportation and board in Plainview, Texas, would be the responsibility of the athlete.

I still have the letter telling us we would be expected to pay for four meals per day, which came to $2.55 per day, and rooms at area motels were available at $14 per night to be divided among four per room.

I was surprised to get the invitation and wanted to go even though by then, I was a full-time administrator at Kansas in addition to being the women's basketball coach. Tryouts were a week long, and the trip to Russia would last more than three weeks. That was a lot of time for me to miss KU. Chancellor

Archie Dykes and Vice Chancellor Del Shankel supported my going. They thought it would bring prestige to the university. I was happy to have their backing but made it clear I wouldn't hesitate to decline the invitation if they didn't want me to go.

Young Marsha Sharp, who would go on to coach for 24 years at Texas Tech and was a 2003 Women's Basketball Hall-of-Famer, picked me up at the airport in Texas to take me to tryouts. I confess my memory of meeting Marsha is fuzzy, but she shared it with me years later.

I had never played for a male coach, and it was a challenging tryout, especially because most of the women were from Wayland Baptist and knew Coach Weese's system. Coach Weese did a lot of things different from Bert. In some ways he was more technical, Still, I did well enough to be selected to the 11-player team that left for Moscow from New York on May 13, 1975. Six of my teammates were from Wayland Baptist, a program that won 10 AAU National Championships.

I was excited to travel to the Soviet Union. It was the first time in my life to play games in Moscow, Rita, Frunze and Alma. Russia was a powerhouse. For years they seemed unbeatable. Many of their players were older, and they were subsidized by their government, which allowed them to stay together year-round.

At that time I wore an Afro. After we landed in Moscow, I went looking for my bags. I wore a heavy coat with a fleece lining. Two women who were going through our luggage kept looking at me and trying to say something to me. They were speaking Russian. One of the women came toward me and opened the inside of my coat, first touching the fleece and then my hair. Apparently, she was saying that my hair was curly like the fleece in my jacket. They obviously didn't see a lot of Afros in Russia in the 1970s. Two of my teammates were also Black, and we drew a lot of attention whenever we went out. It was quite a sight for the Russian people to see three tall Black women walking together, sightseeing.

Everywhere was cold and gray. Moscow had little color, and many people seemed to busy themselves with boring jobs. We had an interpreter who let us ask questions. She said that everybody had a job, some big and important, some basic chores. I saw a woman mopping concrete steps and wondered how in the world someone could do the same thing over and over again like that. Our interpreter shared some personal information about herself. She was waiting for the government to approve a marriage license for her and her fiancé. She had been waiting for months. It was possible their marriage wouldn't be approved. I could not imagine living in such a strict, controlling society. That was the life of many people there at the time.

The Russians were far better than us at basketball — their government supported them financially, and they became the best in the world. I defended the tallest woman in the game at that time, imposing 7-foot center Uljana Semjonova, and she just about knocked my teeth out! When she caught the ball inside, she extended her elbows and simply drop-stepped to the basket. I'd try to steal the pass to her because there was nothing I could do if she caught it except foul her. One time she reached to catch a pass and was already in her "catch-it-and-go" movement when I stepped in front to intercept. Well, I got hit in the face so hard I saw stars! Her elbow caught me in the face, and I ended up spitting out granular particles of teeth. After intercepting the ball and passing it to a teammate, I jogged up the court trying to clear my head. Semjonova tried to apologize but I shook her off. Normally I would not have done that, but I needed to get my composure back. After the game I tried to let her know there were no hard feelings.

We didn't win any games in Russia. The closest we came was 13 points in the last one. It was clear that to be competitive internationally, the U.S. had to find a way to spend more than two weeks training.

Along with the memories, I came home with souvenirs. Even though I am not an alcohol drinker, I brought home lots of wine. I brought matryoshka dolls, nesting dolls of decreasing size placed in another, for Josie.

That trip ended my basketball playing days, and with my job at Kansas becoming more demanding, that was good. Yet I got an unexpected invitation, one more attempt to make an Olympic team despite it being in a sport I had no history of playing.

The coaches for the 1976 Olympic Team Handball team wanted basketball players. They thought basketball players could easily transition to the game. Team handball wasn't popular in the United States, but in many other countries, it was one of their national sports. It's a combination of other sports played with a ball about the size of a volleyball on a court a little larger than a basketball court. It's a game of seven on seven.

I didn't know much about the game, but I had enough talent to compete. I didn't have much time to perfect it, but I understood my position if not all the rules.

I made the team along with several other strong athletes, including Carmen Forest, Reita Clanton, Mary Phyl Dwight and Linda Lillis. Peter Buehning and his wife, Renate, were our coaches.

I joined the team for trips to Denmark and Iceland to play games in those countries where team handball was more established. I had an unforgettable experience in Iceland in a public swimming area with a large, heated pool and three or four hot tubs around it. I couldn't imagine getting in the water. It was snowing, for gosh sake! My teammates knew I was not comfortable swimming, but they kept pushing me, so I reluctantly joined them.

We showered inside before all of us tiptoed to the pool. Then I took the plunge. From my shoulders down I was submerged in the warm water, happy to remain at the shallow end. We stayed in the pool for a while before making our way to three hot tubs, each one warmer than the other. I remember walking back to our hotel with my winter coat wide open, snow crystallized on my hair. It was such an incredible feeling. The combination! My body was still very warm from the last hot tub, and the cold air seemed so perfect cooling me off.

In Denmark, I enjoyed watching the free spirit of the people and thought that if I had been born in another lifetime, I might have enjoyed being a hippie! Hippies just seemed to love life. Knowing my tendency to worry about most things, that was a refreshing thought.

I joined the team for the World Championships for team handball in Russia right before Christmas in 1975. I had to go alone because I was unable to get away from Kansas in time to catch the flight with the team. After landing, I walked around the terminal hoping to find someone from my team. Instead, I saw two burly Russian men holding a sign with my name on it. They beckoned me to follow them. It felt like something in a movie. I got in the back seat of their car, and they took off down some back roads. I had no idea where we were going. Just like I remembered from my first trip there, Russia was dark and gray. They dropped me at a train station and handed me a ticket and some money. God was with me, and I was thankful as I stepped onto the train, trying to figure out where I was going.

The conductor led me to a sleeper car with bunk beds on both sides. A couple was facing me. The only thing I wanted was for someone to wake me when we got to Riga, where the rest of the team was. The couple didn't speak English. We communicated with hand signals. I never understood one word they said, but they seemed to like me and I liked them. They sliced pieces of cheese and meat. It looked like a log of bologna, and not the quarter pound of bologna I grew up eating. Then they sliced me a big piece of hard bread. Finally, we tried to get some rest. I was so grateful they remembered to wake me when we got to Riga, 922 kilometers from Moscow. Riga is right on the beautiful Baltic Sea.

The Russians trounced us on the court — one game was 35-4 — and we finished 11th among the 12 teams. (We beat Tunisia!) When the 16 of us returned to the United States, we scattered, unable to practice regularly, which left us in the same boat as basketball back when Bert coached, never enough time to practice and play together.

Team handball was set to debut in the 1976 Olympics in Montreal, but the United States lost in the qualifying round in Milwaukee. I hadn't been playing that long, so losing didn't hold the sting of what happened in 1972 with basketball. I was thankful for the opportunity to experience competition at the highest level, even though we fell short of the ultimate goal. I was happy to return to Kansas, where I introduced team handball into the health and physical education department as a class.

In my mind, the curtains came down for me after not getting the chance to compete with the National Team in the 1972 Olympics. Everything I did after that athletically was a bonus. The invitations to play here or there were pleasant surprises. I had confidence in my athletic abilities going back to running races on the playground in grade school. God blessed me with enough athletic talent to play several sports at a high level and I am grateful for those experiences that shaped my life.

As I began to coach I realized how athletics could launch other young women to learn to be confident in who they are. As an athlete, you learn how to win. You also learn to handle losses and mistakes, searching to find determination within to work harder and try again.

I was driven to remain upbeat even during the most trying times. No doubt that being an athlete prepared me well for the next chapter, the most storied one of my life.

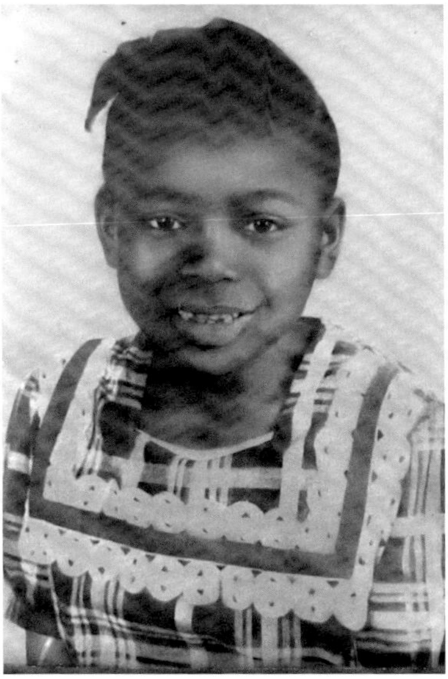

Me in third grade, missing teeth and all. I was so happy Mom parted my hair on the side and not down the middle! My mother had this photo enlarged and framed and gave it to me as a Christmas gift. I was so happy I cried.

My parents, Goldie and Marian Lomax Washington, on their wedding day

Mom, Dad, Butchie and me in a rare family photo. We were visiting Dad's family in Washington, D.C. Notice Dad's long fingers! I was probably 6 or 7 here and it doesn't look like I wanted my picture taken. Mom and Dad look so happy.

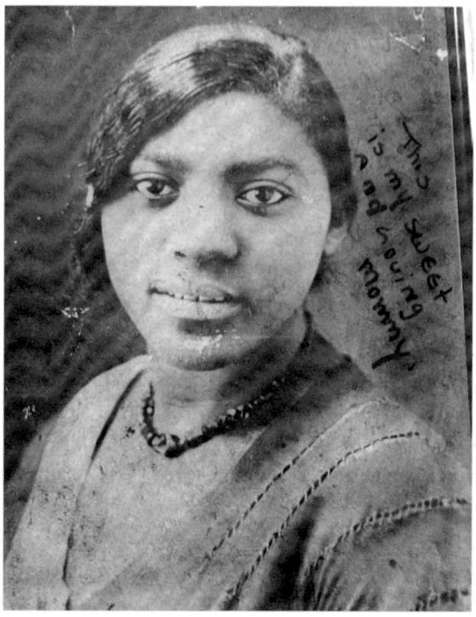

That's my mother and I'm not sure why I decided to write on her photo with a marker. I remember being so nervous I would smudge it and I was telling myself not to misspell anything! Mom is only 19 here.

My adventurous grandmother, Grandmum, Bessie Lomax. She threw me my first and only birthday party when I was little. My grandmother was soft-spoken, the opposite of my mother's fiery spirit.

That's me on the left with the first young girls I really got to know. All of us made up the Delvatones singing group. We would practice our "Doo Wop" and enter singing competitions. We usually finished second behind my friend Barbara Watkins.

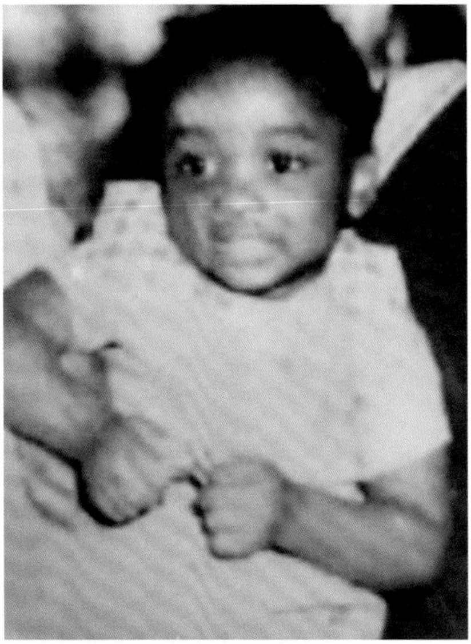

My beautiful daughter, Josie — Marian Josephine Washington. I was only 14 when she was born.

My 1965 high school graduation picture. On the back of this picture is the "letter" I wrote to myself that became the first words of Chapter 1. My necklace is a gold medal from one of my track and field events. I took off the ribbon and put it on a chain.

One of the few photos of me in action at West Chester State. Note my uniform: a tunic with bloomers.

photo courtesy of West Chester University Athletics

I wish I looked happier in this picture because I was. Winning a national championship in 1969 at West Chester State, today West Chester University. Seeing the best teams in the country come to our gym was the best experience I had as an athlete at that point in my life. I'm standing next to coach Carol Eckman.

Me with a young Josie visiting B. Reed Henderson High School, formerly West Chester High School, my alma mater. West Chester High was renamed in 1968. Henderson inducted me into its Hall of Fame.

My patriotism was on full display as a member of the National Team.

I made it! The 1969 United States National Team. Top row, from left, Ellen Mosher, Mary Tope, Pat Ramsey, Myrna DeBerry, Cherri Rapp and me. Bottom Row, from left, Colleen Bowser, Lynn Gamble, Margaret Propst, Judy Schneider, Carol Bollinger and Susan Britton.

Marching with the National Team into the World Championships in São Paulo, Brazil, in 1971. I think Bert made us line up by height. The place was packed and this was a thrill.

I'm sitting next to Alberta Lee Cox, who coached the U.S. National Team. Most likely Bert was trying to calm me down in a game in South America. Bert was a pioneer, associated with many firsts in our sport, including being the first woman to coach a U.S. women's basketball team on foreign soil when she did so in 1965. Assistant coach Carolyn Moffatt is beside her.

Nobody cleaned up better than the Raytown Piperettes. This was probably taken in Gallup, New Mexico, where the AAU held its national championship. Bert gave all of us matching purses but we had to sew on the beaded peacocks. I needed a lot of help sewing mine.

Ellen Mosher and I clicked from the first day we met. Ellen and I were both on the National Team. Whenever all of us went to dinner with members of another country's federation, Bert would look to Ellen and me for entertainment. Here Ellen and I are singing. Ellen went on to have a successful coaching career at the University of Minnesota.

My ninth grade math teacher, Ruth Redding, who helped change my life.

What fun I had coaching the first women's track and field team at Kansas. There were only a few competing at this meet at Kansas State. We didn't win, but we weren't last, either. It must have been a windy day!

I look so young here in my first year as KU's new women's athletic director of intercollegiate sports. This was taken in front of Allen Fieldhouse in 1974.

photo courtesy University of Kansas

My expression says it all. It was difficult to hear the Kansas Student Senate voting down an increase in the women's athletic budget. I had a chance to address the Student Senate before the decision. Before Title IX, women's athletics depended on partial funding from the Student Senate.

That's Josie and me when she was at Lawrence High School. This was one of the first times we had our picture taken by a professional.

A plaque that hangs in Allen Fieldhouse of my first basketball team from 1973-74. We played our first game in the Fieldhouse on Dec. 12, 1973, beating Haskell University 69-29. It was the first time a women's basketball team ever played on that court.

photo courtesy University Daily Kansan

From the University Daily Kansan, April 1, 1976. Clyde Walker was the athletic director during the five years when I was building the women's intercollegiate athletic program at Kansas. The Black hands you see emerging from the rubble are supposed to be mine. Even though Clyde was never receptive of supporting women's athletics, it was shocking to see this. But he couldn't bury me. I would rise and so would women's sports at Kansas.

photo courtesy Kansas Athletics

That's Adrian Mitchell, my first All-American, holding up the "Big Eight" championship trophy in 1979. The Big Eight didn't officially recognize women's basketball until the 1982-83 season, so all the women's sports administrators at each of the eight schools worked together to recognize conference champions. Lynette Woodard is behind the little girl, Shalaun Hogan, daughter of Bill Hogan, Associate Executive Vice Chancellor at Kansas.

photo courtesy Kansas Athletics

Early in my coaching career, I was able to work out a deal with Nike that gave my basketball players shoes. That helped me allocate the small budget we had toward other pressing needs.

photo courtesy Kansas Athletics

A fierce expression, wouldn't you say?

photo courtesy Kansas Athletics

Celebrating another Big Eight Conference championship with my players, from left, Lisa Baker, Sandy Shaw, Lynn Page, Evette Ott (holding the trophy) and Mesho Stroughter.

photo courtesy Kansas Athletics

We won the inaugural Big 12 Conference championship (1996-97), and I was named Conference Coach of the Year. All smiles with my starters, from left, Shelly Canada, Jaclyn Johnson, Jennifer Trapp, Tamecka Dixon and Angie Halbleib.

It was an honor to be an assistant to coach Tara VanDerveer for what many consider the best women's basketball team ever assembled — the 1996 U.S. Olympic team that won gold at the Games in Atlanta. This photo is Josie's souvenir autographed by everyone.

photo courtesy Adrian Mitchell

Adrian Mitchell, my first All-American.

Lynette Woodard, who held the Division I scoring record for 43 years. A four-time Kodak American and first female Harlem Globetrotter.

With Kathleen Sebelius, 44th governor of Kansas and 21st U.S. Secretary of Health and Human Services.

photo courtesy Kansas Athletics

I was usually serious standing on the sidelines during a game.

photo courtesy Kansas Athletics

After 31 years, I resigned as the Kansas coach in 2004 to address my health. I returned to Allen Fieldhouse on Feb. 28, 2004, to say goodbye.

My beautiful grandchildren, Lauren and Ricardo, escorted me to the podium when I was inducted into the Women's Basketball Hall of Fame in 2004.

With Josie, Lauren and Ricardo.

My mother is between Josie and me. Three generations of Washington women named Marian.

My granddaughter, Lauren, is between Josie and me. This is right after Lauren became a mother to twins, my great grands, Carter and Cameron. Another snapshot of three generations of my family.

The last photo taken of my brother, Butchie, and me. We lost Butchie in 2004.

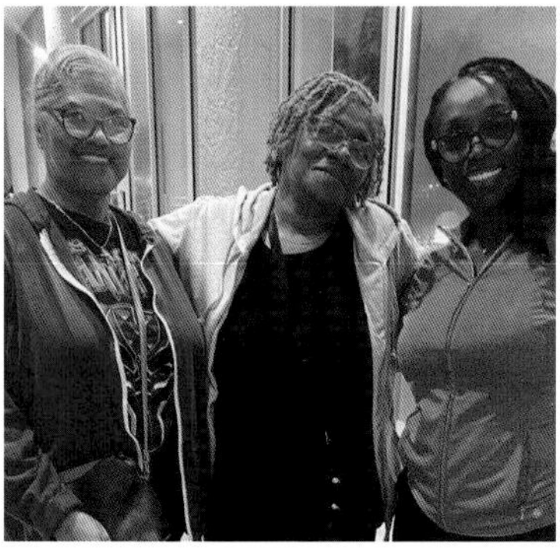

My sisters Cathy and Janet with Josie.

With Josie and her husband, Rick, and my grandson, Ricardo, celebrating the newly named Marian E. Washington Women's Basketball Suite at the dedication ceremony on Oct. 22, 2021.

photo courtesy Kansas Athletics

What a blessing!

photo courtesy Kansas Athletics

Marking my 25th year coaching at Kansas.

Me and Bella

Chapter XII

Land of Oz

I believed there was room for excellence in both men's and women's sports. My constant mantra to anyone questioning women's capabilities was that female athletes were capable of bringing visibility, great success and pride to a university. If given an opportunity, women could contribute to what was already an excellent athletic program. I wanted female athletes at Kansas to feel important and supported for their accomplishments. It wasn't men vs. women in my eyes. They both deserved to be recognized.

In **1974,** I was ready for a terrific career opportunity that came my way. Josie and I would be moving to East Lansing, Michigan, to work under Nell Jackson, the first director of women's athletics at Michigan State. Nell, who 17 years earlier had become the first Black woman to be head coach of an Olympic track and field team and had been an Olympian herself, offered me the chance to work in a physiology of exercise lab and coach softball my first year. She promised I could coach basketball the next season. I interviewed at Nell's home, and she pretty much offered me the job on the spot. The combination of coaching and teaching appealed to me, and Nell was encouraging when she talked about building Michigan State's women's intercollegiate athletics and the role I would play. I had such respect for her and felt she would be a great mentor.

I was excited to go, though I also had applied to be the assistant women's athletic director at Kansas. I hand-delivered my application to the chancellor's office on the last day the job was open. I never thought I would be considered, but friends encouraged me to go for it. I was so nervous when they called me for an interview.

Interviews were held at Robinson Gymnasium, home to KU's Department of Health, Sport and Exercise Sciences. What is today Robinson Center sits directly across from Allen Fieldhouse.

I arrived early and tried to relax. When it was my turn, Dr. Wayne Osness, who chaired the department, came to get me. He could tell I was nervous. With a smile on his face, he beckoned me to come into the room, where I sat at an elongated table, seeing faces from the chancellor's office as well as the men's athletic department. The only other Black person in the room represented the Board of Regents. I kept telling myself that no matter what happened, I would learn from the experience of being interviewed by such an important committee.

After introductions, I remember talking about my teaching background and my international athletic experiences. My master's degree was going to be in Administration, Biodynamics and Physiology of Exercise. It's hard to remember what I was asked, but before I left, I stressed that nobody would work harder than I would. The one thing I was worried about, which I thought could eliminate me, was that I had not yet completed a postgraduate degree.

The hiring process stalled after that. Nell was waiting for an answer. She had extended an offer while Kansas had not. My lease was up at the apartment complex in Kansas City. I didn't see myself returning to teach at Martin Luther King Junior High.

My bags were packed and boxes lined the hallway of my apartment, so I had to decide quickly. Should I take the job at Michigan State or wait on Kansas to make a decision? My mind was spinning over all the possibilities. What if Kansas didn't offer me the job? How long could I ask Nell to wait? I decided to rescind my application at Kansas because I had not heard from anyone. I called Vice Chancellor Del Shankel and explained that my lease was up, and I had a job waiting at Michigan State.

I hung up thinking I was finished at KU. The next day, Chancellor Archie Dykes called to invite me to his office, where he and Del asked me to have a seat on a couch while they sat in chairs, facing me. Chancellor Dykes spoke first, telling me how much he wanted me to remain at Kansas. He talked for a few more minutes. Del sat smiling and nodding, agreeing with what the chancellor was saying. Then I heard the chancellor say, "We want you to be the assistant athletic director who will start our first intercollegiate women's athletic program."

"Thank you," I heard myself saying. Inside, I couldn't believe it. Oh, my God, *Hold it together,* I thought.

The chancellor went on to add that I could keep my position as head women's basketball coach. My salary would be $14,000, far more than I had ever made in my life. (For reference, gas was 38 cents a gallon, eggs were 78 cents a dozen and a 12-inch pizza in Lawrence was $2.40.)

It was hard to think clearly, but I found myself accepting the job. I remember very little of what was said after that. Before I left the office, I asked one question because the appointment for the position wouldn't be official for something like six weeks.

"Can I start tomorrow?"

"Go ahead, Marian," they told me, although I would not be paid until the appointment became official on June 18, 1974.

I walked out the door and took the stairs that led to a long hallway and out the main door to a walkway. I went down the steps of Strong Hall to the street. I took a shortcut to my car through a grassy area. If somebody was looking at me, they might have stopped to stare because I was in a daze, unaware of everything around me. *What did I just do? Was I truly prepared to be an administrator in a college athletic department? Is this too big for me?* The thought of it was overwhelming, yet I also felt exhilarated.

I drove to my apartment and called Nell to thank her and let her know I was staying at Kansas. I wanted her opinion: Did she think I could do the job? Nell told me she was sorry I was not coming to Michigan State but she thought I could do the job. That was reassuring to hear.

I went over and over again in my mind about how I ended up with such an important position. I knew I had some support in the chancellor's office, but I never thought I would get the job. I believed, as always, it was in God's hands and he continued to bless me and guide my every step.

My mind was racing 1,000 miles a minute about everything that needed to be done, and I didn't want to waste any time. I was eager to meet Clyde Walker, the athletic director, and his staff and excited to see my office. I kept thinking about what an amazing turn my life had taken.

I was 27 years old when Josie and I moved to Meadowbrook Apartments in Lawrence, a place that, 50 years later, is still my home for part of the year. I didn't know it then, but I was about to begin a turbulent ride that tested every fiber of my being, affected my health, exhausted me regularly and took every ounce of strength I could muster.

I knew what men's sports meant at the University of Kansas. If you're not from Kansas, it's hard to fathom how big a deal men's basketball is and how much it means to the community. The Jayhawks' first coach, James Naismith, was the inventor of basketball and a longtime KU professor of physical culture. Dr. Naismith was from Canada but his family allowed him to be buried in Lawrence.

Allen Fieldhouse, at 1651 Naismith Drive, is named for Phog Allen, KU's men's basketball coach for 39 years who played for and was trained by Dr. Naismith. Everyone local knows the arena as The Phog, which opened in 1955. Allen Fieldhouse had no air conditioning then and millions of dollars of upgrades haven't changed that. It's one of the features that people often talk about, remarking, "Wow, it's so hot in there. Why don't they have AC?" Home court advantage, indeed! It's quite toasty on a cool day and can be sweltering on a humid one. However, many from both inside and outside the state will tell you there's no better place to play and watch basketball than Allen Fieldhouse.

Wilt Chamberlain played for the Jayhawks for two years, debuting as a center his sophomore season with 52 points and 31 rebounds in a victory over Northwestern. (At that time, NCAA rules prevented freshmen from playing varsity sports.) Wilt chose Kansas from more than 200 schools recruiting him. By 1973 the Jayhawks had one NCAA men's basketball championship (1952) and five Final Four appearances (1940, 1952, 1953, 1957 and 1971). They'd go back again in 1974. Adolph Rupp and Dean Smith played at Kansas. For more perspective, in 2008, ESPN ranked Kansas second (behind Duke) on a list of the most prestigious basketball programs since 1984-85.

Although KU football didn't win as many championships as most alumni would like, anyone working in college athletics will tell you how revered football is. It costs more than the other sports, and given that, there's debate about how much money it makes, but athletic departments depend on it to bring in revenue. Kansas' storied football history includes Gale Sayers starring for two years and racking up 3,917 all-purpose yards. Gale, by the way, was KU's director of fundraising for special projects when I was hired.

Being aware of Kansas' rich sports history for men, I did not see starting an intercollegiate sports program for women threatening that. I believed room existed for both men's and women's sports to excel. My constant mantra to anyone questioning women's capabilities was that female athletes were capable of bringing visibility, great success and pride to a university. If given an opportunity, women could contribute to what was already an excellent athletic program. I wanted female athletes at Kansas to feel important and supported for their accomplishments. It wasn't men vs. women in my eyes. They both deserved to be recognized.

I can't say in the beginning that Title IX, which prohibits discrimination based on gender, played a role in my thinking. Even though it had been signed into law in 1972, schools were still fighting it, and enforcement of the law was lacking. While I had some awareness of that legislation, nobody knew how it was going to be implemented or enforced.

In 1974, schools looked at Title IX in one of three ways. A few embraced it — that's when you saw programs such as Delta State, Old Dominion, Stephen F. Austin and Louisiana Tech win championships in women's sports. Others acted as if it didn't exist, likely thinking it would eventually be overturned. The majority of schools, including Kansas, did just enough for fear of losing federal money. Even after several of our women's sports programs were doing quite well, we could never do enough to gain the respect and financial support we needed.

The negativity toward the idea of females competing in college athletics was unnecessarily harsh. The girl dads who support their daughters today in women's sports were few and far between, and the administrations of these colleges overwhelmingly thought having a women's program threatened the success of the men's program.

In addition to Title IX, women's athletics was also under new governance. The Commission on Intercollegiate Athletics for Women (CIAW) that presided over that first national championship at West Chester State was replaced by the Association for Intercollegiate Athletics for Women (AIAW) in 1971. Composed almost entirely of women, it sought to avoid what it considered the mistakes in men's college athletics. The AIAW embraced championships, but it did not feel the same about giving scholarships until faced with both a court challenge and the possibility of being in violation of Title IX by not affording female athletes the same opportunities as men.

That was the backdrop when I was hired, along with the racial tension that made it all the more startling to some that Kansas would hire a Black female for a leadership position. This wasn't Philadelphia or Baltimore or Washington, D.C. This was the Midwest, and Kansas had sundown towns — all-white municipalities that discouraged Black people from remaining in town after sunset – as late as the 1960s. I saw very few Black people on the street, and few businesses were owned by Black people. I could find a barber to edge my hair in Lawrence, but if I wanted something more, like a Wave Nouveau as opposed to a Jerry Curl, I drove to Kansas City, Missouri.

The students at KU were almost all white and none of the women's teams had a Black player. I knew in my new role at Kansas I would frequently be the only Black woman in the room. I knew I would have to face discrimination being Black and a woman — that double-edged sword.

I scheduled my introductory meeting with Clyde Walker, hired the year before, whom I was expected to work under. The first time I walked into his office, I brought a smile and extended my right hand.

Clyde brushed past the tips of my fingers. Nothing was collegial about those few minutes we spent together. A true Southerner, he made it clear that he wanted no part of helping me build anything. I was basically on my own.

I encountered an iciness that leaves me cold 50 years later.

Not long after that, Clyde spoke to *The Kansan*, the campus newspaper that was read throughout Lawrence.

Passage of Title IX, he said, could be "the ruin of college sports," adding, "Ninety percent who contribute to our program could care less about women's athletics."

Clyde offered to help women's athletics — as long as it wasn't financial. He added, "There aren't any women who can compete with men and they readily admit it."

I was stunned to see those comments from a man with the responsibility to represent an entire athletic department.

What did I have to say in response? a reporter asked.

I countered with candor.

"I had never read something so negative toward women's athletics, which should have a place as part of a university that should be committed to all students, not just its male ones," I said.

I questioned Clyde's proof for the 90% reference and noted that it wasn't going to help me to have the athletic director say people cared nothing for women's athletics.

When I picked up *The Kansan* the next day and saw my comments in print, I realized I certainly had been blunt. *What have you done?*

I walked to my car and drove to the outskirts of Lawrence. Was I running away? I pulled into a gas station and spent a few minutes talking to my mother on a pay phone. I don't remember what we said. I just needed to hear a comforting voice. I hung up and said a prayer. Despite my fears and even though I was scared and angry, I returned to my office to finish my day.

I received a call from Clyde's office with a time to report there. I feared losing my position before it had begun. When I walked into his office, and this time you can bet there was no attempt at a handshake, he told me to have a seat. He sat holding the newspaper.

Leaning back in his chair, looking down at the article, he mused, "We get misquoted a lot." And then he read my own words back to me. When he was finished, he looked up.

"Did you say this?"

A moment frozen in time. My twenty-something self facing this 60-plus serious-looking man who seemed powerful, menacing almost, behind his desk. I found the courage to be truthful, "Yes, I did. I was not misquoted," I answered.

A pause.

"I can't have this," he said.

I looked him in the eyes and responded, "I agree." I got up and walked out of his office.

The next morning, Chancellor Dykes and Del asked to meet with me. As I parked behind the office of the chancellor, I took a deep breath and said a long prayer.

As I readied myself to be fired, I heard them offer an idea. They said they thought it was best if the men's and women's athletic programs operated separately so they would be better able to assess each in terms of resources.

I would not be an associate athletic director reporting to Clyde.

I would be the first Women's Athletic Director for the University of Kansas and report directly to the chancellor's office.

What? Am I hearing this right?

I can do this — launch a program that didn't exist before. A program that to me was as much about advancing women as it was about advancing women's athletics.

I recalled that Mrs. Redding didn't talk to me about how high I could jump or how far I could throw a discus. She told me I was smart. She believed in me. She encouraged me to achieve so I could realize my potential as a person. That was the gift I wanted to pass on to other women. That was the gift I wanted to pass on to other women *of color*. Athlete comes second in student-athlete. Having women graduate and take the life lessons that athletics teaches to apply to their professional and personal lives was my mission.

To accomplish what I envisioned took money, and luckily by July 1974 women's athletics earned a significant fiscal victory from the Kansas legislature and the Student Senate: We received an athletic budget of $120,000. With the threat of Affirmative Action looming, women's athletics received $63,860 from the Student Senate compared with the 1973 budget of $9,300. It wasn't without a fight. Clyde wanted all of it to go to the Kansas Athletic Corporation, which supported men's sports. But he lost that battle. The men, by the way, had a budget well over $2 million.

While it was a paltry sum in comparison, I remained firm, *fierce* in my determination of what women's athletics could and should be at the University of Kansas. Second to none. My education — a teaching degree and the graduate classes toward my master's degree in administration — laid the foundation for me to devise a road map to follow because we needed everything. When I was teaching physical education, I had to break down a skill into a series of small steps toward the larger goal. That's how I approached this tremendous responsibility.

I had my own office, on the ground floor with white cinderblock walls on one side and a window air conditioner on the other. It was ideal — for an equipment room, not an administrator's office. It was on the opposite side of the Fieldhouse. Clyde made sure I was as far away from his office as possible.

I turned the small area into an office within an office. I soon realized I needed a place to have a private conversation or be able to close the door when I was on the phone. So I put up walls, which I had to pay for out of my meager budget. When construction was complete, my office was so small I could almost touch both walls when I stood up. I had an all-purpose carpet glued down on the concrete floor. I found two desks, one for me and another for a secretary. I brought in chairs, a filing cabinet, telephones and a typewriter. I found two more small desks and chairs for coaches who dropped in and out. I had students serve in secretarial roles until I was able to pay for a full-time secretary.

I was forced to prioritize. We needed lockers, uniforms, coaches, equipment and offices. I made a list of short-term and long-term goals. KU women's sports had no presence in Allen Fieldhouse in 1974. Nothing. Many of my counterparts across the country faced resistance at their respective institutions, which were also responding to the changing athletic landscape because of Title IX. But at Kansas, before tearing down the walls of inequality, I had to build walls. Literal walls had to be constructed in Allen Fieldhouse for the sake of progress.

I had to find space anywhere I could in this building, create something where there was nothing.

Could a curtain be put up under this stairwell to stow equipment? Could walls and showerheads be added to this empty corner? Is anyone using this file cabinet?

"This is the space I need to have. Nothing is here. Is there a reason I can't have this area?"

I made it very difficult for someone to tell me no.

Female athletes needed a place to shower and dress. Their coaches needed a room for meetings and phone calls. There was no weight room for women, no area for them to be taped.

All of our teams initially dressed and showered in Robinson, where they used lockers that were part of the Health and Physical Education Department. I rationalized that as much as I wanted the coaches to have offices rather than having to come in and out of my office to do what they needed for their programs, a real locker room was more important.

It would mean our athletes would have a place to store their clothing during practices and games and be able to shower afterward. It would mean I would no longer have to huddle in the public restroom with the Lady Jayhawks at halftime and after games. I found yet another corner in Allen Fieldhouse to build an actual locker room for our sports to share. I had to be patient whenever walls had to go up. While renovations always seemed to be ongoing at the university, women's athletics wasn't a priority for state construction crews. But I kept pushing for the women to have a locker room to call their own.

In the meantime, I had to rotate sports usage. My budget allowed me to purchase two banks of half lockers. They were really little bins that were only large enough for a pair of shoes and maybe a change of clothes. They were nothing like the full-size lockers that players personalize today. Dr. Osness and I came up with an idea and joined forces. The PE department did not have money for additional lockers. By getting the extra lockers, I could move more sports from Robinson to the Fieldhouse. Tennis and golf moved along with basketball, track and field, softball and volleyball. The swimming and diving, field hockey and gymnastics teams continued to use the lockers in Robinson. Moving these six sports out of Robinson freed up lockers for Dr. Osness to accommodate his intramural and club sports programs.

Uniforms were all hand-me-downs. The athletes who played fall sports passed those uniforms to those who played winter sports who passed them to the spring sports athletes. Cynthia Kelley, who was a senior during my first season as head coach of the basketball team and played three sports, had never worn a uniform that had KU written on it until I was able to purchase warm-up jackets for the teams. She told me wearing that jacket meant the world to her. As far as cleats and socks, she bought them herself.

We needed a weight room, too. The male athletes had a state-of-the-art weight room. Men's basketball and football each had weight coaches. Our first weight room was what was called a Universal Gym. It was one piece of equipment that had multiple stations for doing exercises. It reminded me of a merry-go-round. I put a chain-link fence around it to prevent anyone from taking it and gave each coach a key to our fenced-in training area. It was another small step toward helping our sports program improve. We didn't have a strength and conditioning coach for our teams. Coaches or assistant coaches were responsible for their team's strength-training programs.

I remember our first athletic trainer, Jackie King, a physical therapist. I read later that she was the nation's first trainer for women's sports. I found a vacant office for Jackie with a desk that was left behind. That desk became our medical table for her to tape the athletes. They sat with one leg dangling while Jackie taped them up.

I decided to brighten things in my office as best I could, so I had a Jayhawk painted on a wall. It wasn't a little Jayhawk. I had the image painted as large as possible. And it wasn't a Jayhawk people were used to seeing. It was a Lady Jayhawk. A Jayhawk with a skirt. I felt it was important that female athletes have their own identity. Other schools were also using "Lady" before the names of their mascots. At the end of the year, I awarded watches featuring a Jayhawk in a skirt to the seniors on the basketball team.

Many of my former players still wear those watches with pride. Today, most athletic programs have dropped the "Lady" in front of their nicknames with the idea of creating unity within athletic departments. But in 1974, I thought it was important for women to have something of their own. Because at that time, we literally weren't one department.

In addition to women's basketball, I was in charge of field hockey, gymnastics, volleyball, swimming and diving, golf, tennis and softball. Hiring coaches for all those sports came out of my budget. I could afford to give stipends of no more than $1,700. Let's just say nobody was quitting a day job to be a full-time coach!

I hired John Weltmer to be the inaugural sports information director for women's athletics. John was meticulous in his record keeping and received national recognition for his work. Without computers, he wrote out all the box scores by hand.

Before 1974, women's sports had been part of KU's physical education department, and professors often rotated coaching them. If you had played the sport, you were a candidate to coach, and agreeing to do so came with a small stipend. But the truth is you might never have even played the sport you were coaching.

I retained several of the coaches from the PE department and hired a few new ones. I found a volleyball coach, Jack Isner, who was a lawyer in Kansas City. He had a successful club team in Missouri. I was lucky to have an alum, Gary Kempf, coach swimming and diving.

As much as I wanted to hire female head coaches, I couldn't find enough qualified women who could afford to accept my small stipend. But I instituted a rule for the male coaches I hired. They had to have at least one female assistant. It was important to me to help groom women so they would be prepared for head coaching positions.

In the middle of all of this, something was missing. It was glaring to me that we didn't have a track and field program. Not only had track been my first love, Kansas men's track dates to 1900, when Dr. Naismith was the first coach. The men's team was elite with an illustrious history. Before he was an Olympian, Al Oerter was a two-time NCAA champion in the discus. Likewise for Jim Ryun, a two-time All-American with five individual NCAA titles in the mile, and Billy Mills, a three-time NCAA cross country champion. When you first think about Kansas' athletic program, you think about men's basketball. But the men's track and field program had a rich tradition as well.

I couldn't find a coach, but that didn't stop me from starting a track program. I hand-wrote a sign that read, "Who wants to help start a women's track team?" and tacked it up in Robinson. The only hand up was my own — yes, I would coach women's basketball and track and field, serve as the director of women's athletics, and to top it off, my daughter Josie was about to be a teenager! Nope, I wasn't going to let myself think about it all. I just had to do it.

You probably think I slept great in those days once I finally put my head to a pillow, but the truth is quality sleep eluded me (and still does). Before FOMO became a term for "fear of missing out," I lived it, constantly worrying I might have forgotten something. I would replay, in my mind's eye, all that happened that day. Maybe I forgot something that needed to be done. There was always a problem to fix. More to do. And never enough hours to do it.

All of KU's men's sports competed in the Big Eight Conference along with Colorado, Missouri, Iowa State, Kansas State, Nebraska, Oklahoma and Oklahoma State. The conference did not recognize women's athletics championships until the 1982-83 season, even though each of the Big Eight schools started women's intercollegiate athletics in 1974.

Every conference school hired a female administrator to oversee its women's sports programs. I was the only one with the director title, so they called me the "Dean." I was able to build some camaraderie among the Big Eight administrators. We would support each other, sharing marketing strategies on how to get fans to our events. Even if the conference headquarters in Kansas City didn't recognize us, the coaches of all Big Eight women's sports programs were of accord that we would come together and feature our own championships.

At the end of every season, each sport held a small celebration with mostly family members in attendance. I decided to have an all-sports banquet for the women's athletic department. First-year athletes received certificates. When athletes lettered in a sport, they got a big K. Upperclassmen who previously lettered were awarded bars to attach to the K.

Our inaugural awards banquet was held on April 27, 1975, in the ballroom of the KU Memorial Union. Micki King, who won an Olympic gold medal in diving in 1972, was the guest speaker. The coaches brought their entire teams to the stage and talked for a few minutes about their accomplishments, and each athlete was introduced. If an athlete achieved something special, she was recognized. When those women stood on the stage, I wanted them to look out at all the people who would hear about their accomplishments. Their families, friends and fans were there. I made sure the chancellor was there so he could see and hear about everything each team had achieved. By having him attend, the women knew they were representing something much larger than themselves. They represented the University of Kansas.

It grew to be quite a large gathering that turned into a long night annually but worth it! This was the beginning of our intercollegiate program. Our sports programs became an intercollegiate program by playing against schools they hadn't competed against before. We weren't winning all of our games or matches, but we were doing a good job representing KU. A lot of people were proud of what was happening. I would hear good things from people I didn't know when I went to the grocery store or walked around Lawrence. We were beginning to build a fan base of people keeping up with one or more of our sports. Finally!

At the same time, it was a challenging period for Josie and me. We ate a lot of chicken and spaghetti, meals I could make in a hurry. I remember apologizing to her when I'd come home after another stressful day. I never wanted her to feel she was the reason for my frustrations. She'll tell you, I was very strict with her. I knew where she was at all times. At least I tried to know. Josie was very active by then. She played volleyball in high school, and I was able to get to a few of her matches. But I could see Josie blossom when she was singing or on stage acting. I stopped pushing athletics when I saw Josie memorize her first script with no hesitation. She loved to perform.

I know it was difficult for the teenage Josie to share me with so many young women. I think she resented the time I had to be away from her. I reminded her she was my only daughter, and no one was more important to me. Sometimes your children have to go through their own challenges before they can better understand. As a mother, you wait for that moment when your child says she is proud of you and understands what you went through. That happened for us. That's my Josie!

But back in the early '70s, I felt the weight of the task on my shoulders. It helped when I could see we were making progress, even if it was slower than I had hoped. The coaches were delighted about being able to use the Universal Gym. It was wonderful to have a locker room that was ours in Allen Fieldhouse.

We were only just beginning. It should have been full speed ahead, but let's just say there were bumps along the way that kept us from hitting full stride.

Chapter XIII

Turbulence

I was proud of everything I accomplished as director of women's athletics. I was also grateful that I had the spirit to embrace all the good of those five years. I never allowed the negativity around me to harden my heart. I kept the burden of the battles to myself. Many of my players were unaware of all I had endured, some until years after they graduated, and many, no doubt, are reading about my life experiences for the first time here.

My **days** were so stressful I often thought I might get sick. Progress was slow and funds were tight. I knew my budget would be slim, but I grew impatient waiting for our simplest needs to be met. What I didn't anticipate was that everything, from the small decisions to the big ones, would be a fight. Nor did I realize that my biggest battles would be within the walls of my own institution, and not all of them pitted me against white male leadership.

Some of my biggest battles came from a faction of women who turned what should have been a positive time into a toxic one.

I knew change would be hard, and I looked younger than my years. I was the only Black face in the athletic department. Being a woman new to the department actually hurt me among the other women, who weren't used to seeing a female in a leadership role, especially when it pertained to athletics. Add to that I was Black and all of them were white. The professors who I retained as coaches only knew me as a graduate assistant. I didn't have any experience with inner office politics and that was what I encountered at every turn.

My intent was to build camaraderie while building a women's athletic program, a journey for us to share as one department. I did not see this as *my* journey. I wanted it to be *our* journey. I thought together all of us could focus on the larger goal of making Kansas women's athletics among the strongest sports programs in the nation. I welcomed suggestions, feedback and any input that would get us moving in that direction. My door was always open.

I would go to work every day with a smile, hoping for a fresh start, seeking common ground, trying to pull us together as a team. But most days I would leave work feeling deflated by their negativity.

It reached a low when some of the coaches went around me to seek support from the chancellor's office. The ugliness filtered down to the student-athletes. Things got particularly contentious with the softball coach. Even though she was successful on the field, we didn't have a positive professional relationship. One student-athlete who was on her softball team and my basketball team tried to create divisions among the basketball players. It went beyond favoring one coach over another. One of my first-year players would later tell me that she was harassed by some of her teammates for her loyalty to me. It saddened me to have any student-athlete involved in a professional conflict.

I tried to rise above it. I made a point of attending the AIAW Women's College World Series in 1974 to show my support for our Lady Jayhawks after their excellent season. I drove 400 miles round trip to Omaha, Nebraska, but it was clear I was not welcome. The coach kept her players at a distance. I could feel the snub. I didn't regret being there; it was the right thing to do as athletic director, but I wished I could have joined them in celebrating their season. I knew I had to find a way to end the animosity.

Back at KU, I overheard gossip about myself, including a ridiculous statement about how could I work such long hours? *She must be on drugs, they said.* Pat Collinson, my administrative assistant, heard that from a worker in the maintenance department. I couldn't imagine why anyone would spread such nonsense.

I reached out to a longtime female senior administrator on campus. I was hoping for support and suggestions from a leader who fought for change regarding women's issues. Faculty and students respected her. To my surprise and disappointment, she was just a step up from a Clyde Walker kind of greeting — a real lack of warmth. I thought she might be willing to introduce me to a few of the women's groups on campus so I could connect with them. It was clear she wasn't interested in helping me in any way, shape or form. As you might guess, I never went to talk to her again.

I was stunned to learn that a petition asking for my removal as athletic director circulated within the department and was sent to state legislators. I read the word "dictator" associated with my name in a *Lawrence Journal-World* article. I don't know who started the petition or who signed it, but I didn't see it coming. I met with the university lawyer, who told me not to worry about it. I was thankful that no one from the chancellor's office talked to me about it. Only one person ever mentioned it — a young, white Kansas legislator.

When he asked to meet with me, I thought we were going to discuss how KU could receive more money from the state for women's athletics.

Instead, he said, "I'm concerned about your program. I've had a lot of people come to me with complaints. I've decided to monitor your program."

I cut him off quickly. "You must be out of your doggone mind!" I said. I wanted to add a lot more to this man who knew nothing about my program, but I refrained from cursing him out, and truth be told, I rarely cuss. I made it clear he was not going to be monitoring anything and left him sitting alone in Strong Hall.

Oh, and I did see him again. Years later, running for re-election, he came to my neighborhood looking for votes. He rang my doorbell. I opened my door and waited. When he realized it was me, he could not have turned more pale. He shuffled around standing on my porch. Then he finally got up the nerve to ask for my support at the polls. I looked at him, smiled, and said I would have to take a look at his record.

I didn't do myself any favors when one of the first things I wanted to do was return field hockey to the physical education department as a club sport. Now remember, I played field hockey and certainly had nothing but respect and love for it. I was an all-conference field hockey goalie for goodness sake. Nor did I want to cut any sport. I felt for the athletes. I could feel their pain at the loss of opportunity. But I had to look at the larger picture. Geographically, Kansas was at a disadvantage. Field hockey wasn't a high school sport in the state. The best teams were on the East Coast. KU field hockey was strong at the state level, but entering the intercollegiate era meant scheduling tougher competition, and it didn't make sense to travel that far beyond the state to play on a shoestring budget.

It got particularly hairy with my last field hockey coach. I certainly understood she didn't want field hockey to be a club sport, but I knew, if she was honest with herself, she understood why I needed to cut it. Instead, she went to the chancellor, asking him not to allow me to eliminate the sport. Then she turned to the Student Senate for money for her program. Once again, I had athletes thinking I was the bad guy. As had happened before, Chancellor Dykes or Vice Chancellor Del Shankel would quietly ask me to keep field hockey. It was a mistake because divisive attitudes within a department snowball into larger problems. Field hockey was ultimately cut in the 1976-77 budget, following a trend at other Big Eight schools.

Years later, that same field hockey coach came to me and applied for a job as equipment manager for women's basketball. I interviewed her, remembering all I went through. But God can make your enemies your footstool, so although I hadn't forgotten what happened, I silently forgave and decided to hire her. She worked for me for a lot of years and did a good job.

I was constantly accused of favoring and rewarding my basketball team over the other sports. Basketball, volleyball and softball carried more athletes than golf and tennis, for example, and were allocated more money. It was a matter of making what we had go the furthest. I tried my best to be as fair as possible. I learned early on that just because some things were not equal didn't mean they weren't fair.

Many days I felt alone. I'd go into my office and close the door. I found solace praying and reflecting on the positives. Trying to push away all the things I had to do that week or month. Sometimes I would reflect on growing up in West Chester and how nice it was to see people of color who knew me and my family from the inside out. I longed for that comfortable feeling of belonging. People saying hello to each other with smiles and warmth. I didn't have a lot of that in my early years in Lawrence. There were only a few Black faces in Allen Fieldhouse — maintenance staff and a few assistant coaches on the football team. The men's equipment manager and I would stand and talk for a few minutes, but conversations with others would be limited. I became aware of the cultural differences between the East Coast and the Midwest. In the East, there were many more sports programs for women, and definitely more Black women participating. Racism existed everywhere, but it was blatant in the Midwest.

I prayed similar words every day: "Lord, if you do not want me here, it's OK. Just move me." I waited for a sign. I started to attend a little church on 4th Street under Pastor Ronald Yates and his wife, Ruby, who became dear friends of mine. They would think about me and out of the blue, call to ask how I was doing. Before they hung up, they would pray with me. When I would share those times I was struggling, asking God to move me, Sister Yates usually responded, "We don't feel God is ready for you to leave yet."

I made some unpopular decisions, but they ended many of the problems that plagued my first two years as athletic director. I accepted a lunch invitation from a close friend of the softball coach, hoping for some input to improve my relationship with her. Instead, I got an earful about the softball program not getting what it deserved and how unfairly the coach was treated. It didn't take long for me to get up and leave. It was clear I couldn't work with the softball coach and relieved her of her duties.

I dismissed a few others, including a trainer, who continued to perpetuate negativity in the department. The newspapers wanted me to talk about it, but they were personnel matters, so I didn't offer details. The dismissals had nothing to do with wins and losses. We needed a department of people willing to work together in support of one another. I had the backing of Archie Dykes and Del Shankel. The elimination of these people was a turning point. I saw my coaches and staff come together and be happy for each other's successes, no matter how big or small. It was a relief when attitudes improved around me. It was what I hoped for in the very beginning, all of us working together. I silently wished that positivity extended to the men in athletic administration.

My days were long. They started the night before by laying out Josie's clothes for school and making sure she had all her books and lunch money. I set an alarm and had a backup — an assistant would call me to ensure I was up. Getting out the door, especially on winter mornings before 6 a.m., was painful because it was so cold. During the first week of basketball conditioning, I was on campus by 4:45 a.m., in time for the five-mile run that was part of a preseason conditioning program for the team.

Back then, I jogged the five miles with my players. After a week we'd drop to four miles, then three, and finally they needed to achieve a certain time in the mile. No matter how old I got, I refused to finish last, so when the team got faster, I started jogging with my post players, who started their run ahead of the rest of the team. At least I could always keep up with them!

All day I juggled all the details of overseeing nine sports. That included preparing budgets for each sport, meeting with coaches and staff, writing and answering correspondence and brainstorming to find fresh ways to market our programs. Raising money was a daily concern. Sometimes I'd step out of my office, put on a hard hat and check out how our physical projects were progressing. Basketball practice was later in the day. I never wanted to miss practice. I could probably count on both hands the number of practices I missed, even while I was the athletic director, though sometimes Pat would be looking for me to leave practice for a quick meeting.

Josie was always on my mind, and she knew to call as soon as she got home from school. She was what was called in those days a latchkey kid. She knew to immediately lock the doors behind her as soon as she got home and grab a snack waiting in the fridge. She was expected to start her homework before turning on the TV. When road trips became overnight ones, I made arrangements for her to stay with trusted families if she was not traveling with us. If I'd get home late, I would make a simple dinner – often something microwavable. When I wouldn't make it home for dinner, Josie would have to settle for a Salisbury steak frozen dinner. If I had made fried chicken the night before, she ate the leftovers. My fried chicken dipped in vinegar is one of her favorites. I'd usually walk in and she'd be doing homework or starting a chore. I'm guessing she often started one or the other only when she heard my car in the driveway!

During the turmoil of those early years, I found joy in coaching the first women's track and field program in 1974. Track and field had been my first love, and here I was at Kansas, which had one of the top men's programs in the nation, but where was its women's program? Even though it meant the responsibility of wearing another hat as track coach when I couldn't find a coach, I did not want to wait another year to start the program. Allen Fieldhouse had an indoor dirt track that circled the perimeter of the basketball court. I had only an hour to run practice – beginning at 6 a.m. – because a faculty run started at 7. That's when faculty members walked or jogged on the track, and they had priority over us.

My first KU track team was a positive group of four runners, a shot putter and a javelin thrower. Blond with braids, Carrie Weltmer was one of the sprinters. She still lives in Lawrence and has fond memories of the days when she'd be a second driver, following my car to away meets in her brown Buick. The javelin hung out her back window! Carrie remembers a trip we took to Arkansas with me driving a station wagon ahead of her. She and her teammates got a $6 stipend for lunch and were out of luck when that wasn't enough to include a Coke. She didn't get any reimbursement for gas mileage, yet she didn't think a thing about it. Like the rest of the team, she was happy to be competing.

It was something of a milestone when I arranged for the coaches to use state vans for travel instead of their personal cars. Each van could carry 15 people. Since many departments on campus also used these vehicles, we needed to reserve them as soon as possible or we would be out of luck. If we didn't get one, another option was to rent a car, but any vehicle we rented had to be paid for upfront out of our own pockets. Afterward, we could submit a request for reimbursement, but the state took its time giving our money back. Sometimes we waited weeks to be reimbursed, which is not ideal when you're counting your pennies. What was worse, if you forgot to get a receipt or lost it, you were out of luck. I learned that the hard way while traveling with the basketball team. Quite often I misplaced a receipt. I might stuff it in my pocket and eventually lose it because I was in a hurry. After that happened a few times, I wised up and delegated one of my assistants to keep track of receipts.

My coaches impressed me with their commitment. Tom Kivisto, my tennis coach, remembers taking the tennis team on a West Coast swing through New Mexico, eating fast food the whole way and sometimes arriving an hour before match time. At night, three women shared one room that had one double bed and a cot. Home matches were played on cement courts without wind protection. The ball barely bounced. On blustery days the players had to deal with dust from the nearby unpaved parking lot. They were the same courts students used for recreational tennis, so Tom had to be careful about kicking people off them for team practices. Sometimes he'd let them finish rather than stir something up. With obvious disadvantages, Tom made the very best of it and went on to win the women's Big Eight championship in 1977, defeating Oklahoma. Every player on the roster was from Kansas, something Tom touts fondly.

I saw the landscape changing and knew Kansas had to adapt to keep up. I knew to be nationally competitive we had to start offering scholarships, even if they only paid for books. In women's basketball, we were already losing ground to programs like Stanford and Tennessee. There were no scholarships my first year, but I believed we had to start giving some form of aid for the 1975-76 season. I told that to a reporter before I left for an AIAW convention in California, and the next thing I knew Del Shankel was calling me.

"We just read you're going to be offering scholarships," he said.

I was chipper in my response. "Yes, that's true!"

"How are you getting this money?" Del asked.

"We're going to make sure we have the money," I assured in my best positive voice. "We have to have scholarships. I will find a way to raise the money."

I flew back early to meet with Del. Pat remained at the convention with my instructions on how to vote on the AIAW initiatives on the agenda.

One way we raised money for scholarships was through summer camps that I encouraged my coaches to run. A portion of the proceeds went into their scholarship funds. My first basketball camp attracted 35 girls.

We sponsored other fundraisers, like car washes, and yes, I was out there with a hose in one hand and a sponge in the other. We held campus events and accepted donations. One fraternity agreed to take a coach and put him or her in a mock prison. Breaking him out of "jail" required donations. I was grateful for any student support.

By 1975, KU handed out its first athletic scholarships to women when the Ruth Hoover Scholarship Fund was established. Many people who contributed to the fund did so to commemorate Ruth Hoover, who began at KU in 1921 and headed the Women's Physical Education Department for more than 25 years. She excelled in field hockey and was known for starting the Quack Club, essentially the first official women's swimming program at KU.

By 1976, 25 women were on partial scholarships, all paid for through donations. My budget was $144,000. Remember, the men's budget was well north of $2 million with 191 athletes on partial or full scholarship. After two years, I got our scholarships funded through the Williams Fund, which solicited alumni for donations.

While media coverage was scant for women's sports results, all kinds of opinion pieces were written about the impact of Title IX. Many of them suggested men's sports would suffer because women's sports had to be funded. It would have helped institutions if the law presented a road map, a blueprint for everyone to follow. But we were given a blank page as how to implement the law.

In 1976, *The Kansan* published an editorial cartoon that I would not forget. In response to the talk of a merger between the men's and women's athletic departments, the drawing featured a muscular and larger-than-life caricature of Clyde Walker. He had a sledgehammer in hand, grinning broadly, while tearing down the walls between the two departments. You could see Black hands — mine — sticking out from the construction debris. The rest of me was buried under the rubble. The caption read, "Just getting a head start on a little remodeling, Marian." The accompanying letter from the female associate editor of *The Kansan* noted the ridiculousness of truly separate but equal facilities, suggesting another Allen Fieldhouse would have to be built for women's sports. As if that was what anyone was asking for. I didn't appreciate the cartoon of Clyde hovering over me with a smirk. It was offensive, insensitive and a visual reminder of the attitudes I was up against.

By 1977, our budget was up to $197,000 with 37 partial scholarships, and I was one of five full-time employees in my department. An article in the *Leavenworth Times* reported that Title IX was "alive in Mid-America." That same story noted that I preferred the "Ms. designation," which made me chuckle. Consider the times. I thought it was the right balance between Miss and Mrs.

KU established a University Committee with Compliance for Title IX, but nobody was sure whether the enforcement deadline of 1978 would or could be met.

Meanwhile, fresh challenges emerged. On more than one occasion, I also had to deal with unwelcome sexual advances of men in authority positions, mostly white men. They flirted or tried to kiss me. Most of the time I learned to be creative in my rejections.

In one of my early meetings with a well-respected white administrative leader at the university, I got up to leave and he gave me a hug. Then he looked down at himself and whispered in my ear, "You see what you do to me." I immediately stepped away, patting him on his back. I didn't know what to say. I tried to control how shocked I was as I made a quick exit. I kept thinking no one would believe me, but I found out I wasn't alone. Two other women in senior administrative positions had also been on the receiving end of unwanted attention from him. I was concerned that any negative publicity about him would affect the women's athletic program.

The harassment continued. He visited my office after home games, but I made sure I was never alone with him. I remembered what happened to me as a child with men finding ways to corner me when Mom and Dad were not around. After games I would have Pat return to the office with me, and we decided that after five minutes or so she would call me on my office phone so I could make an exit. I finally reported him and found an ally in Bill Hogan, the associate vice chancellor, who was also Black. He promised me if he had to sit on my lawn to stop what was happening, he would. He assured me it would not happen again. And it didn't.

Then there was another incident with a well-known former KU track athlete. He was a friend who flirted with me at times, but I thought he was harmless enough. Both of us were scheduled to be at a banquet in Missouri. Several important people were going to be at the event, including Lusia Harris, a Black woman and one of the early pioneers of women's basketball. I felt it was important for me to go to gain exposure for our program. The track alum was also invited and owned and piloted his small plane. He invited me to join him to fly to the dinner and to return to Lawrence early the next morning. I didn't have the time to drive an eight-hour round trip. Flying with him seemed like a good alternative, though my plan was to pray every moment because I still did not like to fly. Shortly after we were up in the clouds, he put the plane on autopilot and made unwanted advances. Let's say he had no concept of personal space! I was no longer subtle. I was angry.

"You've got to get back to flying this plane," I said with a voice and body language that told him exactly that.

The whole thing turned into an unpleasant experience. It made for a long trip back to Lawrence.

While Clyde was public in saying no one was interested in watching women's athletics, I stayed focused on finding ways to let people know about upcoming games. Athletic departments today amplify their events through all the platforms available, ranging from social media to their own networks. We didn't have a Big Eight Network (and if we did, it wouldn't have broadcast women's sports). The newspapers didn't print our game times. People didn't know about our events until the day of or after the fact. When I was out in the community, people would tell me they didn't know we had a game. "How do we find out about your games?" they asked. I relied on the parents of my players to spread the word, but that only went so far. I wanted a marquee in front of Allen Fieldhouse that would list everything going on inside and around campus, but there was no momentum behind that idea.

I tried to grow the fan base with the help of supporters who dubbed themselves the Courtsiders. They were fans — women, men and their families — who were eager to welcome our players back to school and support them throughout the season. Every fall they held a picnic and cooked everything homestyle. It became a smorgasbord of wonderful food. After we ate, each player introduced herself, sharing where she was from and something about her family. The fans asked questions about the upcoming season. Many of the Courtsiders became lifelong friends of mine.

I was always on guard about people disrespecting my players, and that included a visiting radio crew. I was on the sideline during a game when I heard a broadcaster refer to us as "jungle bunnies." I was more than steamed. When he packed up his equipment and made his way up the stairs, I followed him. I got so close to his face that I think he feared I might punch him in the mouth. I made sure he knew I planned to report him to his supervisors.

We as coaches encouraged our student-athletes to sit in the front rows of classes as often as they could, not in the back rows. I wanted their professors to see them in class and get to know them. I provided signed letters for each player to give to her professors with information about scheduled events. I wanted the professors to recognize the student-athletes as responsible students. Most appreciated the communication. A few started coming to games and matches, supporting student-athletes from their classes.

Complaints mounted as we neared the July 21, 1978, deadline for Title IX compliance. The Office of Civil Rights had to respond to every complaint, and this was at a time when most athletic departments were not in compliance, so change was slow if at all. One suit brought by a Kansas junior called our athletic department out of compliance in almost every category. Another complaint specifically mentioned cutting field hockey. One of the first trainers I hired filed suit about the lack of proper facilities to tape athletes, noting that some were taped in the public restroom and others in the smoking lounge of the locker rooms at Robinson.

I got to know the lead investigator for the Office of Civil Rights in our region. She was sympathetic but overworked. She documented the ways KU was not in compliance, but Kansas did just enough to avoid losing federal funding. I later learned that coaches from other universities were telling young prospects that Kansas had a history of not supporting women's athletics. One rival school even sent a postcard with a copy of a newspaper article talking about lack of support at KU for women's athletics.

Yet with every passing year, it became clear that women's athletics was only going to grow, not go away. When Iowa State announced in 1978 that it intended to merge departments within a year, Kansas was the only Big Eight school that continued to separate its athletic departments. The idea of having one fund for all of athletics gained traction, and it made sense, though I worried women's athletics would play second fiddle if both were under one umbrella. But I knew a merger was coming and that my role would change.

I made sure I didn't lose sight of what we had accomplished in the five years since I started. All of the sports had excellent coaches and each had assistants. We had a trainer and a strength training room. We had uniforms that weren't hand-me-downs, and warmups. We were giving women scholarships. We had a locker room so our players didn't have to leave Allen Fieldhouse covered in sweat to shower in their dorms. We traveled by vans, not cars, and every so often, we flew. During overnight trips we went from cramming four into a small motel room to two players sharing the space. Coaches could fill out a form estimating the money they needed to make a trip and get an advance. No more having to use your own funds.

We had women from all over the state and many parts of the country wanting to come to the University of Kansas. And unlike when I started in 1973, we had Black female athletes competing for KU.

We had a lot to be proud of. Kansas women were in Allen Fieldhouse, on the track, on tennis courts and on the fields. At least one sportswriter from the *Lawrence Journal-World* was assigned to cover Kansas women's sports, and articles began appearing on the sports pages instead of fans having to read about us on the society page.

I knew a merger would end the camaraderie we had built in our department after the turbulent beginning. With every passing year, my relationships with the coaches on my staff became stronger. I held an annual retreat away from campus that included a meal and spending time reviewing new AIAW rules, budgets and planning for the coming season. We talked about goals for the teams and the department. Before we packed to go home, we finished our retreat with something fun. I remember ending one retreat with a trip to a roller-skating rink. I was holding onto a rail on the side, struggling to keep myself upright on skates while coaches double my age flew by me on their wheels.

A merger would mean instead of all the women's sports reporting to me, every assistant administrator in the athletic department would be assigned certain sports, much like athletic departments are organized today. It also meant that the Big Eight would officially embrace women's sports and their championships as part of the conference, which was long overdue.

Perhaps that's the biggest reason the Clyde Walker era — all five years of it – ended. In May 1978, Clyde was hired at North Carolina-Charlotte, and later that year Bob Marcum became Kansas' new athletic director.

From day one, nothing about the new athletic director suggested to me that he was open to growing women's athletics. But he couldn't overlook Title IX, which gained momentum when the federal regulations called for men and women to receive equal scholarships in proportion to their participation in sports. Colleges were told they had to comply or risk losing federal funding. Many major college athletic programs insisted they were being crippled by Title IX enforcement while the country was also facing rampant inflation. Shortly after, Bob Marcum suggested Kansas might have to drop its Division I-A status. Unfortunately, gymnastics got caught in the fire, eliminated for a $40,000 budget savings.

The NCAA filed suit questioning the legality of Title IX. The suit was dismissed in 1978.

The KU men's and women's athletic departments officially merged on July 1, 1979 — submerged, is what I called it at the time. I was made an associate athletic director and given 18 months to decide whether I wanted to continue in administration. But I decided almost immediately.

It was a good time to step aside. I had no interest in working for Bob. I had gotten the women's athletic program off the ground, and women's basketball demanded more of my attention. My Lady Jayhawks were becoming nationally relevant.

The toll of the long hours was catching up with me. I hadn't taken vacation for years. Nobody wanted to do anything without my approval, so my phone was constantly ringing. I remember going to Litchfield Beach on the coast of South Carolina for a few days — finally, time away — and my phone rang every day. I cut my time short because I couldn't relax. My eyes had dark circles under them. I remember leaving with my players for a road trip, and before we got out of Lawrence, they waited on the team bus while the bus stopped in front of my doctor's office. I ran in to get a quick B12 shot to lift my energy, hopped back on the bus and away we went.

I was grateful that I had the spirit to embrace all the good of those five years. I never allowed the negativity around me to harden my heart. I kept the burden of the battles to myself. Many of my players and most of the other female athletes and coaches in the department were unaware of what I faced. I didn't want them to know. I needed the athletes to focus on earning their degrees, and the coaches to help their teams achieve.

Although my days as athletic director were over, my coaching career was just getting started.

KU women's basketball finished 30-8 during the 1978-79 season. We were winning behind excellent talent. One student-athlete, Adrian Mitchell, had not played in high school because there wasn't a team. Another, a sophomore named Lynette Woodard, was pretty good, too. I'm not alone in believing she was the greatest to ever play college basketball.

Chapter XIV

Rock Chalk

I wanted to build an elite program, but at the same time I wanted to give young women the opportunity to win, to advance, to pursue their dreams, to find their potential through a college education. In most cases, it was a future they could never have imagined without basketball as the launching pad. I wanted to show young women how to believe in themselves, just as Mrs. Redding helped me as an eighth grader believe in myself.

It was a modest beginning on Nov. 23, 1973: Kansas 48, Rogers State 38 in a game played in Springfield, Missouri. The result was recorded as Win No. 1. I had no idea 559 victories would follow. It was the start of what would turn into 31 years of coaching women's basketball at KU. When you're 26 you can't imagine doing any one thing for 31 years. Yet, 923 games later, I was still walking the sidelines in Allen Fieldhouse.

By the time I coached my last game in 2004, the career numbers added up to a .607 winning percentage, 11 NCAA Tournament appearances, two NCAA Sweet 16s, seven regular-season conference titles, six conference tournament championships and three AIAW Sectional finishes. Kansas went from not being recognized in the Big Eight to winning the conference tournament four times. I was named the last Big Eight Coach of the Year in 1996, and when Kansas joined the Big 12 the next year, I was honored as the conference's Coach of the Year.

But for me coaching was more than numbers. I wanted to build an elite program, and at the same time give young women the opportunity to win, to advance, to pursue their dreams, to find their potential through a college education. In most cases it was a future they could never have imagined without basketball as the launching pad. I wanted to show young women how to believe in themselves just as Mrs. Redding believed in me.

I was a natural mentor. My office door stayed open for three decades. Most of the time, the after-hours sessions weren't about breaking down X's and O's. I was an ear, making sure my players knew they could come to me any time about literally anything. I know a lot of coaches delegated to their assistants many responsibilities I shouldered. I knew that my players, especially my Black players, trusted me. In me they saw someone who looked like them. It helped that I was approachable and easy to talk to.

As much as I appreciated my college coach, Carol Eckman, she knew nothing about the adversity I faced off the court until that day I became so overwhelmed I began spilling out the details. She said almost nothing in response. In fairness to her, my life was far removed from anything she had experienced. I don't think she knew what to add or how to help. I was describing a world she hadn't ever been a part of and might not have known existed.

Many of my most talented players came from households with only one parent. They weren't sure whether they should stay in college, wondering if they should be at home getting a job to help with their family's financial challenges. When I heard those stories, I reflected on the young woman I once was, trying to play my best basketball while going to West Chester State, holding a job at night and having a child at home. College was just one part of my life. For my peers, it was the biggest part of their lives. I never could say that. Coming home to find we had lost electricity again, to see only a little bologna and cheese in the refrigerator, was a reality that often demanded more attention than what I was studying or how many rebounds and points I could contribute.

Like many of my players, I remember the guilt of going to class while my siblings went to work. When I left home in 1970, I could only watch their lives from afar — Janet had three children, Izzy had four boys as a single parent and Cathy had two sons. All of my sisters worked long hours in nursing homes or in company plants making "chips." Butchie worked around the clock on cars. I remember beating myself up, thinking, "You are weak. You should stop going to college. Get a job and help your family."

Somehow God held me because I just couldn't make myself leave college behind. It was as if sports was the chain that pulled me, sometimes *dragging me* along my journey. As much as I wanted to play basketball, I knew having a degree would ultimately make a better life for Josie and help Mom and the rest of our family. When I encouraged my players to press on through the difficult times, I did so with a genuine understanding of what was pulling them in another direction on their individual journeys. I stressed how important it is to change what can become a repetitive cycle of a broken home, poverty that can lead to drug use and a sense of hopelessness. Someone in families like those has to be willing to step up to chart a different course, to be that role model who inspires the younger generation. Many of my players were the first in their families to go to college, get a degree and be that sorely needed example.

Especially early on, many of my Black players struggled to adjust to life at a predominantly white school. I also could relate to them because I know how vulnerable it feels to be the only Black woman in a room or in a restaurant or grocery store. I experienced culture shock again and again after leaving a part of the country that was drastically different from where I landed. My path would have been more comfortable had I remained in the East and been hired in Washington or Philadelphia. The East was far more integrated than the Midwest in the 1970s. Living in Lawrence was unlike anything I had experienced, even though I had just spent two years less than an hour away in Kansas City. Likewise, many of my players didn't see a lot of peers who looked like them, dressed like them, related to how they did their hair, the music they liked, the slang they used.

I always felt as if I stood out. KU had minority professors, but they didn't have their names in the newspapers as regularly as I did. They weren't constantly protesting some inequity and making waves. I felt like I was on my own island, a Black woman in a leadership position in an athletic department of white men working in their little circles where I wasn't welcome. I would be nervous when I had to speak at country club lunches or to civic groups, even though I usually received positive feedback. Gale Sayers, a KU athletic fundraiser, seemed to thrive in those settings. His job was to raise scholarship money for the Jayhawks. He connected with many well-to-do alumni and Kansas business owners whom he called by their first names. I knew very few people at these events and felt completely out of my element, often asking an assistant coach to join me so I would have someone to talk to when there were no more introductions to be made.

It was important to me that my players be confident, whether they were in class, at a campus event or speaking in public. They could watch how I handled myself in public, but I also made sure all of them were involved when there were opportunities to meet fans at an event and talk to them about our program. I gave them a basic outline with talking points to help them speak at public events, encouraging them to share where they were from and what they aspired to do with their degrees.

I remember when Angie Aycock was named a Kodak All-American in 1995 and she spoke at the Final Four banquet. She and I spent the night before carefully preparing what she was going to say. At the dinner where the Kodak All-Americans were recognized, Angie addressed the audience with poise. When she was finished, she got a standing ovation. I remember many coaches coming up to me and saying, "You must be so proud." And I was!

After years of trying to get the best out of each athlete, walk-ons included, I finally realized not every player was committed to getting a degree or working as hard as she should to improve her game. Hard as it was, I set some boundaries for myself. Those who I felt wanted a degree and who understood what we were trying to accomplish for our basketball program got the best of me. I didn't mind investing time, but I had to see progress at some point. I had to accept I had only so much energy, and I wanted players who *wanted* to be successful.

I faced my own learning curve with my first team. This was a veteran group of women whom I inherited. The core of my team was seniors. I was lucky that these were very competitive women who were hungry to learn. Many played two or three sports at KU. This was a time when athletes could play basketball, volleyball and softball. But the women on my team didn't go to college to become student-athletes; they were students who happened to enjoy athletics. They weren't on scholarship. Most hadn't lifted weights, let alone followed a conditioning program. It took until 1973, my first season as a head coach, for Kansas to sanction its first state high school girls basketball tournament.

We played with no fanfare and without a public address announcer. Players had to find their own meals before and after games. They got pretty good at taping their own ankles, too. We didn't travel with a trainer, so any injury during a road game would have to be addressed once we got back home.

I wasn't much older than my team during the '70s, which meant I could easily get on the court myself and show them precisely what I was trying to teach, whether working on one-on-one moves or showing them how to box out. I could demonstrate what it meant to "step through" rather than just talk about it. I had fun playing one-on-one with my players. I stayed on that court as long as I could. My defensive skills were the last to go. I could still move left or right, drop step and fight over screens. My shot was so-so, but it was no longer about me winning. I was winning when my players kept improving and performed well against our opponents.

The downside was having to draw a line when players wanted to do social things with me. I went with a few to an outdoor concert in Kansas City to hear the band Chicago. I didn't usually do things like that, and as much as I enjoyed them, I realized I could not be both their coach and their pal. I found myself thinking how great it would be when I was 10 years older and not in my 20s. As the years went on, I didn't question myself so much. I could occasionally do things with my team and not be concerned because my young players now considered me "old."

From the beginning, it was always important for me to look professional on the sidelines. I took seriously that I represented the University of Kansas, my players, my family and Black coaches. The little money I spent on myself went to the clothes I wore at games. I tried not to repeat the same outfit, though I'd often mix and match jackets with the same pair of black slacks. I always wore a cross around my neck.

Before every season, I went on a shopping spree at a mall in Overland Park, Kansas. I befriended a saleswoman at Macy's who soon learned the style of clothes I liked and started looking out for me. Whenever there was a sale, she called me at my office to let me know she was holding something for me to look at. I liked the polished look of Ellen Tracy designs. Later, when I made more money, I started collecting St. John's more elegant knits. At first I wore a lot of skirts, but I was happy when pantsuits became fashionable. I remember creating a little excitement when I came out wearing form-fitting leather pants a couple of times! I wore basic black but wasn't shy about putting on my red and royal blue leather pants. The first time I wore leather was during a Big Eight tournament in Salina, Kansas. When I walked toward the bench, heads turned. Nothing was said, but the air around me seemed to grow still. Hey, I was in the middle of Kansas, for gosh sake, surrounded by hard-working farm families. I knew I was creating a stir, but I also had the confidence to be myself. My players loved me in leather!

Subconsciously, I think I remembered when I had only one pair of shoes and a few clothes to wear to school. I would always notice how some of my role models dressed. Mrs. Redding looked so regal wearing her African colors and prints. And then there was Bert, immaculately groomed and able to walk easily in five-inch heels. My pumps were two inches, nothing too high, because I paced the sidelines a lot. I often crouched on my heels, almost like a baseball catcher's position. Of course, there was the time I left my house in a rush and stuffed my pumps in my purse, only to realize right before game time that I had put in two left-footed shoes. I had no choice. I wore them the entire game feeling as if everybody was staring at my awkward walk to the sideline and to the locker room. I stood talking to my team at halftime praying nobody would look down at my feet. That's one of the few games where I did a lot of sitting!

My first players couldn't believe they were able to play in Allen Fieldhouse, where the KU men sold out games, packing in crowds of more than 16,000 fans who turned it into one of the game's most magical venues. It is special walking inside and seeing that iconic banner that reads, "Pay Heed All Who Enter: Beware of The Phog," which commemorates Phog Allen, who coached there for 39 years. My players loved being on the same floor where Wilt Chamberlain played for two seasons in the '50s. It was largely empty for our games except for family members and friends. Quiet as it might have been, I was excited to watch my team compete on this grand stage. I wished we had more people to share it with, but all I could think was, "We are finally here! Right now, we are in Allen Fieldhouse playing a basketball game." Women weren't just sitting in the stands cheering on men anymore. They were the athletes!

There was no admission fee for our games, and fans were handed pieces of paper to jot down players' numbers and have fun keeping up with scoring. When I asked KU to help us get a program for our games, they told me the men had programs only because of advertisers. They insisted that no one would be interested in advertising for a women's game. I was able to get a team poster made with the help of an art student I found on campus who agreed to sketch the faces of my key players on a block of wood. We then made a 9x10 poster and ran off copies to sell at our games.

In 1977 I finally got a small stipend to add an assistant coach — Kathy Meek, the daughter of a wheat farmer from West Texas. It wasn't easy to find good assistants when you couldn't offer much in the way of a salary. Kathy, though, applied and qualified for a graduate assistantship that gave her additional money. She had been a standout high school basketball player, so she knew the game and could help teach. She also took care of details such as making travel arrangements and overseeing the equipment and uniforms. Most importantly, she made sure she didn't leave the practice floor without my clipboard, which I was always misplacing.

The first KU women's game-day program didn't happen until 1977, and it wasn't connected to our athletic department. One day in a Lawrence grocery store I met a little woman with a big smile and lots of energy. She introduced herself and asked if I would be interested in her helping me get game programs and possibly developing a "Marian Washington Coach's Show" on the radio. Of course! I answered. I soon learned that Peg Witmer was a creative genius and the marketing manager at a local radio station, KLZR. She went to banks and stores and sold enough advertisements for the Lady Jayhawks to have regular game-day programs. A player's picture was always on the front. The rosters of both teams and spaces for fans to record points, rebounds and fouls were on the back. That same year, Peg got me my own cable TV show, which lasted for one season, and she got my radio show started, which lasted until my retirement.

Once KU administrators saw that business people were willing to advertise in our programs and on radio, they took over Peg's initiatives and managed them through the marketing office. KU never thanked Peg for the work she did, but her efforts did not go unnoticed. Other Big Eight women's coaches wanted to talk to her about how to get their coach's shows off the ground. Peg is one of my best friends, and I appreciate all she did.

Even after the athletic departments merged and the whole country debated Title IX, many in the athletic department still treated us as if we were intruders in their space. The scales remained tilted heavily to accommodate KU men's basketball and football. The men's basketball team practiced in the afternoon when its players were out of class. We were forced to practice late in the evening or early in the morning, and it was never just us. We shared the Fieldhouse with track and volleyball. During inclement weather, it got even more crowded when football came in.

Football never made a quiet entrance. Out of the blue, I would hear a coach yell, "Football's coming in!" The next thing you know, players would be running the stairs. Footballs would be tossed back and forth over the court while we were in the middle of a drill. During bad weather, the baseball team was there, too.

It was like being part of a three-ring circus. It was obvious we needed an indoor facility for football, baseball and track, but it wouldn't be built for years.

Once, men's basketball "asked" me to cut my practice short. The coaches demanded we get off the court so a visiting team could practice. I didn't want to make a scene in front of my players, so I told them we were ending practice early. But I was not going to let that happen again. I kept asking myself: Why such disrespect? The administration knew what Title IX said about that kind of treatment. Yet getting the administration to change its attitude, to accept that women's basketball should have priority over a visiting team, was not easy in the 1970s. But I didn't back down. I made sure, from that point on, the administration scheduled the visiting team's practice around us or I was going straight to the chancellor.

During some major renovations to Allen Fieldhouse, construction workers with jackhammers breaking concrete made it nearly impossible to hear anything. I resorted to a bullhorn and then a portable microphone. I was screaming to be heard. No matter what I tried, my players couldn't hear me.

I had my suspicions, so I asked my assistants, who were white, to talk to the construction workers. The crew said they were told to use the jackhammers during certain times of day — the exact hours when women's basketball practiced. I went straight to the KU senior administrator overseeing construction. He denied that was true. Before I returned to my office, I saw him talk to the foreman. Suddenly, no more jackhammers during my practices.

If we played a doubleheader with the men's team, our shootaround time was early. If the men's game was televised, the broadcast crew came in early and acted oblivious to the fact that women were on the court, preparing for their own game. The media crew would set up equipment with cables lying all over the court. It never failed. I would have to walk to the other side of the court to the men setting up cameras and microphones and ask them not to be so loud because we were practicing. I also had to tell them they needed to move their cables off the court so athletes did not trip over them.

"You *will* be responsible if any of my players get hurt," I cautioned in a stern tone. As soon as they heard the word responsible, the crew immediately moved the cables until we were finished.

Then there was the game that nearly interfered with the start of a men's game. I believe we were in overtime when the former baseball coach-turned-administrator dared to come to my bench to tell me he was going to have to stop our game so the men could warm up for their game. I shot him a look and assured him we would not stop playing until our game was over.

Because women's basketball usually practiced late, the dining halls were closed by the time we finished. That left my players with nothing to eat. I met with the dorm managers and arranged to have them hold bagged meals so the players would at least have something in their stomachs at night. But it wasn't a hot meal like the men got. All they could do for us was make up bags with maybe a sandwich, drink, chips and a cookie inside. They would also leave a bowl of fruit. The cafeteria staff left these bags sitting on a countertop when they were closing for the night. I worried a student in the dorm might walk by and grab a bag or two. We were lucky that happened only a couple of times.

Football and men's basketball feasted on steak and roast beef, hearty sides and more at what was called the training table at Burge Union. None of the women's teams was permitted to use the training table until it became a Title IX complaint. Bob Marcum, the athletic director, claimed there was no issue, pointing out in a newspaper article that men's non-revenue sports could not eat at the training table either. He said football and men's basketball set aside money from their budgets to pay for the food. That was ridiculous — this money was added to their budgets in the first place. And, of course, there was no extra money put in my budget to pay for the training table, so the women continued receiving bagged meals in place of a real dinner. It took until the early 1980s for the athletic department to rectify that inequity.

Late practice times and subpar meals weren't the only issues we had to contend with. The men's basketball players benefited from academic support, thanks to student tutors who were designated academic coordinators. Our women weren't getting tutored or being advised for classes, so I brought in my own person, Professor Renate Mai-Dalton, who became a dear friend and was the last person to see my mother alive.

Renate, a professor emerita from Germany who is in the KU Women's Hall of Fame, established tutoring for minority students in the School of Business. Her program resulted in an extremely successful graduation rate. She also connected students to major companies offering internships and job opportunities. Renate agreed to help my players plan their schedules and recruited other professors to tutor female athletes. However, she was something of a taskmaster and a lot of my Black players couldn't relate to how she talked to them. I knew they could get more help from her than anyone else in the department, but there was clearly a communication issue with some of the athletes, so I became the go-between. When the athletic programs merged, the director of the entire academic program for KU wanted all of the players to work through his academic department. He didn't want Renate to continue working with my players. I decided those who didn't need as much help could receive tutoring through the academic center, but I knew I could count on Renate to work closely with those having a more difficult time. No one was happy with the arrangement, and I was often playing referee, but all of us accepted that the student-athlete came first.

We went without many of the amenities teams take for granted today. We rarely watched much film before games. Those times when we did, the quality was far inferior to today. Early on, I purchased a Super 8 camera and had one of my managers film our games. Try to visualize large circular reels of game film recorded by inexperienced filmmakers. My student managers often forgot to follow the play because they were cheering for our team. Eventually we graduated to a VCR, still primitive compared with today's digital world.

We couldn't slow the film down or speed it up because we didn't have the equipment. The men had a more elaborate setup and a knowledgeable staff member who broke down tape any way the coach wanted. We had to wait years before we could afford anything close to the equipment they had.

We had our share of adventures on road trips during those early years. I liked playing at Minnesota when my friend and former teammate from my national team experience, Ellen Mosher, coached there. The first time we went to Minnesota we experienced blizzard conditions. I drove one of two 15-passenger vans, and after we stopped to eat, the vans were buried in snow. All of us dug out the vans so we could get back on the road. It was difficult to see, so I followed the backlights of cars in front of us, sometimes inching forward at 5 mph. We passed cars and trucks in ditches. There were times when I gripped the wheel, praying we would not wind up in a ditch ourselves. We arrived safely just before tipoff and then won the game. I sat and had a long prayer, thanking God for protecting us and asking God to help us get home safely. Somehow we did.

The next time we went to Minneapolis we flew — two small planes, with me traveling with one group of players and Kathy the other. We arrived safely, but after the game, we took off for home in a snowstorm. I remember our pilot inspecting the flaps on the wings with a flashlight. Now you can guess how I was feeling watching a pilot with his flashlight, given how much I hated to fly under normal circumstances. The second plane got delayed, and Kathy and her group ended up being diverted to Kansas City. I was relieved when I learned they had landed safely.

Recruiting was limited under the AIAW's strict rules. The national body didn't want women's sports to fall prey to the money many felt corrupted the men's game, although by denying scholarships they were taking away opportunity. It took the threat of a lawsuit in 1973 to change that. But AIAW rules still didn't allow reimbursing a recruit's travel costs for what today would be called an official visit. That made campus visits almost impossible for players from low-income families. AIAW rules further prevented college coaches from talking to players in their homes or on the phone. Initial conversations had to go through a high school coach.

I knew we needed talent — outstanding players with potential — to put KU on the map. In my second year of coaching, I recruited my first great player — Adrian Mitchell, who remains one of only two KU players to score more than 2,000 points and grab more than 1,000 rebounds. Hers is one of four women's jerseys hanging in the rafters in Allen Fieldhouse.

Even though Adrian grew up 40 miles east of Lawrence, she never considered attending KU. I walked into a Kansas City gym for an AAU game, planning to watch another player. The game started, and the first time Adrian touched the ball I could not take my eyes off her. She could score. She could rebound. And could she ever move! Her athleticism separated her from the other players. I knew immediately she would make a difference in my program.

Adrian remembers the first time we spoke. After the game I talked to her coach, who introduced me to Adrian. "Would you be interested in coming to KU to play basketball?"

She couldn't believe the question. Adrian was 21 years old and never played at Central High School, which didn't have a girls team while she was there. She was working in downtown Kansas City in the purchasing department at City Hall.

Adrian's life looked a little like the one I once had. She was a single parent with a 2-year-old daughter named Monique. Going to college never crossed her mind, and her high school counselors never brought up the subject. No one from her family had attended college. She would tell me years later that talking to a Black woman who was both a coach and an athletic director at a major university left an impression she wouldn't forget.

In her quiet voice, Adrian answered, "I would *love* to come play at KU."

The next week, Adrian made a surprise visit to our campus. Afterward, we talked in my office and before she left, she signed to come to KU. Adrian wanted Monique to live with her, so I made arrangements with the housing department. KU offered off-campus housing for families with a husband and wife. I needed them to recognize that a mother and daughter are also a family. I had a fight on my hands again, but through persistence, I finally secured a spot for her in Stouffer Place, which contained student apartments, not dorms. It was the first time a single mother was permitted to live there.

Adrian needed all the financial support she could get, so I worked with her to apply for food stamps and find affordable daycare for Monique. Adrian qualified for financial aid, so she didn't have to borrow money.

Adrian, along with Kelly Phipps and Viette Sanders, became my first scholarship players. They each received about $600, which was worth more than it would be today but still wasn't much. Soon afterward I signed a shooting guard from Missouri, Cheryl Burnett, who would go on to coach at Southwest Missouri State. Now we could compete with stronger teams even though we still had a number of walk-ons.

Adrian went on to earn All-Big Eight honors and twice was named a finalist for the Wade Trophy, given annually to the best player in women's college basketball. She was invited to try out for the World University Games team in 1977 and was selected as an All-American her junior year. In 1979 she was drafted in the second round by the Chicago Hustle of the short-lived Women's Professional Basketball League.

Adrian fondly recalls ending her freshman season in Las Vegas — the first plane trip for KU women's basketball.

UNLV officials wanted a home game with Kansas, so they agreed to help us financially. We didn't have enough money in the KU program in 1976 for that kind of trip. UNLV paid for most of our meals and got us a significant discount on lodging. We played the first part of a doubleheader, with the men's Runnin' Rebels following us.

We experienced what "home-court advantage" really meant. It wasn't just two teams competing. Fans became the sixth player, and they were loud, rowdy and rude during the game. When I challenged some of the officials' calls, UNLV coach Dan Ayala and I got into it. He got animated, which fired up the crowd. I could feel the heat in my face as I confronted him at midcourt. It wasn't just about losing the game. We were experiencing an ugly environment, and it didn't help that I felt some of it was orchestrated by him. We lost 99-84.

My players loved being in Vegas. Most had only read about what went on in the desert. A couple of parents joined us. I had never been to Vegas, but sure enough, as we got off the plane, it was just as pictured in magazines. We saw slot machines everywhere and could hear the *cha-ching* of coins raining down on the holding trays. I knew I was going to have challenges keeping the team focused and away from playing the nickel, dime and quarter slots.

Although I didn't want the players gambling, when I saw their parents having so much fun I decided to try. I bought a book to learn how to play blackjack. After reading a few chapters about when to hold and when to fold, I sat down at a $5 table with a $20 bill. I applied my beginner's knowledge and was shocked to have won $200 after a few hands. And then I started to lose. Remember, I don't like to lose, so I put most of my winnings in my pocket. The moment I lost a few hands, I stopped playing. For some reason, I thought about Dad and his belief in saving as much money as you can, when you can. The experience was good because it confirmed I was *not* a gambler. I didn't enjoy putting money in a machine, pulling a lever, never to see it again.

Yet in 1977, I hit the basketball jackpot by signing a 6-foot center from Wichita.

Every coach who saw Lynette Woodard play wanted her. She could do anything on the court, even in high school. I had never seen a young girl handle the ball so effortlessly. And could she score! She could find space between players and pop in holes quickly and easily. Lynette outran players while dribbling. She made the game exciting with how easy she made everything look.

Wichita North High School went 59-3 while Lynette was there, which included two state titles (freshmen could not play varsity at that time). She averaged 33 points and 20 rebounds in her final high school season and was named a Parade All-American.

I actually heard about Lynette from an unlikely source — Josie. While Josie was attending Lawrence High School, the Girls 5A state tournament was in Lawrence. Lynette was just a sophomore. After watching Lynette in a game, Josie made a beeline for her. "You have to play for my mom!" she insisted. Josie even went to the hotel where the team was staying — the Holiday Inn on Iowa Street — and found Lynette again, telling her, "You have to go to Kansas where my mom coaches." My daughter grew up around talented women so she recognized how skilled Lynette was.

I was lucky enough to hang medals around the necks of Lynette and her teammates when Wichita North won state her senior year.

Because of AIAW rules, Lynette's exposure was somewhat limited. I was so thankful! But I had to overcome a major hurdle — Lynette had determined she was not going to attend a school in Kansas. Like so many kids, she wanted to leave her home state. She had adventure on her mind. I remember Lynette calling me to say, "I would play for you, Coach, if you were anywhere else."

I responded saying, "I'm not somewhere else, Lynette. I'm here at Kansas."

Fortunately, I persuaded Lynette to make an official visit to KU. It meant she had to take a bus to Lawrence from Wichita, about 163 miles. The bus makes a lot of stops, so it was close to a four-hour ride. Remember, AIAW rules prevented reimbursement for expenses, so KU couldn't pay for her trip.

Lynette called me the morning she was supposed to come and said she didn't think she could make it. I don't know if I sensed she was making an excuse, but I was disappointed. I let her know that I had arranged several activities on campus just for her. I held my breath for a few minutes, praying she would change her mind. She hung up saying she would take the next bus to Lawrence.

I tried not to drive too fast to the bus station, but I was running late. I had gotten held up in a meeting and here I was, rushing. Lynette was waiting in a bus station, by herself, after riding for hours. What a way to start her visit! As soon as I saw her, I jumped out of the car and apologized for being late. She was surprised when she realized everything that was on my plate — coach and director of women's athletics. She didn't know that about me until then.

We stopped for a bite to eat. We didn't order much because she had to pay for her own meal. Afterward, I showed her the campus, which is especially beautiful at night. The first place I drove to was Campanile Hill, where there is a tall monument dedicated to those in the KU community who died in World War II. The clock on top of the monument rings every 15 minutes with a special bell chime. Just like a church bell, the stroke of each hour is heard while students walk to and from class. At commencement, KU graduates wearing caps and gowns gather at the top of the hill. They walk through the base of the monument and down the hill to the football stadium for the ceremony. Along the way, family and friends cheer. It's a special tradition. I wanted Lynette to see herself in that moment, to imagine where her parents would sit, and I wanted her to think about how she would feel walking down this famous hill to accept her diploma.

The next day, I had arranged for all the Black professors on campus to attend a reception for Lynette. It was amazing how many professors came. Everyone was upbeat and excited to talk to her about what it was like to go to school here.

Little did I know that Lynette was a young militant. She believed in Black pride. She wanted to be in an environment where she could be comfortable being a Black woman. I could see she was having a good time. I know receiving such a warm welcome helped me recruit her to KU. The reception room was decorated with Kansas banners and balloons, and finger food and drinks were provided. Pictures of the Jayhawks were all around the room. She met the chancellor and Del Shankel, too. Her entire experience that day was geared to academics and how she could further her education at KU. I learned other schools had taken her to parties and given her athletic gear, which was against AIAW rules. As much as I wanted Lynette to sign with us, I wasn't going to break rules to get her.

Lynette and I didn't talk much basketball during her visit. This was a 17-year-old who was told again and again how athletically talented she was. I wanted her to understand she was more than just a basketball player — she was also an intelligent young woman who would succeed as a college student at KU. She needed to see herself capable of anything she put her mind to.

I would later learn what was most important to Lynette. Dorothy Woodard was the glue to Lynette's family. Lynette's mother made sure her children went to church every Sunday. She would later tell me the story of one day searching for her little girl. Across the street in the park was a tent full of holy worshippers. Mrs. Woodard said as she looked around the tent she saw two long pink tails bouncing up and down. They belonged to 6-year-old Lynette, who was singing and dancing with the members. Lynette stayed involved with her hometown church for a long time after college.

I felt good after Lynette left Lawrence, but I knew she was going to make at least one more visit to a school in Texas. Of course, I was nervous, especially when she called and told me what a good time she was having there!

Several days later, she told me she was coming to KU. I was thrilled! I had some talent on my team now, and adding a player like Lynette would help us become a nationally recognized program. This is *amazing*, I thought. Finally, I was getting closer to that vision I had for the program.

Lynette didn't want to publicly announce her commitment at first because she was scheduled to be in a couple of all-star games and she worried coaches would limit her playing time if they found out she was KU-bound.

Seeing Lynette in a Kansas uniform for the first time — her No. 31 now hangs in Allen Fieldhouse — was a splendid sight. The best high school player in the county was a Lady Jayhawk. KU now had two elite players in Adrian and Lynette. Our team would be able to compete with the top programs in the country.

Lynette immediately lifted Kansas Basketball to another level. People started coming to our games just to see her play.

Even on the road she was a draw. She wasn't just good at the game, Lynette was great at every part of basketball. Sheryl Swoopes was a terrific scorer. Nancy Lieberman was a beautiful passer. Lynette played all five positions. She was first or second in almost every major statistical category in the nation for the years she played. Think about that. Every year she led in scoring, rebounds and/or steals. In her senior year, she played point guard and climbed into the assists column.

It was almost like she was floating when she handled the ball. She had a sophisticated court vision so she could see plays develop. She could rock a defense to sleep. She was so creative, a scoring machine who was dangerous all over the floor. She and Adrian combined to be a potent offense right away. KU won nine of its first 10 games behind Adrian, a junior, and Lynette, a freshman.

We took our lumps during an East Coast swing, the first time Kansas had ventured that way. I lined up games against some of the best teams in the country in Immaculata, Maryland, Rutgers and George Washington. I knew to be the best, we had to play the best, so I wasn't worried about early-season losses.

Behind Lynette and Adrian, Kansas debuted in the national rankings on Dec. 14, 1977. My Jayhawks came in at No. 18! We reached postseason for the first time in 1978 after a 20-7 regular season. The AIAW broke the country into 10 regions that were geographic because teams did not have the money to travel far for the early rounds. Kansas was in Region VI, which was hosted by Kansas State.

The regional winners advanced to the national tournament, and a selection committee chose six additional teams to round out the field of 16.

KU won its first-ever tournament game, defeating Northwest Missouri State 66-63 at Ahearn Field House in Manhattan, Kansas. The next day we lost to Missouri, but our season continued even after we dropped the third-place game to Drake.

Kansas was invited to the 16-team National Women's Invitation Tournament (NWIT) hosted by the Amarillo Chamber of Commerce in Texas. (For some historical perspective, Wayland Baptist won the first nine of those.) The NWIT waited until after the AIAW regional round to pick its field, so teams got to participate in two postseason events if they lost in the first one. Kentucky beat us in overtime in the first round in Amarillo; we then beat Minnesota and lost by one to Drake to end our season at 22-11.

By Lynette's second year, when Adrian was a senior, I was dealing with attitudes on my own team. There was jealousy because Lynette scored so much. She averaged 31 points as a sophomore and had gained name recognition. Media who covered us only wanted to talk to her. Her name was almost always the only one in the newspapers. This did not help the morale of our team. During interviews I consistently discussed the team's performance. Yet as much as I tried to get writers to do a more thorough job reporting how other players contributed, the articles were small and mentioned only the high scorer.

It got to the point where Lynette came to me and said nobody would pass her the ball.

I looked at her and said, "Well then you'll just have to focus on your defense and steal it!"

Team dynamics are different today. Most players understand and accept their roles because they want to win. When I think about a few of my early teams, I know we had players who missed out on consistently winning because they were so focused on individual goals. Adrian admits today that she struggled initially when her scoring dropped because Lynette took so many shots. I even kicked Adrian out of the gym one practice, but that was the only wakeup call she needed. I was hard on my best players. They set the example and sometimes I had to call them out, especially if I thought their work ethic was lacking. They were my leaders, and I needed them to understand the impact they had on their teammates, who looked up to them. I remember telling one player to run the track until I got tired! Another time I left one of our starters home from a trip. As a head coach, I drew a hard line so that everyone understood what was acceptable and what was not. Not working hard was something I simply refused to tolerate.

In 1979, Lynette led the nation in steals during a season that saw Kansas win the Big Eight tournament for the first time. We as Big Eight coaches recognized the honor; the conference, remember, didn't start counting women's championships until the 1982-83 season. That started a string of three consecutive conference championships. Three! We beat Mizzou in the first championship game and the next year nipped Kansas State. Those were big victories over two bitter rivals. Men's basketball had all sorts of conference banners from multiple leagues, and they had the national title banners. But finally we as women had something of ours hanging in Allen Fieldhouse. Big Eight champions 1979. Big Eight champions 1980. Big Eight champions 1981.

Those were significant milestones. The Rock Chalk chant — Rock-Chalk-Jay-Hawk-K-U-U-U — wasn't just for men's basketball anymore. We started hearing it at our games, too.

In '79, KU swept the AIAW Region VI tournament, three wins that included beating Nebraska for the fourth time that season, ousting top-seeded Missouri and then K-State in the final behind 26 points and 17 rebounds from Lynette, who was named tournament MVP. We earned a trip to Carbondale, Illinois, for the Central Sectional playoffs. It was an achievement to get there, where we needed to win twice to reach the national semifinals.

In Carbondale, we were tripped up by a dominant Louisiana Tech team that held Lynette to a season-low 15 points. The Lady Techsters routed us, 100-61, on their way to a national runner-up finish.

We finished 30-8 — the first time we won 30 games in one season. With Adrian graduated, I moved Lynette to point guard for the next two years to free her up a bit.

KU went on to win 29 games the next season, and again we went 3-0 in the Region VI playoffs, surviving our first game against Central Missouri by a point. We defeated Kansas State in the championship game behind Lynette's 37 points. For the second year in a row she was named tournament MVP.

By 1980, the AIAW Tournament had expanded to 24 teams. We beat a Cheyney State team coached by C. Vivian Stringer in the sectional playoffs, a huge win for us behind Lynette's near triple-double and our press that forced 27 turnovers. We found ourselves pitted again against our nemesis, Louisiana Tech, in the next round. We had come close to the Lady Techsters in the Wayland Baptist tournament earlier in the season, losing 76-74.

But in Ruston, with all five starters in double figures, Louisiana Tech ended our season again, 81-73. The Lady Techsters advanced to the Final Four.

We had one more season with Lynette, and heading into 1980-81 I knew she was close to becoming the all-time leading scorer in the collegiate game. Now there wasn't an online record book to call up, and national media coverage was still scant. Newspapers covered their home teams, but the scoring record didn't receive nearly the attention it would warrant today. The AIAW discouraged individual accolades, believing they took away from the team concept, and kept records for national championships only. But official records were available, and they were precise. Both coaches signed a scorebook after each game to make it official.

Initially, newspapers reported that Carol Blazejowski of Montclair State held the record. "The Blaze," as she was called, won the inaugural Wade Trophy and had amassed 3,199 career points. She was a fantastic shooter. Lynette had scored 2,888 points going into her senior season, already the most by a male or female in KU history. We were playing at Madison Square Garden in the Hanover Spring Classic when new information came to light. Mel Greenberg, the longtime guru of women's basketball reporting who started the national women's poll, reported that Tennessee's Cindy Brogdon, with 3,204 points, was the scoring leader.

Lynette left no doubt, eclipsing Brogdon's mark with a jump shot that was part of a 22-point night during a regular-season game at Allen Fieldhouse against nationally ranked Stephen F. Austin on Jan. 6, 1981. After her first basket, the game was stopped for Lynette to receive the ball and an ovation. Her parents and siblings came to the floor to embrace her and congratulate her. She didn't know they were in the stands so it was a happy moment for her. I felt it was fitting to see her get the record at home.

On Feb. 3, 1981, Kansas was No. 3 in the AP poll, the highest the Lady Jayhawks had ever been ranked. We had been picked preseason to go to the Final Four. However, we just never seemed to get a break.

After going 4-0 in the Region VI playoffs and having just three losses all season, I was disappointed when Kansas was seeded sixth and matched against No. 10 UCLA in the sectionals. The Bruins were 29-5, coached by Billie Moore, and had a superstar in Denise Curry, the other candidate besides Lynette being mentioned for the Wade Trophy. If we were going to meet the Bruins, it should have been later in the tournament. I called the AIAW committee to protest the seeding. I was told one of the teams seeded higher than us had a couple of injured players returning. So what? What about my team that worked so hard to finally get a top seed? I couldn't believe what I was hearing. I even got a call from a coach whose team was seeded in the top four agreeing that our seeding was too low. I couldn't get the slight out of my mind. I was so tired of fighting for the right to fairness. Looking back, I felt I let the team down, wishing I had been able to focus more of my emotions on winning the game in front of me.

We lost 73-71 at Allen Fieldhouse. UCLA went to the free-throw line 34 times. We shot 16 free throws. It's a game we should have won. I was so sad. The team was heartbroken. Lynette's remarkable collegiate career had come to an end.

Lynette stands alone in KU history as the career leader in points, rebounds, steals and too many categories to list. No female player in any era has matched her versatility. Her handle was so good that it was no surprise to me when the Harlem Globetrotters invited her to join their world-famous team, the first woman to hold that distinction.

She is the gold standard in college women's basketball, amassing 3,649 points without the benefit of a three-point line, playing with the larger men's ball and being part of a Lady Jayhawks team with just three players on full scholarship. Yet I'm certain that most young players today don't know Lynette's name, let alone realize her achievements.

Nor do they know the names Cindy Brogdon, Carol Blazejowski, Denise Curry or Susie Snyder — the two through five top AIAW scoring leaders.

Almost nobody acknowledges AIAW records. The NCAA dismisses them. These incredible players and coaches who should be celebrated are treated as if they barely existed. They are not considered as significant as NCAA players and coaches, and the NCAA disregards AIAW championships.

But women's basketball didn't start with the NCAA. It only continued.

I can't deny what the NCAA has given our sport. Nor can I overlook what it has diminished. I have a lot to say on the matter, enough to start this next chapter about why history is important and why failing to recognize it isn't just arrogant.

It's plain wrong.

Chapter XV

Buried

Only a few of today's athletes know the real history of women's sports, and in particular women's basketball. Not only has it been dismissed, but it's been replaced by a selective record book that is insulting to anyone who played before 1982.

In the movie "The Burial," Jamie Foxx plays an unconventional lawyer named Willie E. Gary who represents a small-town Mississippi funeral home against a behemoth corporation. In one scene, Willie Gary gazes around a peaceful wooded plot of land and is asked by an older Black man if he knows anything about where he is standing. He shakes his head ... *no*! The man reveals they are atop a slave burial ground. There are no headstones because slaves were buried without them.

Willie Gary listens intently when the man tells him that nobody talks anymore about what used to be there. The history of those slaves, which is part of a larger history of Black people in America, is buried deep underground. In fact, the man says, in the South many slave burial grounds have statues and monuments on top of them commemorating the Confederacy.

It's like taking one history and putting it right on top of another. It's like taking one man's legacy and putting it on top of another. 'Til one day it gets

> *pushed down so deep, buried so deep, can't no one ever find it no more.*

The new history becomes repeated so often that the old history falls into an abyss.

That's what has happened to the history of our sport, women's basketball. We are forgetting pioneers, the young women of the past who played this game with all their hearts. Pioneers who played without fanfare are why we are where we are today. Not only has the game's history been dismissed, it has been replaced by a selective record book that is insulting to anyone who played before 1982. The NCAA counts records only in its own era.

Just because the NCAA blessed it doesn't make it so.

In the early 1970s, the NCAA wanted nothing to do with women's sports and went to court to argue that Title IX didn't apply to athletic departments. It was only in the latter half of that decade that the NCAA realized it was going to have to play ball — women's athletics wasn't going away. The NCAA's decision to introduce championships for women's sports spelled the demise of the AIAW. The NCAA had power and money, offering payment of expenses for teams in postseason competition, expanded television coverage and relaxed recruiting and eligibility rules.

I was part of meetings when we as coaches were promised that AIAW records would be protected. We were told our statistics, our accomplishments, would be carried forward. But somehow it became a handshake deal. Nothing was written down. It's amazing that such a huge chunk of our history was treated so lightly.

I'm upset with the NCAA's treatment of the AIAW, just as I was frustrated with the AIAW for not recognizing the accomplishments during the AAU era. Think about the title of Brenda VanLengen's upcoming documentary series on the history of women's basketball: Where would we be "If Not for Them"? That pretty much says it all.

I became aware of how the NCAA was treating the AIAW's accomplishments during the 2000-01 season, when Jackie Stiles of Southwest Missouri State was said to be on pace to break the NCAA women's scoring record. At some point, I realized they weren't talking about Lynette's record.

Jackie was given credit for the scoring mark after passing Patricia Hoskins of Mississippi Valley State, who finished her collegiate career with 3,122 points. Jackie finished with 3,393, which is certainly extraordinary but short of Lynette's 3,649. Lynette chased the scoring records of Carol Blazejowski and Cindy Brogdon, both also forgotten names.

Then history started getting buried even further. Kelsey Mitchell from Ohio State passed Jackie, and Kelsey Plum from Washington passed Kelsey Mitchell. Neither player scored more career points than Lynette.

During the 2023-24 season, the dominant storyline was Iowa's Caitlin Clark and her pursuit of Kelsey Plum's record. This was again an opportunity to tie the past and present together. To point out that women played using the men's ball before 1984 and that there wasn't a three-point line until 1987. Lynette scored 3,649 points, shooting .525 from the field, during a career that spanned 1977-1981, all AIAW years ignored by the NCAA.

When Caitlin scored her 3,650th career point in Iowa's game at Minnesota on Feb. 29, 2024, the game wasn't stopped. There was no official acknowledgement. Iowa coach Lisa Bluder criticized the NCAA that night for not recognizing Lynette's legacy and what she called "the real record." I was happy when Coach Bluder invited Lynette to an Iowa game a few weeks later. Lynette was introduced in Carver-Hawkeye Arena to a standing ovation, but that's just a moment. We need the official record to reflect that moment or we'll lose it.

Why doesn't college women's basketball recognize *one* scoring leader? Division I women's basketball needs one record book. Why are the accolades and milestones achieved by the AIAW's greatest players reduced to a separate section of another record book? *Pre-NCAA records,* it says, which almost sounds prehistoric to me. The Division I Women's Basketball Records Book online is 145 pages long. But the name is misleading. It contains NCAA records only. The Pre-NCAA Record book online is in an entirely separate section. It's all of nine pages.

Why is the NCAA selective about what counts and what doesn't? Coaches' achievements were carried forward when the game transitioned to the NCAA in 1982. Players' achievements were erased. When Pat Summitt became the first coach to record 1,000 victories in 2009, that number included 175 victories she achieved during the AIAW era. I believe that's how it should be, but I don't understand why those victories "count" in the NCAA record book, but the statistics for women who played in those games are relegated to another section of the record book.

Why does the NCAA celebrate coaches while diminishing the accomplishments of athletes? All the records should be together. One set of records. One history. Put an asterisk, if necessary, to identify which governing body, AAU, CIAW, AIAW or the NCAA, the records fell under, but don't hide our history. No one is denying that the game changed, but those pioneers left a legacy that should be reflected going forward.

Burying history is a dangerous precedent. Having an organization decide history isn't right. I'm seeing the same kind of injustice where I live now in Florida. History happened. It's not something to be interpreted later by people who were not there. In our sport, we're burying legacies, forgetting those who paved the way. Just as politics polarizes, we are creating divisions between our past and present.

I've been upset with the NCAA for many years. It's such a powerful group that could do more to advance women highlighting our achievements. Instead, it's cutting us off at the knees. It should have been more generous in acknowledging the AIAW and what it contributed.

It makes me incredibly sad that many women playing today don't know Lynette's name. Or for that matter, Anne Donovan, who as of 2024 is the leading career shot blocker (the NCAA recognizes the talented Brittney Griner, who starred at Baylor from 2009-13). Anne, who played from 1979 until 1983, crossed both eras. How crazy is it that the NCAA recognizes only the blocks she recorded her last two seasons? How about the fact that in 1982 Lynette Woodard was the first female athlete to receive the NCAA's Top V Award, an honor recognizing the top five athletes of the year? Yet her statistics continue to be buried by the NCAA.

My West Chester State team won the first national championship under Coach Carol Eckman. Carol's name isn't even listed under *coach* in the record book; that space is blank. I'm not sure why.

We've forgotten Delta State's glorious past, Old Dominion's championships and Louisiana Tech's dominance, all teams that carried the torch before Tennessee and Connecticut.

At times I've felt as if I'm the only one beating the drum, but I was happy to learn about a nonprofit called Legends of the Ball Inc., which is passionate about remembering and celebrating our history and connecting the past with our present between the AIAW and the NCAA and among the WBL, the ABL and the WNBA. My former player Adrian Mitchell sits on the board of that organization. Liz McQuitter, its president, won a national championship with Temple Junior College and became part of the first scholarship class at UNLV before being drafted by the WBL's Chicago Hustle.

Liz sums it up: "There is no greater agony than burying a story that's inside your soul."

Liz is determined to have her nonprofit educate the women's basketball audience about all that came before. She calls the pioneers of our game "the new forgotten" and contrasts the way we treat our history with the men's sport that, in her words, "remembers and reveres records, and honors" its trailblazers. Liz would like us to connect the dots as the men do.

Two legendary coaches, Tara VanDerveer and Muffet McGraw, also support having one record book, and former Iowa coach Lark Birdsong, when interviewed by a Wall Street Journal reporter as Caitlin Clark drew close to the NCAA mark, said women's college basketball statistics should begin in 1972 with the passage of Title IX. She added in that Feb. 8, 2024, article that Tara's record of winning the most games of any man or woman in college history, a milestone the NCAA recognized on its website, includes victories from her time coaching Idaho during the AIAW era.

Major League Baseball accepts the records from the Negro Leagues and from the 19th century. The NFL recognizes all American Football League statistics.

We as women don't do enough to keep our history alive. Together we must find ways to educate people who love women's basketball. Why haven't women with positions in the media — sportswriters and broadcasters — been willing to educate the public? Do they know the history? How can they broadcast that viewers are watching the race to break the Division I scoring record and leave out that it's only the *NCAA* mark? If we don't help ourselves, it may never get done.

What about today's women's basketball coaches? Why don't they know more about our history? They are standing on the shoulders of past coaches who were paid little if anything. Carol Eckman couldn't make a living coaching women's basketball, but today some coaches earn more than a million dollars a year. They should know the names of coaches who paved their paths.

I am thankful and extremely proud of the progress we've made in growing women's sports. Let's celebrate our history and make sure it is told accurately. Don't let the NCAA bury the stories and the stars and especially the accomplishments that grew the game into what it is today.

KPOP .... Keep the Past in Our Present!

Chapter XVI

Sisterhood

The bonds I established with my players continue. I can pick up the phone and talk to many who played for me and feel as if no time has passed. The sisterhood they share with one another is beautiful. It makes me happy that they love each other and work hard to keep the sisterhood strong.

I **coached 923** games at Kansas. People often want to break down a play from one of them or know more about a big win or one of our tough losses. Those memories aren't so fresh for me. But the relationships I formed, friendships with the women who played for me, are ties that I will cherish forever.

Some of my best teams had what we today would call swagger. I think of Lynette Woodard, Lynn Page, Evette Ott, Vickie Adkins, Tamecka Dixon, Adrian Mitchell, Jennifer Jackson, Cynthia Kelley, Charisse Sampson, Lynn Pride, Angie Snider, Shebra Legrant, Angie Aycock, Jennifer Jackson, Angie Halbleib, Shana Waters, Jennifer Trapp and Lisa Braddy, to name a few. They were beautiful, kind women off the court, but on the court they were tough! They were never intimidated. You could see that whenever they played, especially their relentless defense.

I pushed to get the best out of my players in every drill, in every game, but I wanted more than that for them. I wanted them to excel academically and grow personally. I wanted to give them experiences they had never had.

Lynette remembers going with her teammates to see "The Wiz" on Broadway during an East Coast swing. I don't think anyone on the team had been to a major stage play. They got the chance to see one of our most gifted singers, Stephanie Mills, perform. As part of that trip, we played at George Washington University, and I arranged for the team to have dinner in D.C. with some of the Philadelphia 76ers. Maurice Cheeks had just been drafted, and he was there. I can't tell you how I pulled that off, but my assistant Kathy Meek was blown away.

Later teams went to SeaWorld in California, and in Philadelphia we ran up the same steps as Rocky. When we went to Alaska in 1999, we had a sled tour pulled by Siberian Huskies. Once, I took the whole team to see Janet Jackson in concert. Getting those tickets was tricky, and all credit to my assistant coach Pam DeCosta. Seeing Janet live was epic and worth having to cut back on a couple of meals.

During a trip to Hawaii, the players decided to play a joke on Pam. Lynn Pride bought a bunch of lottery tickets and gave one to Pam. I didn't know anything about it.

I saw Pam on the bus scratching the ticket and then motioning me to come over. She couldn't believe it: She had won $10,000! Then she told me Lynn had given her the ticket. I thought, "Part of this jackpot belongs to Lynn." But Pam pointed out that was against the rules. When Lynn hopped on the bus, she wanted to see Pam's ticket, but Pam wouldn't let it go; she clutched it as if it were gold. Lynn urged Pam to read the back of the ticket, which she finally did. It turned out to be a prank ticket! Pam couldn't believe it.

Oh, she was upset! She was on such a high, and it came tumbling down. I tried to hold a coaches' meeting back at the hotel, but I walked in and just fell out laughing when I looked over and saw Pam. The shock of the prank for all of us came tumbling back to me. I couldn't stop laughing!

Trips like that help build team chemistry. Lynn Page remembers her senior year, 1989, and how upset I got when I was told our budget didn't include enough money for us to play in a holiday tournament. When I found out our men's team was going to Hawaii, I promised my team we were going somewhere tropical.

Many travel groups specifically worked to coordinate trips abroad for college teams. It was ideal if you could get into a tournament that provided financial support. Those years when we were nationally ranked, we were offered a lot more money to participate, which helped my budget. We were fortunate to find one of those tournaments that day.

I waited until the end of practice to give my players the news that we were going to Aruba. They could not stop singing, *"Aruba, Jamaica, ooh, I wanna take ya...,"* from the Beach Boys' popular song "Kokomo."

When I started recruiting, we had almost no budget, so most of the players were from Kansas or the surrounding area. When my budget increased and home visits were allowed, I traveled from coast to coast and as far north as Alaska and south to Florida to find players. When I started recruiting farther away from Lawrence, it was vital to show off the KU campus, considered one of the most beautiful in the country. If I was recruiting a player from the East or West coasts, her vision of the Midwest was often cowboys, Indians and farmers. That's what you often saw on TV — cowboys riding horses and herding cattle in wide-open spaces. Getting young women to identify with the University of Kansas was challenging until they saw it up close. They were surprised to see that our campus wasn't all flat land. In fact, it's full of rolling hills.

Getting to know families during recruiting was important. I could identify with the struggles of many of them and with the concerns mothers had about sending their daughters away. My players were so important to me, and I want to share more about a few who helped transform Kansas into a nationally competitive program.

When Lynette was at Kansas, her support system included the "three musketeers": her mother, a cousin and a friend of her mother's named Lucy, a fun woman with an oxygen tank. They regularly traveled from Wichita to Allen Fieldhouse.

Lynette gave me no trouble because if she wasn't in class, she was in the gym. Sometimes she'd practice by herself, but the guys were always challenging her one-on-one. She'd join any pickup game.

For all four of her years, Lynette hung a poster of the Harlem Globetrotters she got from Burger King above her locker. "I want to be a Globetrotter," she told me, and I thought, why not?

Lynette grew up with that dream, inspired by her cousin, Hubert "Geese" Ausbie, a Globetrotter for 24 years. The idea of the Globetrotter travel schedule, 175 games a year, sounded cool to her. Lynette loves to travel and speaks a couple of languages. She was one of 18 women to try out for the Trotters in 1985, one year after she captained the U.S. team that won gold at the Olympics.

When the Globetrotters announced the final team in Sherman Oaks, California, Lynette's family and I were in the stands eagerly waiting. The president of the Globetrotters took the microphone and announced, "The first female Harlem Globetrotter is Lynette Woodard." Lynette was escorted to midcourt by one of her new Globetrotter teammates. She got a standing ovation.

Wherever she went, she made sure her family and friends had tickets to their games. What fun it was for me to take my grandchildren to those Globetrotter games. She even brought the Trotters to Allen Fieldhouse to help raise money for women's basketball. However, the administrators wanted to spread those monies to the other non revenue sports.

Lynette spoke to almost all of my teams over the years and later became one of my assistants. She is family, godmother to my grandchildren, and while she has stacked up accomplishments over the years, her heart has always been in Kansas, nurturing the sisterhood that links generations of Jayhawks.

When another of my players, Jennifer Jackson from Tuscaloosa, Alabama, signed with us her mother commented, "Who would have thought that a Black coach would be able to recruit a white player from Alabama?" But I wanted her to be my point guard. We later laughed about it, but Jennifer's mother let me know that as soon as she met me, she thought KU would be the best place for her daughter. Jennifer took pride in dispelling the stereotypes about how Southerners feel about Black people. She was a talented guard who started every game but one in her four years at KU.

I recruited Angie Halbleib out of Wisconsin, the first time we signed a player from there. I went to Middletown, Wisconsin, to watch Angie play at her high school. I remember looking for a minority in the crowd and finally saw a Black woman managing a concession stand. The gym was packed with some of the nicest people. A postal worker told me what a great kid Angie was. Church people welcomed me. By the end of the night, everybody knew who I was. Angie had a lot of schools recruiting her. But as soon as I went into Angie's home, her mother said she knew KU was right for her daughter. Leenar Halbleib and I became great friends. We saw each other only a couple of times after Angie graduated, but we had a lot of love for each other. Leenar was a brave and beautiful person who left us too soon.

Lynn Page, who stood 6-4, was one of my tallest post players. I went to Oklahoma to meet her mother, who was almost as tall. They invited me to dinner with the family. I remember a great meal, and for dessert, we had ice cream — it was the first time I had tasted cookies and cream.

Evette Ott was from Flint, Michigan. She was one of the best point guards in the country. I got to know many people at her high school, even her track coach. The way Evette tells it, once I left her home, her mother knew that Evette would be OK at Kansas. Her mother wanted Evette to be a student first and athlete second, which was fine with me. Evette intended to go farther south to play somewhere warmer, but she fell in love with the campus and connected with Lynette, one of my assistants at the time. Evette had one visit left after coming to Lawrence, but she didn't take it. I was a happy coach.

I had my favorite places to take recruits when they visited. Many couldn't afford to eat steak regularly, so steak it was. I believe I was recruiting Charisse Sampson and Keshana Kedet from Los Angeles when we went to a popular Lawrence steakhouse. I saw something new on the menu, a cheesesteak sandwich. I missed the cheesesteaks from Philadelphia that combined shaved meat and melted cheese with onions and peppers on a hoagie roll. I was so excited to get my meal, but after the waiter placed my food on the table, I had to blink twice. In front of me was a thick steak between what looked like two pieces of Wonder Bread. This was their version of a cheesesteak sandwich! I was shocked, and after explaining to our waiter what I was expecting, he took it back.

Charisse was a special player, a Parade All-American who grew up in central Los Angeles. She tells stories of looking out her window at home and seeing drug addicts. She could have been a victim of the drug scene there but instead was inspired to do more with her life. Charisse was a consistent long-range shooter. She has one of the sweetest temperaments. Always respectful and a pleasure to coach.

Of course, every coach in the country wanted a home visit with Dawn Staley. I appreciated that Dawn agreed to let me meet with her and her family. I liked her mother, and my Philadelphia connection made me hopeful, but Virginia won this talented point guard. Dawn was an incredible player who already has three national titles as coach of South Carolina.

I felt fortunate when Angela Aycock chose KU. After meeting with her high school coach and AAU coach at her school, I met her mother and sister. I thought Angie was leaning my way. But she had one more visit — to Nebraska. Coach Angela Beck and I are friends to this day. Coach Beck took Angie horseback riding. It was all Angie wanted to talk about for a while. Even though I started to worry, I continued to stress academics. I was thrilled when she signed with us. Angie became my second Kodak All-American and played two years in the WNBA.

I signed Tamecka Dixon while Angie and Charisse were still playing. Tamecka had a lot of interest from ACC schools. UConn was building its program and wanted her. My assistant Reneé Brown had built a relationship with Tamecka that led to the two of us going to her house in New Jersey for a visit. Tamecka's whole family was there — aunts, uncles, two grandmothers and more. By this time, Reneé had gotten to know even the mayor and anyone important to Tamecka.

Tamecka's father was a great college player until he tore up his knee, so he was familiar with the recruiting process. We ate dinner with her mother and helped with the dishes. Kansas was the first school Tamecka visited, and she'll tell you today she decided on the spot that she wanted to become a Jayhawk. She didn't change her mind when one of the top programs in the SEC opened a trunk full of gear and invited her to take whatever she liked. Tamecka's father made her send everything back to that school because he knew it was an NCAA violation.

In 1994, Tamecka, Charisse and Angie played in one of the most memorable games of my career. Our opponent was Colorado, which had lost only to top-ranked Tennessee. Payless Shoes agreed to promote the game by sponsoring a campaign to fill the Fieldhouse. I was nervous and excited at the same time that night. As I began walking toward the court, I slowly raised my head to see rows and rows of people in the stands. I kept walking, looking upward, expecting to see empty seats. My throat got tight and tears started to fall because it was like a dream. The Fieldhouse was packed. One of my assistant coaches put her arms around me and led me to the bench. It was magical. Tamecka would later say winning that game was her greatest memory as a Jayhawk.

That game set the Big Eight attendance record for women's basketball with 13,532 cheering fans! I thought back 20 years to when our program drew only a handful of people. It was a crowning moment when we won 59-57. I thanked God over and over again for his many blessings and for giving me that gift.

Behind Tamecka, we reached our first Sweet 16 in 1996. As a No. 4 seed, we hosted the first and second rounds, beating Middle Tennessee to open the tournament. No. 5 Texas was next, and I was 0-3 against Hall of Fame Coach Jody Conradt, the winningest coach in our game at the time.

KU led almost the entire way against the Longhorns in that second-round victory. Our defense was outstanding, and all five of our starters scored in double figures. What a feeling to be in the Sweet 16! I remember soaking it in with my assistants, Maggie Mahood, Misty Opat and Tim Eatman, before walking into the joyous locker room.

Tamecka became my fourth All-American later that year. She went on to be a three-time WNBA All-Star who played on two championship teams. I flew to California to be in the stands at her first professional game. I was so proud of her.

KU got back to the Sweet 16 two years later behind Lynn Pride, one of my most gifted athletes and among the most talented players in the country. A highly recruited player from Texas, she had height, quickness, tremendous jumping ability and an instinct for the game. Lynn was talented enough to be an All-American.

After beating Tulane in the first round of the NCAA Tournament in 1998, we upset Iowa in Iowa City in front of a hostile crowd. We came from behind to do it and sealed it with free throws. It would have been nice to get to the Final Four in Kansas City that year, but Arkansas beat us in the Sweet 16. I said after we lost that I had never been prouder of a team. We were young and weren't very deep. The Kansas men had lost in the first round that season, surprised by Rhode Island. It was the first time in school history that the KU women's team had advanced further than the men's in the national tournament.

Those were some of the highs over my three decades. Any coach who has done this for a while will tell you about the lows, none worse than losing a player unexpectedly.

We lost Jennifer Trapp too early. Jennifer was from Lawrence, a real workhorse on the court. She was a Lady Jayhawk from 1993 to 1996. She played briefly in Finland but didn't like it there. I wanted to bring her on as a staff member but couldn't work it out with the administration. I've always wondered if it would have made a difference for her. Jennifer ended up taking her own life.

Danielle Shareef was just 36 when she was killed in a car crash in Tampa. Danielle played for me from 1989 until 1992. She was getting her doctorate at the time of the accident, hoping to open a school for young boys. She was such a sweet and gentle person.

Jackie Martin from Macon, Georgia, played for me from 1984 until 1988. We had an incredible relationship. Now, Jackie did *plenty* of things to fire me up! Sometimes I would pull her out of practice to do some running, but she had the best heart and I adored her. Jackie missed one game in her collegiate career. She had shoulder surgery and could barely lift her arm, but she never wanted to come off the floor. There would be times her shoulder would pop out and she had to leave the game long enough to pop it back in. After Jackie graduated, she became a volunteer assistant, and we worked out together regularly until she became too tired to do it. It took her a while to see a doctor, but when she did, he diagnosed her with leukemia.

She stayed in Lawrence with the team during her treatments and lost all her hair. Jackie, Lynette, Evette and Stacy Truitt, a really strong guard for us in the early '90s, stayed at her bedside and prayed. When she passed at the age of 26, I was sitting with her family when Lynette wanted me to come into the hospital room.

I walked back, and I'll never forget the smile Jackie had on her face. That's what Lynette wanted me to see. That's what she wanted me to remember.

Two talented sisters from Oklahoma, Barbara and Vickie Adkins, signed with Kansas in the early 1980s. When their mother became ill, Barbara went home, and Vickie remained. She was a three-time All-Big Eight selection who ranks sixth today on the all-time scoring chart. We lost her suddenly.

Shebra Legrant was a junior college All-American who played only two years for Kansas but scored more than 1,000 points behind an intensity she brought every game. When I received the call that she passed away, it was hard to believe.

I've lost others who were way too young. Any time I lose any player, it leaves a hole in my heart.

Today I can pick up the phone and talk to many who played for me and feel as if no time has passed. The sisterhood they share is beautiful. My door is open to them anytime. My home today is about a mile from the ocean. At least once a year I have two, three or four players staying for a few days or weeks. Lynette, Evette and Lynn Page were just here, and the four of us never stopped laughing. I used to think when players visited, I had to entertain them. Now we enjoy each other. They come and go as they please and find joy in making meals together or helping me with small household chores.

When I was inducted into the Women's Basketball Hall of Fame in 2004, I had no clue so many of my players planned to attend. The older players decided ahead of time through group chat to wear black, while the younger players decided to turn out in white. The Hall has a lovely winding staircase, and I remember seeing them all — nearly 50 women — wrapped along that staircase. They were in their black and white, and there I stood — wearing black and white! I was so emotional I could hardly talk. God is so good. I was so proud that these young women cared enough to demonstrate their love and support for me.

My players are like family. I'm so thankful for everything we achieved together. They are now parents, doctors, lawyers, physical therapists, business owners and more, but when we're together, we're all Jayhawks. I love receiving Christmas cards with pictures of their growing families. I get phone calls out of the blue from players who say, "Just checking on you, Coach. How are you doing?" But what I really want to hear is how they're doing. It's always been about them.

Chapter XVII

Gold

As someone who was always challenging and questioning the United States Olympic Committee, I certainly didn't expect to be the first Black coach chosen for an Olympic staff.

I **was making** my bed when I got a call from Tara VanDerveer. We had been friendly in coaching circles, but she had never phoned me. I was surprised to hear her voice.

After exchanging hellos, she said she wanted to ask me a question.

"I think you should sit down," she suggested.

I sat on the bed. I knew Tara was our Olympic coach and taking a one-year leave from Stanford to coach Team USA. No coach had ever made that level of commitment.

"Would you like to be one of my assistant coaches for the Olympics?"

Am I hearing correctly? I wondered.

It was November 1995, nine months before the Summer Olympics. "Yes, *yes* I would *love* to be on your coaching staff," I answered, thanking her profusely. After all these years, I was finally going to be part of an Olympics. God works in mysterious ways.

It was a proud moment. I had long ago given up my dream to go to the Olympics. Tara later said she chose me to be one of her assistants because she thought I was the best person for the job. She didn't realize that, just as Bert had, she made me a first. By accepting Tara's offer, I became the first woman of color on an Olympic women's basketball coaching staff. A quarter-century before, Colleen Bowser and I became the first Black women to represent the United States in international competition – on a national team coached by Bert.

Although neither milestone received a lot of attention, I take pride in that legacy, something my grandchildren and great grandchildren can relate to. When you're the first, you pave the way for others to follow. In 2021, Dawn Staley became the first Black woman to be named head coach of a U.S. women's basketball Olympic team. She made us all proud, especially coaches of color.

Thinking back to 1982, I broke another color barrier when I was asked to coach a select team for the Williams Jones Intercontinental Cup in Taipei, Taiwan. I was the first Black woman to coach a U.S. team in international competition. Again, I didn't know I was breaking the color barrier. Nobody talked about it. Very little was written about that or the Jones Cup in general, but it was a special experience for me.

I coached 14 all-stars, including Paula McGee of Southern California, Valerie Walker of Cheyney State, Lea Henry of Tennessee and Valerie Still of Kentucky. We spent two weeks training at USC before leaving for Taiwan. Joan Bonvicini, hired to coach Long Beach State two years earlier, was my assistant. Joan went on to win 700 games in her decorated career.

Together, we discovered the culture of Taiwan. I chuckle when I remember mopeds carrying entire families. I'm not kidding. I saw as many as five or six people — mothers, fathers and children — on one moped bringing home groceries. I also remember our interpreter telling us how strict Taiwan's legal system was. A rare bank robbery occurred there that year. The culprit was executed. Let's just say Taiwan didn't have a lot of crime. My players could walk the streets using the buddy system and not be fearful.

This was a young team that ended the tournament with a 7-1 record and won the silver medal behind Canada.

Over the years, I continued to be involved with the United States Olympic Committee (USOC), traveling to the National Training Center in Colorado Springs as part of the player selection committee for the 1984 and 1988 Olympic teams.

I was vocal about the lack of minority coaches at the grassroots level of USA Basketball. There was no one of color on any staff unless she was a manager or trainer. Every Black player was coached by a white person. You can't dream it until you can see it. I knew we could do better. We *had* to do better. My concerns extended into the 1990s when I joined the Black Coaches Association (BCA), hopeful that as a group we could address USA Basketball and achieve equitable representation.

The BCA was mostly men. While serving on the BCA board, I was surprised when BCA founder Rudy Washington nominated me for president and all these hands went up. Somehow in 1992, I became BCA president, the first female in its history to hold that role and the only one to serve two terms in office. I took the role seriously. I wanted to provide more resources to minority female coaches, many of whom thought their issues weren't being heard by the Women's Basketball Coaches Association.

The BCA offered workshops on strategy, marketing, recruiting, job opportunities, concerns about officiating and more. I was disappointed when many of the Black men's coaches weren't interested in sharing their basketball knowledge with the women. I thought it would be wonderful to learn from coaches such as John Thompson and George Raveling. But they didn't want women to be a part of their little group that shared strategies. Could we sit and listen? They didn't want that, either.

They were few, but we were fewer, and their attitude bothered me. Here was an organization trying to combat racism that was propagating sexism.

I was introduced to Carol Callan, the women's national team director, at a Final Four. Standing on the concourse, I told Carol I thought it was important for every national coaching staff to include a Black coach. I pointed out that national teams always had Black players, and it only made sense to have minority representation on the coaching staff. Carol promised to talk to Bill Wall, executive director of USA Basketball.

I followed up by writing a letter to USA Basketball using my platform as president of the BCA. Truth be told, I never mentioned anything about it to the BCA members. I knew it was the right thing to do, so I did it.

Lo and behold, USA Basketball announced a policy change. Every USA Basketball coaching staff would include a coach of color starting in 1996. I still have the letter I received from Carol telling me the good news. I took pride in helping bring about this change in policy.

As that person *again* who was always challenging, questioning and pushing the envelope, I didn't expect to be selected for an Olympic coaching staff. That all changed with Tara's call. Ceal Barry from Colorado and Nancy Darsch from Ohio State were the other assistants, but all three of us were the second set of assistants for the team that had been together for a 52-game pre-Olympic tour around the U.S. and Europe. My own assistant coach, Reneé Brown, who had been on Tara's staff before taking the job with me at Kansas, was an assistant for those games.

The 1996 a Dream Team was touted as the best ever assembled. It included Jennifer Azzi, Ruthie Bolton, Teresa Edwards, Nikki McCray, Dawn Staley, Rebecca Lobo, Katy Steding, Sheryl Swoopes, Katrina McClain, Lisa Leslie, Venus Lacy and Carla McGhee.

This U.S. team had an important mission. The United States won bronze in 1992 behind the Unified Team of former Soviet republics and China. That wasn't acceptable. The 1996 team, with the home-court advantage in Atlanta, wasn't tasked with just winning gold. Anything other than gold would have been considered a failure. The '96 team also shouldered the responsibility of laying the foundation for the start of two professional leagues in the United States, the ABL and the WNBA.

The players became household names. Lisa Leslie, Sheryl Swoopes and a few others were in commercials. They were on magazine covers. Their task was bigger than themselves, and all of them bought in.

When it was time, we were more than ready.

Standing in a holding area at the opening ceremony in Centennial Olympic Stadium, we watched the delegations from all over the world on TV like the rest of the country, the men's Dream Team standing with us. "Guys. Look at this. It's amazing!" Charles Barkley said, staring at the screen.

We could hear the crowd noise from television, but once it was our turn, everything sounded much louder. When we marched into the stadium, the roar from the home crowd was deafening. Honestly, it gave me chills. Tara tapped me on the shoulder and shouted in my ear, "Can you believe this?"

Here I was, walking out as a coach all these years after missing out in 1972. From my days watching Wilma Rudolph on a snowy black and white TV to actually being part of sport's greatest spectacle just a few weeks shy of my 50th birthday, I had made it!

It was mesmerizing to see swimmer Janet Evans taking half a lap around the track, carrying the torch. She headed up a ramp where a figure dressed in white appeared. It was a breathtaking moment when Muhammad Ali, suffering the early effects of Parkinson's disease, took the torch from Janet. America and the rest of the world watched as The Greatest lit the flame. A moment and a night to savor.

After the opening ceremonies, we were all business again.

Being a head coach so long, it felt odd to step into an assistant's role, yet it was fascinating to be a student. I was excited to learn how Tara went about drills and preparation. She broke down film differently than I did, and ran drills I had never seen. I learned things I was able to incorporate into KU practices.

While I had duties related to drills and scouting, I also found myself in a familiar role with many of the minority players who needed an ear, a sounding board. I was good at being able to relate to them and be an encouraging voice, whether their issue was playing time or something personal.

We were unable to be with the other athletes in the Olympic Village because of security concerns. Like the U.S. men's team, we stayed in the Omni Hotel in downtown Atlanta. That's where Shaq held my granddaughter, Lauren, in his arms. My sister Cathy and my mother made the trip. I was happy whenever Mom could be part of my special experiences. Josie was disappointed when her job made it impossible for her to join us.

We talked easily with coaches and players from the men's team during meals and in elevators. Their rooms were on one side of the Omni. We were on the other. Lennie Wilkens, who coached the men, thought I looked like a relative of his. He was awesome. Many of the men came to our games and cheered us on. We cheered for them, too. Men's basketball was the only event we attended at the Games.

I remember the U.S. Olympic mascot that year was named Izzy, a cartoon character. That made me happy, because it reminded me of my sister Isabel who we affectionately called Izzy.

The arena was walking distance from the hotel, but we never walked. We took a team bus that had a hard time moving because we were mobbed by fans and television cameras.

I didn't hear the pipe bomb that exploded in a park near our hotel, a domestic terrorism incident that killed two people and injured more than 100 others during the first week of the Games. The balcony to my room overlooked the area that was bombed. Before that tragedy, I had smiled watching the athletes having such a good time with music playing. The bombing was the only stain on that amazing Olympic experience.

I met a young couple who shared that they had taken part in a lottery for tickets. They wanted to attend men's basketball and were disappointed to receive tickets to women's basketball. After coming to one game, they told me they loved it and were cheering hard for us. It was nice to hear that.

The U.S. won all eight of its games in Atlanta, beating Brazil 111-87 in the championship game to cap a 60-0 mark (counting the pre-Olympics tour). I remember thinking throughout the final game, "We are going to win the gold medal!" There was never a doubt.

Coaches don't take home medals in the Olympics. Those go only to players. But I got an Olympic ring. Throughout the two weeks, I exchanged pins with athletes from other countries. Everybody wanted the American pin.

I felt it was absolutely an honor, a blessing, to have been a part of that Dream Team. You talk about the right team and the right coach at the right time. Everything came together in 1996. The players represented their country flawlessly by carrying themselves professionally on the court and off.

We've had reunions in Knoxville and Las Vegas, and I remain in touch with many of the women. It was nice for Ceal and me to develop a friendship off the court. We had been involved in so many heated battles in Big Eight games. Finally we were on the same side.

I hear from Teresa Edwards and Venus Lacy, who check in on me regularly. Teresa told me later I was a calming presence. She was nearing the end of her career, and we talked more about life than basketball. We still do today. Venus and I have good memories of sharing fish and chitlins, real Southern dishes, when we were at the National Training Center.

Sadly, we lost Nikki McCray recently. She was such a joy, someone who bridged gaps between the generations of players.

Dawn Staley played overseas after graduating from Virginia, and watching her in Atlanta I was certain she would be a star in whatever American professional league she chose.

I was proud to see the WNBA launch the next year, and happy for Reneé Brown, the league's inaugural director of player personnel. Reneé stayed on for 20 years before stepping down as chief of basketball operations. I was proud that someone from my coaching staff held such a major position in that organization. Reneé was the glue who helped keep everything moving forward, especially when it came to building trust with the athletes.

It was fulfilling for me to see KU players succeed in the WNBA. I tried to travel to at least one game for all of my players in the league. I was at Tamecka Dixon's first game in Los Angeles. Angie Aycock and Charisse Sampson played in both the ABL and WNBA. Lynette was 38 when she got drafted by the WNBA, where she played for two years. Lynn Pride, Nakia Sanford and Jaclyn Johnson also spent time in the WNBA.

For me, seeing women's basketball reach heights I always imagined was extremely satisfying. I always believed women would play in front of big crowds and on grand stages.

I was proud Bert lived to see it all. We stayed in touch until she died in 2015 at the age of 83. She asked to see me near the end of her life. She couldn't speak. I held her hand and updated her on what was happening in sports. I let her know how much I loved her. I had such respect for her. She laid the foundation for the United States winning gold 25 years later.

General (R) Marty Dempsey, Chairman of the Board — Jim Tooley, Chief Executive Officer

September 8, 2021

To the University of Kansas women's basketball community:

It is my pleasure to acknowledge Marian Washington and her contributions to USA Basketball, particularly in the area of coaching. As you know, Marian served as an assistant coach for the 1996 USA Basketball Olympic Team, the first coach of color on any Olympic Women's Basketball Staff. This was the culmination of a change in the policies and procedures precipitated by a conversation that occurred several years earlier with Marian as she advocated on behalf of all black coaches. I would like to give a personal account of that conversation and recognize Marian's efforts to strengthen every USA Basketball team as a result.

At the time, I was an officer on the USA Basketball Executive Committee and chair of the National Team Player Selection Committee. During one of the NCAA Women's Final Four games, Lynn Barry (National Team Director at the time) introduced Marian to me on the concourse in the arena. With a calm persistence, Marian suggested that it was sensible and necessary that there be a black coach on each national team staff, noting that national teams included black players and there should be similar representation on the coaching staffs. Not only would the players sense this importance but all coaches of color would understand the significance of inclusion on national team coaching staffs.

Marian, a member of the Black Coaches Association, was an influential advocate for all black coaches. Her efforts led to a policy that every USA Basketball coaching staff would include a coach of color. Marian's coaching talents and this policy led to her selection as an assistant coach on the 1996 Olympic Team, also insuring similar opportunities on all coaching staffs. During the 2020 Olympic Games in Tokyo, the head coach of the Olympic Team was, for the first time, a black coach who happened to be a player on that 1996 Olympic Team. This is all thanks to the conviction of Marian Washington and USA Basketball is the beneficiary. Marian, we thank you.

Sincerely,

Carol Callan

Carol Callan
Women's National Team Director

27 South Tejon Street, Suite 100, Colorado Springs, CO 80903-1542 · Telephone: +1.719.590.4800 · www.usab.com

The letter I received from USA Basketball's Carol Callan acknowledged my role in a significant policy change. As Carol notes, "With a calm persistence," I suggested it was sensible and necessary that there be a Black coach on each national team staff.

Chapter XVIII

Parting Ways

When you're coaching, you don't know how it's going to end, but you hope it's not too painful. For me, it was extremely painful.

The **he wheels** came off in a lot of ways after 2000. I coached Kansas in the NCAA Tournament for the last time, a double-overtime, first-round loss to Vanderbilt in Ruston, Louisiana, where things never seemed to go our way.

Tied near the end of regulation, I can still see Lynn Pride coming off a back screen to the basket for what should have been the winning play. Lynn had great timing to catch the pass in front of the rim for an easy layup. It was like slow motion seeing the pass fall short, bouncing off the rim and out of reach. Oh my goodness, unbelievable. That would have won it. We had another opportunity to win in the second overtime but missed a three-pointer.

Two seasons later, Kansas finished 0-16 in the Big 12.

Until that point, most of my teams felt like an extension of me. They were competitive. We didn't always win, but we left everything out on the floor. We no longer had an entire team effort. I definitely had a few players who played hard, but I didn't have an entire team committed to each other and to the program.

When my health declined, I didn't realize it at first. Gradually, I could no longer hear my players on the court. I used to maintain a running conversation with my point guard during games.

Suddenly, I couldn't do that anymore. Repeatedly I had to turn to my staff and ask, "What did she say?" I knew something was wrong, and it was frustrating.

Other times I would start to say something, but I couldn't find the right word. I tried to figure out what was happening. Maybe I wasn't getting enough sleep. Or was it my diet? My energy level wasn't where I was used to it being. I was just 57 years old, yet I stayed tired all the time.

Twice I was hospitalized for chest palpitations, once while on the road and another time in Lawrence when Mom was in the hospital a floor above me. Her health was failing significantly. I was constantly addressing my own anemia. Often I was so exhausted I barely made it out of bed. I took vitamin B12 shots to increase my iron levels for more energy. I decided not to share anything about my health issues. I tried to keep going.

That's when Mom, who was living with me, did not want to be alone even for a second, and she would call my name throughout the night. She would talk about saying goodbye. I wasn't ready for Mom to leave us. I didn't want to hear or think about her dying.

Suddenly, a few weeks before the 2003-2004 season started, my baby brother Butchie died. One sadness after another.

Kansas opened the season with a loss at Missouri-Kansas City. We should have easily won that game over a much smaller program from the Mid-Continent Conference. "Here we go again," I thought. "It's time to retire."

When I told Pastor and Sister Yates I felt it was time to step away from coaching, they agreed. "We feel God is telling us that, also," Sister Yates said. "You have stayed the course all these years, but it's time for you to rest. God wants you to rest now, Sister Washington."

I talked with my assistants and told them I was done. They didn't want me to step away and persuaded me to continue coaching.

"We have some really strong athletes who are interested in the program, Coach. We have to hang in there," I remember Tim Eatman saying.

"We're going to keep working for you, Coach," Lynette said.

Maggie Mahood agreed. "I know they can play better, Coach."

Gary Kempf, whom I had hired all those years before to coach swimming and was now an administrator in the athletic department, rode on the bus to Kansas City and told me he was rooting for me.

Once conference season began, we weren't just losing games. We weren't fighting or playing the way we were capable. It was breaking my spirit. I had some players who really tried, but I no longer coached a full team that understood and appreciated what we had built at Kansas. The results showed again and again.

We weren't getting the same type of player that I was used to coaching. I didn't have a strong connection with the team. Things change. Generations change. My expectations didn't change. I was challenged by a different type of kid. Basketball got them a scholarship, yet it wasn't as important as other things in their lives.

All through my career, my players had personal relationships. I was never about nosing into any player's business, but when relationships start to affect team chemistry, that's a problem. I never wanted to judge what my players did or didn't do, as long as the behavior wasn't hurting someone else or the program. My last four years, the outside priorities of some of my players hurt the program.

In mid-January, we played at Missouri and made national headlines when the teams became involved in an on-court scuffle. Five players were suspended by the Big 12 — three from Kansas. The conference also reprimanded one of my players. It was another uncommon situation, a headache I wasn't used to dealing with.

Add to that a problem with a parent. Nearly all parents had trusted my judgment when it came to their daughters. They understood when I enforced rules or made tough decisions on playing time. You didn't play if you didn't attend class or if you broke a team rule. There were no excuses.

One father wrote me an ugly letter because he thought his daughter wasn't playing enough. My assistants didn't want me to see it, but it was addressed to me. I read the first page before I laid it on my desk. It was truly disgusting. He wasn't involved in his daughter's life, yet his letter was full of vicious attacks. He didn't care if his daughter went to class. She came in highly ranked. He wanted her to play. He wanted me to turn a blind eye to everything his daughter was doing no matter how outrageous.

That letter was the breaking point. I left my office and walked past my staff down the hall to talk to Lew Perkins, the athletic director.

As soon as I sat down, I told Lew I was done, and, uncharacteristically, tears fell. I think he was surprised. He placed me on medical leave, but I knew in my heart I had coached my last game.

I shared with Lew that my physical problems had become overwhelming. He said he could get an appointment for me right away at the Mayo Clinic. I asked him to allow Lynette, who had been my assistant, to finish the season as interim coach.

We announced my retirement at a press conference soon thereafter. Kansas arranged a small celebration for me before the game against Nebraska on Feb. 28 at Allen Fieldhouse. A few thousand fans turned out. I was handed flowers, and there were more tears when the band played the fight song I had heard so many times. Then I walked away — for good.

It wasn't long before Lew invited me to lunch. We exchanged hellos, and he said he missed me. After we ordered, Lew told me he was going to hire Bonnie Henrickson from Virginia Tech.

He said Pat Summitt and Geno Auriemma recommended her. I think Lew was preparing me for all KU was giving Bonnie. Her contract included incentives, making her total package worth almost $1 million. I hadn't made anything close to that.

I didn't begrudge Bonnie, but I thought Kansas gave her the tools to be successful that I was denied. The administration was never encouraging about hosting home games during the non-conference season in my years. In Bonnie's second year, KU played its first 12 games in Allen Fieldhouse. I would have loved that luxury. Bonnie took Kansas to the postseason WNIT five times. I was told more than once that no money was in the budget for my teams to accept a postseason bid when we didn't make the NCAA Tournament. Kansas' men's basketball had a consistency that I wanted to establish. Fans expected a certain level of achievement with the KU men. We worked hard for that level of consistency for the women's program. Playing in the postseason, while great for your current team, also helps recruiting.

I spoke to the Board of Regents about KU women's basketball losing ground to other programs. I told them not investing in our program contributed significantly to our downward spiral. We had been a nationally ranked program that was never supported. I remember seeing a friend on the board shaking his head in agreement.

It wasn't long after I left before news came down of an NCAA investigation into KU for violations that largely had to do with football and men's basketball. The NCAA ended up penalizing both sports and cited Kansas for a lack of institutional control.

In the midst of that, Kansas conducted an internal review and self-reported violations related to my program and pointed the finger at Tim and Lynette. The violations related to two prospective student-athletes receiving on-campus jobs, tutoring, improper transportation and participation in an out-of-season pickup game with the current team. KU, not the NCAA, announced it would take away two scholarships from women's basketball for the 2005-2006 season.

I was furious. I believed administrators were trying to deflect attention from the major infractions in football and men's basketball. They thought that since I was no longer coach it didn't reflect on me. Newspaper articles quoted them saying, "Marian had nothing to do with it," as if that was going to appease me. It was still my program as far as I was concerned. Kansas should have been proud that women's basketball hadn't committed any major NCAA violations. In its final report, the NCAA criticized Kansas for self-imposing penalties it called "wholly disproportionate" for what were determined to be secondary violations.

Despite living a few miles away from campus, the distance felt far greater.

I quickly got an appointment at the Mayo Clinic. After all kinds of tests, a doctor sat with me and told me everything seemed to suggest I was chronically fatigued. No one said the words Lyme disease.

It was years before that diagnosis would be made.

I kept thinking all I needed was rest — stay in bed longer. I thought I would recover and get my energy back. I had to learn that we are blessed with a certain amount of energy, which was a hard pill to swallow. It's not about getting it back. That's why you need to take care of yourself along the way. I lived as if I had an endless well of energy. I kept pushing myself until my tank was empty.

Without a familiar routine, I grew depressed. Things turned around after a summer visit from my granddaughter, Lauren. She wanted a dog. I was not an animal person. If you remember from my younger days in West Chester, I did not like touching feathers or fur of any kind. But when I saw how much she wanted a dog, I bought a Chihuahua that we named Poppy. I thought Poppy would go home with Lauren to West Chester. I don't know why, but I didn't think to ask Josie about it. When Lauren and I told her together over the phone, Josie made it clear she did not want Poppy. If she was going to get a dog, it was going to be a Bichon. Her husband, Rick, was allergic to dogs. Josie thought a pup that didn't shed would be best.

There I was in Kansas with Lauren, and she was crying her eyes out. I thought, "What have I done?"

I made a deal with Lauren. I told her every summer she returned to Kansas, Poppy would be waiting. (Josie, by the way, ended up at the airport to pick up Lauren with a Vizsla, a hypoallergenic dog that Lauren ended up loving.)

At first, I was going to have a friend keep Poppy. But that didn't seem right. I decided to keep Poppy, a pup I held at arm's length for a while. But it wasn't long before I got a second one that I named Pippin. I thought Poppy needed a playmate. I was getting winded running around the couch trying to play with her.

Funny thing about dogs. You fall in love with them. I've said many times, my pups helped save my life. I had to think about them and take care of them. Walk them. They lifted my spirits. Turns out that maybe I am an animal person, at least if we're talking about a Chihuahua.

My Pippin lived to be 18 and was attached to my hip. My Poppy was attached, too, but willing to share me. Pippin wasn't interested in sharing. Poppy lived to be 16. I have a shrine to them in my bedroom with their ashes that I also wear around my neck. Now I have a rescue Chihuahua, Bella, who likes to linger during her walks and has beautiful, piercing light brown eyes that look unhappy unless she's with me at all times. For that reason, she is.

My grandchildren are a light in my life. I was living in Kansas when Josie had Lauren. I wanted my granddaughter to know me, so I made a deal with Josie. I would come and get Lauren every summer, and she would come back to Lawrence to stay for a few months. That started when Lauren was 4 months old. When

Ricky — real name Ricardo Marion — was born two years later, both he and Lauren spent summers in Lawrence.

Lauren played basketball in high school but found her sport in rugby. She was short with strong legs; it was hard to bring her down. She will tell you I am her best friend. Ricky looks just like me. He was a talented point guard for Great Valley High School in Devault, Pennsylvania. He had a long-range shot and good passing ability. He helped his team win the state championship his senior year.

They're adults now, and Lauren has twin 3-year-olds, Cameron and Carter, my great-grands. I was so happy when I went to West Chester last Christmas and Carter ran over to give me a great big hug. We FaceTime often, but it was the first time Carter came to me. As for Cameron, for now, he is busy shooting baskets.

My sister Janet never left West Chester, and we try to see each other at least once a year. My sister Cathy lived with me for eight years after her husband died and now is just a few hours south of me in Tampa. It's nice to have her close for our get-togethers throughout the year, especially at Thanksgiving when I make sweet potatoes with marshmallows and she brings her famous macaroni and cheese.

Taking care of my health remains a full-time job. I was referred to a doctor up north who graduated from Harvard. She took all the test results from the Mayo Clinic some years earlier and agreed that I had chronic fatigue but also thought there had to be a reason. By then I was dealing with pain in my back, and I had vision problems. She sent my labs to California for an extensive evaluation.

The results indicated I was seriously infected with Lyme disease. I likely had it for decades, almost surely related to working so much outdoors when I was young. Fatigue. Joint pain. Insomnia. When I first moved to Florida, I enjoyed walking the beach. Then my back pain made that impossible. When I think back, I suspect Butchie suffered from Lyme, too. I know he was suffering from PTSD, but he also struggled to get his thoughts out and his heart was enlarged. Lyme disease attacks the brain and major organs.

You manage Lyme. You don't cure it, and that's what I've done since the diagnosis. I receive infusions that help, but I battle chronic pain and the brain fog that sometimes makes it hard for me to recall certain words. When I take my medication, I feel like myself for a while. I'm not nearly as active as I'd like to be, and that saddens me. A visiting nurse gives me regular infusions that increase my energy. I have a hyperbaric chamber in my home that pressures oxygen in my cells for healing. You might recall magazines like the National Enquirer featured Michael Jackson in a hyperbaric chamber. They made fun of him but he was ahead of his time. Hospitals across the country use them, particularly for wound care. You may read about a few NBA players having them in their homes to help them recover from one game to the next.

Living with Lyme, you can never predict how you will feel; each day is different. I deal with flare-ups constantly, and one of them occurred in 2018 when KU announced plans to retire Adrian Mitchell's number, long overdue as she was my first All-American. The ceremony was in January, and I didn't feel well enough to attend, so Josie went in my place.

That same weekend, KU celebrated 50 years of women's athletics. Several of my former players returned to Allen Fieldhouse. So did a former professor, who was introduced as "the mother of KU sports." She had written a book touting her accomplishments as a women's athletic director at KU.

Josie was shocked to hear that. So was I when she told me about it.

One of the biggest reasons I decided to write my story is because I feel strongly about preserving history, and it must be accurate. Intercollegiate athletics didn't exist for women at KU in

1968. Nor was there ever an official appointment of anyone other than myself as the Director of Women's Intercollegiate Athletics at KU. That was documented in November 2019 at a meeting that included Josie and me; Jeff Long, the athletic director at the time; legal counsel for KU; and Wayne Osness, who, if you recall, chaired the Health and Physical Education Department along with the committee that hired me. Even though he was in a wheelchair, Dr. Osness stressed I was the only person ever appointed to the role of Women's Athletic Director.

I certainly don't need to be called the mother of anything. But to let someone else call herself the mother of KU sports is insulting to me.

Kansas Athletics, in my opinion, failed to do its due diligence in making sure its own women's history is accurate. Many of us helped to keep women's sports running in the PE department. It would certainly be fitting if the Department of Education had a Hall of Fame for all the professors and graduate assistants who coached women's sports before 1974. But that isn't the case.

It's 2024, and I still want Kansas to publicly set the record straight about the history of women's intercollegiate athletics. I stayed away from the university for a long time, and although I certainly never encouraged it, many of the players in my program also felt disconnected from their alma mater.

The rift lasted until a new administration under Travis Goff made what I feel is a conciliatory effort to reach out to me and connect the past with the present. The naming of the women's basketball suite was part of three days that celebrated my contributions to KU athletics. Nicole Corcoran, a deputy athletic director under Travis, has been wonderful to me. So has current KU women's basketball coach Brandon Schneider. I am grateful for both of them and especially Josie for being relentless in working with Kansas to protect my legacy.

I've always seen KU as my school. It's an excellent institution.

My players received a great education. So did my daughter. KU is embedded in a warm community that is my community, too. I thank God for those who encouraged me and showed me how much they cared.

Most everything about Kansas is close to my heart. I'm a Jayhawk. Always.

Chapter XIX

Me and Her

By Josie Washington-McQuay

My **mother** was standing in the middle of Melholland Drive, hands at her hips. I was packing my car for my long trip.

I recognized that look. Usually when she was in that stance I had to do what she said. Only this time I knew what I had to do, and I wasn't going to let anything or anyone stand in my way.

I was 21 years old, a college graduate, ready to leave everything I knew behind. Pumped to take on the world and start my journey back East. Ready to leave. Now.

Mom doesn't look happy. Like she doesn't want me to go. Isn't this what you always wanted, Mom? What do you mean, I'm not going anywhere? You taught me to be an independent woman.

I *am* going. We've talked about this for weeks. I can't wait. I'm on a mission and ready to go!

Was that a tear? Mom, are you crying?

My white Toyota Corolla was stuffed with all my clothes, my little black-and-white TV and a few utensils I grabbed from the kitchen. Everything I owned was in that car. It was a stick shift. Mom taught me how to drive a stick, but I'd never driven this far.

I was heading more than 1,100 miles northeast with a stop to see my grandmother in West Chester. I would stay with her while I looked for a job and an apartment in the Philadelphia area.

Goodbye, Lawrence. Bye, Mom. I'm on my own!

As I looked in my rearview mirror, I saw Mom, waving.

So many things I wish I had known earlier in life. Now, as a mother of two to Lauren and Ricardo, as a grandmother of twins, I get it.

My mother has always been here. As much as I like to be front and center — that's the theater major in me — Mom was always backstage. I couldn't always see her. Sometimes I swore she didn't care about what was important to me. That was never the case.

Mom made sure I had everything I needed and a lot of what I wanted while growing up. Only I didn't see it. I didn't see a lot of what was right in front of my eyes.

In Marian Elizabeth Washington, I, Marian Josephine Washington-McQuay, have the mother I was meant to have.

My mother is my ride-or-die. My best friend. My heart. I'm her road dog. Her bodyguard. Her protector. Her one and only daughter.

No, we didn't bake cookies when I was growing up. We didn't shop for shoes every week or play with makeup. Mom made dinner every night — usually in the microwave oven because she was working late, getting ready for a practice, coaching or at one of my events. She was so tired when she got home most nights.

I grew up with Mom's village around me — my Grandmum, her mother, was more core. My grandfather, who I called Pop Pop, adored me. My aunts looked after me, and Uncle Butchie was something of a father figure. Mom was in the center of it all, busy with school and basketball and working at night. But she was always checking with me, making arrangements for me, asking about my day. I remember her picking me up at the sitter's, and I would greet her with this big hug. I was always waiting for her because I knew she was coming to get me.

I loved my bicycle that Mom told me I could ride only so far. And let me tell you, she had a spy, the lady at the end of Wayne Street, who would warn me that if I went any farther than the corner, my mother was going to hear about it.

I always had food in my stomach. My favorite when we lived in West Chester that I could make myself was a ketchup sandwich — a mess of ketchup between two pieces of white bread.

I remember the afternoon she came back from one of her big national trips. I was walking home from Fugett Elementary School with my friend, and this big black car pulled up right alongside us. I didn't make eye contact. Mom told me to keep walking if I ever saw a car I didn't recognize. It slowed down. I sped up.

"Josie!"

That's my mother's voice! She was inside the car! I climbed in and hugged and kissed her. Mom was home. She started telling me about a job in Washington, D.C., where she would be teaching at a recreational center for kids. I was coming. We were moving! Mom and I were going to live together.

Just me and her.

Grandmum didn't want us to go, but Mom said we'd still be close enough to drive back to see her. I was so excited. Grandmum looked sad when we left. We drove around the block and she and my aunts and cousins were still waving goodbye.

We shared a nice townhouse with Mom's friend, and she went to work at The Settlement House in Washington, where a lot of the kids looked like me. It was a center for disadvantaged youth, like a YMCA. I was there all the time, playing ball or tag or soccer. That was a fun time.

We moved to Silver Spring, Maryland, just outside of D.C., into a beautiful house for a while. I liked it there, too. I was a latchkey kid in elementary school, with my own key to the house to let myself in after school every day. Mom would leave a note on the refrigerator door for what I was to have for dinner and to do my homework, which she checked each night when she got home.

I had so many experiences most little girls couldn't relate to.

My favorite movie was "Oliver!" I watched it over and over. I could not stop talking about blond, blue-eyed Mark Lester, who played the title character, the orphan. I talked about him so much, and I didn't think Mom was listening.

We went home to see Grandmum, and Mom told me we were going to New York City, too. We took the train and rode the subway for the first time. I got in a long line with her. I didn't know why we were there, but it didn't matter. I was with Mom. All of a sudden, Mark Lester was standing in front of me! He was having some sort of autograph signing, and Mom took me there to meet him.

Whose mother does that?

It wasn't long before we moved to Kansas City, where Mom taught school during the day and played basketball for the Raytown Piperettes at night. I was practically a Piperette myself. I didn't know until many years later that Mom had it in her contract that I could attend practices and travel during the summer wherever she went.

Some games were far away, in New Mexico even. I got to stay in a hotel with Mom, but all the players let me come in and out of their rooms like I was on the team, too.

They treated me special, especially Coach Alberta Cox, whom everybody called Bert. She let me pet her horses and play with her dog, Babe. Sometimes I spent the night at her house. She made me feel like family. It didn't matter what color I was. I'm pretty sure Mom was her favorite player on the team. I could see their bond. Bert, I think, realized how much Mom had to handle, having a child while holding down a full-time job and playing basketball for one of the best AAU teams in the country. When Mom made me the official mascot, I had two cute outfits that matched the team's uniform. Some of the other teams asked if I could be on their bench as their mascot. Bert said no, I was *their* good luck charm.

When Mom had to go out of the country, I waited at the mailbox for the postcards she wrote. I still keep them in a book. *My Dearest Josie, I'm here in Brazil and I miss you tremendously ...* She brought me a sombrero from Mexico. Nobody else had a doll collection like mine. My room was full of iconic treasures.

When we moved to Lawrence, I was in middle school. It felt different. We weren't in a city anymore. I had to make new friends, and I didn't see a lot of people who looked like me. Sometimes Mom had to leave town, and I couldn't go because I had school. Mom made friends with a family with two girls and two boys who were my age. I stayed with them when Mom went away. Mrs. Mitchell became a second mom to me.

I came home from school and looked for the instructions Mom left me. There was always a snack in the fridge and homework to start.

One of my fondest memories involved visiting Mrs. Easton — Edina, the wife of KU track coach Bill Easton. Mrs. Easton would make me cookies and lemonade while I sat on the grass on the hill of the football stadium and watched Mom throw the discus and shot put. She treated me like a granddaughter.

I had started running track in Kansas City. I trained with a pretty big club. Mom gave me my own set of starting blocks, and I was quite the sprinter in the 100 and 220. She pushed me to run faster than I thought my legs could carry me. I was motivated by a coach who was never satisfied.

Mom came out with me on the track, a whistle around her neck.

She'd blow that thing and say, "Again" right after I was finished.

Off I'd go.

"Again."

I was out of breath.

"Again."

Seriously?

"Again."

"Woman, breathe!" I would scream silently. *Why is she so hard on me?*

"You want to beat Jenny Gore, don't you? Again!"

Why am I not good enough? Even though Jenny was always beating me, I made it all the way to the Junior Olympics. Mom took me to Canada for that.

I was becoming a good basketball player, too. I couldn't jump as high as my mother. No one could. I remember watching her from the stands when I was a little girl. I could not believe how high she could leap. Then it seemed like the other players were tackling her.

"You're hurting my mom! Stop!" I yelled. Mom eyed me and told me to shush, that basketball is a physical game.

Now I was never my mother on the court, but I had real skills because Mom put me in the best camps. Cathy Rush, the coach at Immaculata, held one in the Poconos and Mom let me go. At the end of my week when they handed out awards, I didn't get one for points or rebounds or defense. I won Miss Congeniality!

Hmmm... Marian Washington's daughter is Miss Congeniality? But I guess I got some of her genes. There was no girls basketball team at West Junior High School in Lawrence. But the boys coach let me try out, and I made the team. The parents raised such a fuss about a girl on a boys team that I ended up not playing.

The next year, they started a girls team and I played a lot. Out of the corner of my eye, I saw Mom clapping in the stands. She was always there.

"You could have boxed out," she said in the car going home.

Hadn't she seen me score all those points?

I was a full-fledged athlete at Lawrence High School. Basketball. Volleyball. Track. I was a cheerleader. But I discovered something I liked more than sports. Something my mother knew nothing about. The theater.

I had to sing a solo to audition for what was called Chorale, an advanced chorus with eight members — four boys and four girls. It was like making the starting five of a basketball team. We had our own uniforms. We performed everywhere, and Mom was proud of me.

I came into my own in high school. I liked makeup and fashion. Mom did my hair. She didn't mean to burn it that first time she let me get a perm. I got my first job my freshman year in high school — on roller skates at Sonic Drive-In. Mom became a regular customer because she wanted to make sure I got at least one tip.

There weren't many kids who had their own car at 16. Mom bought me a car so I could drive to work. It wasn't shiny and new. It was pea green, and the steering wheel was just like the teeny kind you'd see in a video game console. I thought that had to be a joke, but I drove it. Pulled up to school the first day and saw smoke from the radiator. That car was an adventure.

Mom took me prom shopping, and we picked out this beautiful pastel blue dress with lace, silk and spaghetti straps. Stevie Walker, a big-time basketball player at Lawrence High, asked me to go. Mom told me she wanted me home by 11. Are you kidding, Mom? It's prom! That's not fair. I'm so embarrassed. Everybody is going to be out until 12 or 1. I'll be the only one ....

"You better be home, Josie!"

I was a little late getting back. I was the only one who had to leave early. I don't think it was even 30 minutes past my curfew. I walked in and saw that look. Mom was on the couch and angry. "I told you to be home on time and you did not listen."

I heard about it. Oh yeah, I heard about it. Mom was stern. A lot of my friends thought as the daughter of a single mother

I could get away with a lot. I got away with *nothing*. My mother meant what she said.

I wanted to leave Lawrence for college, but I listened to Mom. She wanted me to go to KU, so I went to KU. I figured Mom would be too busy to know what I was doing anyway. Even though we lived practically next to the school, she let me live on campus. It's a huge campus, so Mom got me a moped. It was the coolest thing. For $1 of unleaded gas, I could ride all over Lawrence and I could park on campus, which was impossible with a car. I loved it.

During my sophomore year, I went on a date with a football player. Soon after, I got called, summoned is a better word, to Mom's office. When I got there, Mom was sitting behind her desk like a principal. "I heard you were dating ..."

"Mom, it was one date!"

She didn't think he was right for me. Did I mention it was one date?

I can't do anything. I want to be a normal college student!

Her Lady Jayhawks are *so* lucky, I thought. I'm the third wheel. Does Mom even notice me? She treats them better than she treats me. When one of them gets a C, she doesn't come down hard. She finds a tutor or talks to an adviser. When I get a C, it's the end of the world. I wish she cared about me like that. When I get old enough, I thought, I'm outta here!

I had a plan. I was going to be an actress, the next Erica Kane on "All My Children." I auditioned for every production I could at KU.

I was the maid in "You Can't Take It With You." Mom sat in the front row. Don't wave at me, Mom. I'll break character!

I was so excited when I heard KU was going to put on "Grease." I wanted to play Sandy. Only they wouldn't let me audition. I couldn't try out for her tough friend Rizzo, either. They had three roles for Black women, kind of like doo-wop girls.

When "Hair" became a university production, I was told I could play only designated Black roles. I didn't read or sing, but I was cast in a Black role. Wait, how can that be? The same thing happened to my friend who was Black. That was wrong.

Why doesn't the theater department have more plays with lead roles for women of color? I kept asking. That upset me, and I wanted to voice my opinion. I wanted to be heard. But Mom was the athletic director for women's sports. She was iconic on campus. I felt like I needed her permission. I'm not sure she'd want me rocking the boat at the university So I asked.

Is it OK, Mom?

"Do what you have to do," she told me, and I did.

I got the Black Student Union involved. Hundreds of us, Black and white, marched down Jayhawk Boulevard. I was front and center with a big sign. Everything was peaceful. I remember making a big speech in front of Murphy Hall, which housed University Theatre; it was my Jerry Maguire moment. I said that KU was discriminating against Black students by not allowing them to audition for major roles in theatrical productions.

Mom was proud.

They heard us!

The next year I played the Lady in Green in "For Colored Girls Who Have Considered Suicide/When the Rainbow Is Enuf." It's an iconic part in a play that chronicles seven women affected by sexism, racism, abandonment and domestic violence. Part of my role involved performing an abortion on stage. So powerful. I had women come up to me afterward, crying. I remember one woman saying, "It happened to me, too."

It was standing room only. They had to add a show because it was so popular. It was an amazing show. Mom was so proud.

But when I told her I was going to be a professional actress, she said I needed a Plan B. For what, Mom?

She doesn't get it, I thought.

Mom didn't get me a traditional college graduation gift. She handed me an itinerary with everything mapped out for a bus trip to the East Coast. First stop: Penn Station. I was going to New York, Connecticut, Rhode Island and Pennsylvania. Every detail was accounted for — who would meet me at the train station, what friends of hers I would stay with and what I was going to do at every stop. She arranged for me to meet professionals who would talk to me candidly about theater. Brown University had an MBA program and a great theater troupe. I talked to the dean about that program. I met real actors in New York, including Barbara Montgomery, a Broadway actress who was later on a bunch of TV shows.

"It isn't easy," she warned me. "If you think you're going to come in here and audition and get a part, it ain't like that.'

Mom gave me the gift that not everybody gets. To see the real world.

When I got back to Lawrence, I was ready to launch. I knew I wanted to be somewhere else. My mother was a celebrity in Lawrence. I wasn't comfortable knowing how often people tried to get close to me so they could talk to her. I was ready to go my own way.

I packed the car and kissed my mother goodbye. Just like me and her all those years ago when we moved away, I was doing the same thing.

I still didn't know why she was crying.

In a few weeks I had a job as a sales manager in Philadelphia. I had a degree, and graduating from the University of Kansas opened doors like Mom said it would. I managed several sales teams and started growing my career. I worked during the day and tried to do theater things at night.

My Plan B became Plan A when I recognized I could use my theatrical skills in sales presentations.

I can't tell you the day I realized what I should have known all along: My mother really did care. I thought she didn't know what I was doing. She knew everything! From May Day in elementary school to all my games to my theater performances in the front row. I thought she didn't hear me.

Mom heard everything.

I stand in awe of my mother today. As proud as I am of her legacy, I am honored she chose to keep me. Not everyone at her young age would have. I didn't ask many questions about my birth. My mother protected me from what happened to her. I didn't fully understand that it was rape until I read Chapter VII in this book.

I know my father made a terrible mistake, and I am sure he soon realized it. I was his only child and he loved me. I didn't have a traditional relationship with my dad. When I would ask about him, my aunts spoke well of him. My father died young from cancer. As I grew, his family stayed in contact with me and were wonderful and caring when I visited. I had a special bond with my father's mother, my dear Nana.

My father served in the military in good standing. To this day, my goal is to get him moved to Arlington Cemetery so he can be honored properly.

I settled in West Chester, where I live today with my husband, Rick. When I visit Mom in Lawrence, I see former players who thank me for sharing my mother with them. I've always loved my mother, but I loved her even more knowing what she did for them. She was put here to take care of others. When she was inducted into the Women's Basketball Hall of Fame, there must have been 50 players there. They love her. Like a mother.

Nothing was given to my mother. She was a world-class athlete who worked for everything she had. When she went to KU, she interviewed to be an athletic director just like everybody else. She got the job because she was the best person for it. Yet my mother never felt like she was part of the "in" club; she often felt like an outsider, even at her own school and inside her own sport. It was hard to accomplish what she did at Kansas without a lot of support, and yet she's left a truly extraordinary legacy.

As an adult in the working world, I found out what it was like to be alone, too. I remember being the only Black person on my pharmaceutical team during a business trip. I didn't have anyone to go to breakfast with. I remember calling my mother and saying, "Mom, I get it."

Mom taught me to work to be the best I could be. At most of the companies where I worked, I was promoted because I was the top sales manager — at the top of every sales team. Mom taught me — and showed me — work ethic. She pushed me to excel at everything I did.

And at every step along the way, she was there. Sometimes behind the scenes and other times by my side.

Me and her.

Always.

Chapter XX

To Myself

Dear God,

I'm no longer 18 years old. I am 77 and I'm writing this letter on May 17, 2024. I'm home sitting in the big chair by the window. I'm nearing the end of telling my story. After being so private all my life, it has been challenging to reveal so much. One evening a few weeks ago, I felt as if a bucket of ice-cold water was thrown on me.

Wow. Can I do this? I wasn't sure.

I was so conflicted that I shared my feelings with Evette Ott and Lynn Page. They had read a few chapters, so after I finished describing my anxiety, they reminded me how much it meant to them for me to be so open about my life. They said I was a beacon of light and a role model they looked to as an example of what is possible.

They encouraged me to stay with my core values that start with "all things are possible for those who believe."

Thank you, God, for helping me be a difference-maker in so many lives. I am blessed to have coached young women with giant hearts who committed to excellence when playing for me. With the help of a dedicated staff, we experienced real hoop dreams. I wanted these women to achieve and, by example, learn how important it is to do the right thing, even when it's hard. I watch, with pride, a legacy they carry forward. They are women who care about others. Strong, educated women with purposeful lives. Doctors, lawyers, engineers, business leaders, teachers, spouses, mothers and more, eager to mentor the next generation.

I have had a lot of time to reflect on my unorthodox life. Circumstances kept me from a traditional childhood. Getting pregnant at 13, having a baby at 14, could have caused me to follow a different path, but you surrounded me with support. You guided me by the people you put in my life, beginning with my parents. Mom and Dad taught me how to treat people, modeled how to work hard and most importantly, trusted in God as I do. How blessed I was to know Mrs. Redding, who helped me believe I was capable of a college degree. I was lucky to learn under Phoen Terrell at Cheyney State and Carol Eckman at West Chester State. Those coaches, as well as Alberta Lee Cox, helped me reach my playing pinnacle.

To my surprise, God, you took my desire to achieve in athletics and led me to the University of Kansas.

"Why me, Lord?" was my battle cry. I know now I had a purpose to fulfill. I had to build walls so those behind me could build them higher and better. Fifty years later, female athletes at Kansas enjoy elite facilities that include practice courts and fields, weight rooms and locker rooms — one so spacious it's a suite that carries my name. That small group of track athletes I coached in 1974 was the precursor for the Kansas women to win an NCAA outdoor track title in 2013. Stanley Redwine, coach of men and women's track for the last 24 years, will be a head coach for Team USA in track for the 2024 Paris Olympics. It's rewarding to know I laid the foundation of one of the finest athletic programs in the nation.

I cherish the community I built in Lawrence. When I return there every summer, it's as if I never left. Many of my best friends are there. When I'm out and about, I'm often greeted with, "Hi Coach!" I never tire of hearing those words.

I look back and understand why you did not move me for 31 years.

Pastor and Sister Yates, my spiritual leaders, guided me whenever I felt discouraged.

Living with Lyme disease continues to be a challenge, especially in the winter. Every day I give thanks for my neighbors in St. Augustine, Florida. Many are wonderful friends who will learn more about me after reading my story. I enjoy striking up conversations with them about my years at Kansas. Almost every day I wear T-shirts with Kansas written on the front. I am proud to be a Jayhawk!

I leave this legacy to my accomplished, devoted daughter Josie; my son-in-law Rick, the champ; my wonderful grandchildren, Lauren and Ricardo, both college graduates; and my precious great grands, Carter and Cameron. My loving sisters, Cathy and Janet, and their families will always remain close to my heart.

This legacy belongs to all of them.

If I could talk to Little Marian, I would gently advise her with words of encouragement. I would tell her all things are possible. You won't live in a Short Line bus forever. God will have you resting in a peaceful community one day. Just keep fighting. Be unapologetic for who you are — a fierce, beautiful, Black woman. Be resilient. Others might not understand God's purpose for you. Nor will you for a long time. Twists and turns on your journey will test you. Keep love in your heart and keep looking for the best in others, especially when you face those who are against you. Don't let anyone make you feel unworthy. You will reach heights you never imagined.

If I could talk to today's young women and men playing basketball, I would encourage them to have fun and give this game everything they have. Know the acronyms CIAW, AAU and AIAW, and learn why they matter. Celebrate the pioneers in the past and the stars of the present, and avoid making comparisons that diminish who came before. We call the circumstances that surround extraordinary achievements phenomena. Today we're reaping the rewards of the groundwork laid by the sport's most esteemed coaches — Tara

VanDerveer, Shirley Walker, Pat Summitt, Sanya Tyler, Jody Conradt, C. Vivian Stringer and Marsha Sharp, to name only a few. Now we're fortunate to have Dawn Staley. No one in our sport is a better ambassador than Dawn, an outstanding player, Olympian, coach and a positive role model for all young women.

Ora Washington, Nera White, Lusia Harris, Pearl Moore, Lynette Woodard, Jackie Stiles and Caitlin Clark are a few of our phenomenal players who have paved the road to a brilliant future for women's basketball. Appreciate them as outstanding reminders of our past, present and future. Each is a snapshot in time.

I applaud today's players committed to growing a game rich with traditions and storylines. All of us are part of something special.

Recognize history. Celebrate history. Share history. And by all means, tell it accurately so the pioneers and the milestones that carried us into the present era connect. My contributions are part of a rich history that started well before my time.

Thank you, God, for all that you do for me and mine.

Marian

Well, Darling, we've arrived at the now. It's been quite a ride.

Afterword

By Lynette Woodard

What was college, really? I was a senior at Wichita North High School and I didn't know. Mail was coming to my school every day, letters and catalogs from universities all over the country.

Mrs. Friday, who worked in the guidance office, would hand me a stack, saying, "I've got some mail for you!" She seemed so happy. I didn't know why. I remember Mr. Williams, my guidance counselor, trying to explain the process, but it was going over my head.

Nobody explained to me what college was truly all about and why it mattered. No one said that college offers you opportunities, challenges and a chance at a career path that could literally change your life. I would hear guys from our basketball team talk about visiting colleges. They talked more about playing basketball than the educational part. I thought I might get a job after high school with Boeing Wichita. I knew college cost money, and I didn't have it. I couldn't see my parents borrowing a bunch of money to send me to school.

I never thought about playing college basketball. Growing up, if girls were ever on a court, they were escorted out, not escorted in. I usually played only with guys on the playground and at the park until high school, where my teammates played at practice. I played every day, every way, everywhere I could.

My sophomore year, Wichita North played in the state tournament in Lawrence. That was the first time I had been there, but I didn't see the University of Kansas campus because I was sick. We won the state title. I didn't realize how important the coach who congratulated me and placed the medal around my neck would become. Her name was Marian Washington.

Two years later, Wichita North won state again. All these colleges were interested in my joining their programs, and Coach Washington wanted me to visit KU. I knew to get to Lawrence I would have to take a bus and that was going to take at least four hours. I told my mother that I didn't really want to ride the bus.

"Get on the bus!" she said.

My mom drove me to the bus station, and off I went. After a bunch of stops, I got off at this little station in downtown Lawrence at probably 6:30 in the evening. I looked around and thought, "I dunno ..."

Coach Washington wasn't there yet. Next thing I knew, this car came zooming up. Coach jumped out and apologized for being late. I knew she was the basketball coach, but I didn't realize she was also the women's athletic director at Kansas. She was late because she had gotten caught in a long meeting.

I was glad to see her, and my recruiting visit began.

Coach took me on a tour of the campus before dropping me off at Oliver Hall, the dormitory where I would live if I came to KU. That's where I met Karen Jamison and Sheila Vann, my future teammates.

The next morning, Coach introduced me to people from all the academic departments at Kansas, along with the chancellor. They were so welcoming. I could feel they wanted me to be part of the Jayhawk family. Everything was so smooth and organized. It was super cool. It was a great visit.

I knew in my heart I really liked KU, but I had already arranged to visit another school in Texas the next weekend. I had a blast when I got there. My hosts took me to restaurants, parties and the beach. I certainly saw the fun side of college, but no one there talked to me about academics. I didn't see one professor. So, what was my path for the next four years?

I was smart enough to know I needed structure. I knew KU was the school for me. Coach recruited me leading with academics. She offered me a great education. Everyone else recruited me emphasizing basketball, telling me how great I could be and how I could change their programs. That wasn't appealing to me. Coach reinforced my becoming a student-athlete. She knew I had a gift to play the game. Her goal for me was to graduate with a degree.

Looking really far back, the seed to succeed was planted in my mind by a secretary in elementary school named Mrs. Bowser. She knew I loved sports, and she was always showing me pictures of her daughter, Colleen, who was on the U.S. women's basketball team. How amazing is it that Coach Washington was in some of those photos with Colleen! All those years before I ever met Coach Washington, I saw her in pictures. In 1969, Coach and Colleen became the first two Black women to integrate a U.S. national team.

I was finally at KU, in the fall of 1977, when reality set in. All of it was culture shock. I worked hard in class, but when we got to the first round of tests, I didn't feel confident. I went to see Coach to tell her I was going home. I didn't think school was for me.

I remember walking in and seeing her at her desk, which was stacked with papers. She was always working.

"I'm going home," I announced.

She raised her head. "What are you talking about?"

"I'm going home," I said. "I don't know if I can pass my tests."

"Lynette, you can do this. I really believe you can do this," Coach said in that calm voice of hers.

Coach believes in me, I thought.

Coach reminded me that instead of playing basketball and working, I chose to go to summer school at Wichita State before coming to KU. I took nine hours, three classes, and finished with a 3.0 GPA.

"Lynette, continue to do what you did last summer. Study. Read. Take notes," Coach said. Then she confided, "Nobody starts off that great. But you have to stay with it." She also reminded me of tutoring services across campus that I didn't know how to fully utilize.

By the time I left that office, I was so happy inside. At that moment, I believed I could do it. I knew I had the ability to graduate. I started to study more in every class. I was so happy to know in my spirit that I could succeed. I was a college student. I graduated as a two-time GTE Academic All-American and a four-time Kodak All-American.

I graduated from the University of Kansas with a baccalaureate degree in Speech Communications.

I admired Coach. She was so strong. I watched her as she built the entire women's athletic department from the ground up. Not only did she coach the basketball team, she had nine other sports under her direction — softball, volleyball, tennis, gymnastics, golf, swimming, field hockey and last but not least, women's track and field and cross country, both of which she started. I figured that I could help by going to practice every day, being focused and doing everything I was supposed to do to help us win on the court.

Everything with Coach Washington was always about taking care of business in the classroom, playing fair, playing hard and doing things the right way. She was a straight shooter, always truthful. We knew all those times when she would meet with the administration concerning our program it was going to be fireworks. We knew when she went in, she didn't play defense. She played offense. When she came back, the battle was won.

On the court, Coach was an instructor. She taught us what she wanted to see on the floor in a way that we could understand. We never got blamed for making a mistake. It was never personal. We never got showboated on.

"Ladies, we must execute!" she would say. "Take care of the ball. You practiced that. You know you can finish. Now finish it!"

When I saw the movie "Hidden Figures," I thought of Coach Washington. She inspired so many in the women's game and touched so many lives, yet so few know about her accomplishments in her 31 years at the University of Kansas. The women's program had very little money and hardly any support from the administration during my four years — *I challenge anyone to build the KU women's athletic department on the budget she had.* That is why she is the Greatest!

I remember the stationery she used. At the bottom was a quotation, "A Commitment to Excellence." She had it then and she has it now.

Coach would tell us that whether or not anyone calls your name, if you've got belief inside, nobody can stop you. That's the inner strength that Coach has and what she gave to us as players.

She's walked it, lived it and earned a legacy that will never be matched.

Lynette Woodard is a Naismith Basketball Hall-of-Famer, a four-time Kodak All-American from the University of Kansas, a two-time Olympian and the first female Harlem Globetrotter.

Appendix I

Thank you, Jayhawks

Thank you to all the women who played for me at the University of Kansas over 31 years. Our journey together will never be forgotten. And thank you to the parents of these Jayhawks who entrusted their daughters to me. Listed below are letterwinners.

Barbara Adkins
Vickie Adkins
Philicia Allen
Michelle Arnold
Angela Aycock
Carrie Baker
Lisa Baker
Janet Ballard
Keila Beachem
Sue Beattie
Stacey Becker
Susan Berens
Darcy Bieber
Stephanie Blackwood
Brenda Bleske
Shannon Bloxom
Tanya Bonham
Kandis Bonner
Fernanda Bosi
Lisa Braddy
Dalchon Brown
Janet Brown
Kaylee Brown
Ali Brox
Renea Bulmer
Cheryl Burnett
Aquanita Burras
Amy Bybee
Shelly Canada
Amy Carle
Melissa Carman
Theresa Cavanaugh

Misti Chennault
Susan Chlystek
Mary Chrnelich
Tracy Claxton
Laura Cook
Margaret Cortese
Kathleen Cullen
Cindy Currie
Bente Dahl
Sandra deBruin
Jennifer Dieterich
Mary Dietrich
Tamecka Dixon
Tina Dixon
Lisa Dougherty
Margaret Douglas
Tracy Duma
Michelle Duran
Dawn Eikmeier
Rhonda English
Lauren Ervin
Holly Fischer
Heather Fletcher
Sonya Foster
Rodneikka Freeman
Kristin Geoffroy
Gail Goodwin
Tamara Gracey
Gloria Graves
Larisha Graves
Patience Grayer
Susan Haight
Angie Halbleib
Ebony Haliburton
Erica Hallman
Nancy Hanna
Katie Hannon
Geri "Kay Kay" Hart
Cindy Hartshorn
Peggy Hatfield
Kerri Hawley
Kathy Hickert
Kelly "KC" Hilgencamp
Tammy Hoffman
Cynthia Hogg
Shyra Holden
Amelia Holmes
Lindsey Horner
Cheryl Jackson
Jennifer Jackson
Karen Jamison
Marilyn Jenkins
Kelly Jennings
Jaclyn Johnson
Terrilyn Johnson
Sereeta Jones
Sherry Jones
Cindy Kelley

Sue Kelly
Crystal Kemp
Jill Killen
Tasha King
Shannon Kite
Sandra Knox
June Koleber
Nancy Lambros
Jill Larson
Deborah Laudermilk
Michelle Leathers
Keshana Ledet
Shebra Legrant
Doris Lippitt
Ruth List
Lynne Lowry
Liz Luna
Jennifer Lutz
Jackie Martin
Patricia Mason
Kristen May
Marthea McCloud
Patti McFarland
Brandi McGinest
Melaney McWhirt
Connie Means
Leila Mengüç
Valerie Migicovsky
Regan Miller
Adrian Mitchell
Caroline Mixon
Brenda Moffite
Karen Morgan
Donna Moser
Ericka Muncy
Mary Myers
LaTanya Nelson
Suzanne Nicolet
Steph Norris
Evette Ott
Lynn Page
Renea Page
Kathy Patterson
Penny Paulsen
Rose Peeples
Marci Penner
Kelly Phipps
Cindy Platt
Lynn Pride
Casey Pruitt
Ashley Pyle
Valerie Quarles
Tamara Ransburg
Suzi Raymant
Cindy Reed
Erinn Reed
Amanda Reves
Brooke Reves

Heather Rhodes
Alicia Rhymes
Deborah Richardson
Liz Roark
Shandy Robbins
Nichelle Roberts
Lori Roenbaugh
Teresa Anne Rouse
Barbara Rowan
Charisse Sampson
Viette "V.C." Sanders
Marion Sandifer
Nakia Sanford
Ann Schell
Suzanne Schmidt
Grace Schmitz
Karen Schneller
Koya Scott
Megan Scott
Selena Scott
Diane Senne
Monica Sereda
Danielle Shareef
Sandy Shaw
Jamie Shelite
Patti Shields
Caryn Shinn
Vickie Shirley
Alana Slatter
Rose Smagacz
Robbin Smith
Sharita Smith
Stephanie Smith
Angie Snider
Rhonda Spears
Sharonne Spencer
Tina Stauffer
Dameyia Stepney
Kathryn Stevens
Christine Stewart
Sherri Stoecker
Mesho Stroughter
Donna Sullivan
Lisa Tate
Angela Taylor
Leonora Taylor
Kristel Thalmann
Chelsey Thompson
Jennifer Trapp
Jenny Travers
Lisa Treacy
Stacy Truitt
Sheila Vann
Sydney Walter
Blair Waltz
Shawna Waters
Debra Webb
Toni Webb

Olivia "Nikki" White
Adrienne Wiley
Dianna Williams
Dana Wilson
Zena "JoJo" Witherspoon
Lynette Woodard
Tarra Yoder

Appendix II

Marian Washington By the Numbers

1 - **Played on 1st** women's basketball team to win a collegiate national championship; **1st** African American woman to play on a United States national team (along with Colleen Bowser); **1st** African American woman to coach basketball at a predominantly white institution; **1st** Director of Women's Athletics at the University of Kansas; **1st** women's track and field coach at the University of Kansas; **1st** African American woman to coach in the Big Eight Conference; **1st** African American woman to coach a United States international team; **1st** African American woman to coach on an Olympic basketball staff; **1st** female to serve as president of the Black Coaches Association and **1st** individual to serve consecutive terms in that role.

3 - **Conference Coach** of the Year honors (Big Eight in 1992 and 1996, Big 12 in 1997); Jayhawks' AP poll rank during the weeks of Feb. 3, Feb. 10, and Feb. 24, 1981, the highest in program history; **3** college degrees (Bachelor's in Health and Physical Education from West Chester State; Master's in Administration and Biodynamics from the University of Kansas; honorary doctorate from West Chester University).

5 - **Hall of** Fame inductions (Women's Basketball Hall of Fame; University of Kansas Athletics Hall of Fame; West Chester University Hall of Fame (twice); Chester County Hall of Fame; Henderson High School Hall of Fame (formerly West Chester High).

6 - **Players on** the court per team when Washington starred for West Chester State in a 56-39 victory over Western Carolina in the inaugural Commission on Intercollegiate Athletics for Women title game in 1969. It was women's college basketball's first national end-of-season tournament.

7 - **Sports played** while attending West Chester High School (basketball, field hockey, track, discus, shot put, softball, volleyball).

11 - **The** Jayhawks' highest end-of-year AP poll ranking, achieved after going 23-9 and advancing to the NCAA Tournament Sweet Sixteen in 1997-98.

17 - Postseason appearances by the Jayhawks, including 11 NCAA Tournament bids; Kansas seasons with at least 20 victories.

30 - **Wins** by Washington's Jayhawks in 1978-79 (30-8), the most in program history.

31 - **Years** worked at the University of Kansas.

42-3 ½ - Distance in feet thrown in the shot put in 1966, the top indoor mark that year in the nation by an American thrower.

560 - **Career** basketball wins (560-363, a winning percentage of 61%).

Acknowledgments

From Marian E. Washington

I want to acknowledge my daughter, Josie, who was by my side while I wrote my story. Josie helped me correct history at the University of Kansas. She worked closely with Athletic Director Travis Goff and Deputy Athletic Director Nicole Corcoran to recognize my contributions to Kansas. Unveiling the Marian E. Washington Women's Basketball Suite was a moment I'll never forget, and I'm grateful to Josie, Travis and Nicole for that. Writing this book was not easy, and I couldn't have done it without Josie and the encouragement of so many others. My darling Josie, you are a beautiful, intelligent woman and I'm blessed to be your mother.

I would like to express my deepest appreciation to my co-writer, Vicki L. Friedman. For a long time, I could only dream about writing a book about my life. What a wonderful working relationship it has been. I needed someone who could help unravel my complicated life. Someone I could be unashamed and completely honest with. Vicki provided that safe place for me. Vicki is one of the most intelligent, patient and hardworking people I have ever met, and I am blessed to call her my friend. God makes no mistakes. He sent the perfect person at the perfect time.

I want to recognize and thank the rest of my family. I have two beautiful grandchildren, Lauren and Ricardo. Lauren, you started to visit MumMum before you could even walk. Ricky, as soon as you could walk, you came to Kansas with your sister. I am so happy I was able to bond with you both.

I want to thank Lauren and Brian for bringing Carter and Cameron, beautiful twins who are my great grandchildren, into this world.

My sisters Cathy and Janet have known me longer than anyone else. Cathy, I want to thank you for being one of my biggest cheerleaders. Janet, it's been wonderful to talk and visit more with you recently. I love you both.

I thank all of my assistant coaches: Sandy Bahan, Audrey Boone, Reneé Brown, Kevin Cook, Pam DeCosta, Tim Eatman, Kate Galligan, Murray Knox, Maggie Mahood, Tracey Mayes, Kathy Meek, Deb Newkirk, Misty Opat, Lu Sweet, Nancy Van Hoozier, Lynette Woodard and Julia Yeater. You worked so hard to help me build a successful program. You will never know how much I appreciate all you did for me.

I want to thank KU secretaries and staff who were kind and supportive.

I send my love to all my players who played with their whole hearts. You helped me build this program. You helped lift Kansas women's basketball to heights no one thought possible. You proudly represented your school, making history along the way. Some of you never had a uniform or a locker room. Some of you rode all night to travel to games. I was always proud of how you represented Kansas. Thank you doesn't say enough.

Thank you, Peggy Witmer, the first to market Kansas women's basketball. You were there when we really needed you.

Thank you, Renate Mai-Dalton, who worked tirelessly to provide academic support for women's basketball. I also want to thank Paul Buskirk for the academic services he provided to my players.

Thank you, Michelle Reillo, for your friendship and helping me deal with my Lyme disease.

Kayla Ransom, Ailene and Theo Helms, Lynn Page, Evette Ott, Cynthia Kelley and Michelle Reillo. Thank you for reading and providing me constructive feedback on drafts of chapters in FIERCE.

I want to thank all my friends in Lawrence, Kansas, and my friends in Marsh Creek in St. Augustine, Florida. I am grateful for my pups Poppy and Pippin and Bella, my constant companion.

I want to acknowledge Bob Snodgrass at Ascend books and our editor, JimMarchiony. Thank you for helping make this book a reality.

If I've missed anyone, I apologize. Please know I appreciate the role you played in my journey.

I am grateful to the pioneers of AIAW and CIAW basketball and to the 1996 Olympic Women's Basketball Team.

Further thank yous to the following:

Amateur Athletic Organization
Black Coaches Association
Joan Bonvicini
Ron Brown
Ceal Barry
Colleen Bowser
Carol Callan
Cheyney State University
Family of Pat Collinson
Jody Conradt
Nicole Corcoran
The Courtsiders
Abbi Craig
Dial Soap Company
Hester Dorsey
Felice Duffy
Teresa Edwards
Nancy Galloway
Travis Goff
Peggie Gillom-Granderson
Maxine Gregory
Roxanne Hall
Mary Jo Hetzel
Kansas women's coaching staff, 1974-79
Kenneth Spencer Research Library staff
Tom Kivisto
Venus Lacy
Legends of the Ball
Jerry Lewis
Rebecca Lobo
Donna Lopiano
Ann Meyers Drysdale
Bob Milner and King of the Road bus company
Carrie Mayhew
Martin Luther King Junior High School family

Kathy Meek
Members of the 1976 USA Team Handball team
The Mitchell family
Ellen Mosher
NCAA
Raye Pond and Sue with Nike
Nurses who cared for my mother
Family of Wayne Osness
Carolyn Peck
Family of Ruth Redding
Brandon Schneider
Kathleen Sebelius
Doug Self
Marsha Sharp
Dawn Staley
Marianne Stanley
Carol Stiff
C. Vivian Stringer
Student managers from 1973-2004
Phoen Terrell
Brenda VanLengen
West Chester Community Center softball team
West Chester University National Championship team, 1969
Williams Jones Cup team, 1982
Women's Basketball Coaches Association
Women's Basketball Hall of Fame
Rev. Ronald and Sister Ruby Yates

From Vicki L. Friedman

Working with Marian on her autobiography is the professional thrill of my lifetime. And yet it's even more than that. I cherish the friendship and the bond we've developed that is extraordinary. What a privilege and a treat it is to have such a special person in my life.

Warm thank yous to Marian and Lynette Woodard for the days I spent in Lawrence, Kansas, getting to know them both. Special thanks and appreciation to Marian's daughter, Josie Washington-McQuay, for everything she did to make this book possible.

I could not have done this without:

- my first and best editor and treasured friend, Dan Kelly
- Jim Marchiony, our editor, and Bob Snodgrass at Ascend Books
- my friend Paul White for being a sounding board & that cosmic connection
- my sons, Harry and Ben Holtzclaw, who continue to amaze me with who they are
- my husband, Mike Holtzclaw, for reading behind me with care
- Rita Phoenix for her special friendship and for teaching me how fun life can be
- Wendy Larry for sharing her passion for women's basketball
- Mel Greenberg for his knowledge and our friendship that dates back to 1990
- Kisses to my muse and shadow, Romeo, my Master Agility Japanese chin.

About the Authors

About Marian E. Washington

Marian E. Washington, the eldest daughter of Marian and Goldie Washington, grew up in a bus that her father made a home in West Chester, Pennsylvania. She became a mother at age 14 when her daughter, Marian Josephine, "Josie," was born.

Marian played seven sports while attending West Chester High School. Her primary athletic focus, throwing the shot and discus, earned her invitations to the Olympic Trials in 1964 and then again in 1968 and 1972. She also competed in the Olympic Trials in 1976 for team handball.

Marian holds a Bachelor's in Health and Physical Education from West Chester State College (now West Chester University), a Master's in Administration and Biodynamics from the University of Kansas, and an honorary doctorate from West Chester University.

Marian became a two-time AAU All-American and starred on the West Chester State College team that in 1969 won the first national women's collegiate basketball championship. She was the first of two Black women to represent the United States in international competition as a member of the U.S. National Team.

Marian became the first and only Athletic Director for Women's Sports at the University of Kansas in 1974, a hire made after the passage of Title IX of the Civil Rights Act. She laid the foundation for women's athletics at Kansas, in addition to becoming the first African American woman to coach basketball at a predominantly white institution. She founded the first women's track and field program at Kansas, and served as its inaugural coach.

Marian amassed 560 victories in 31 seasons as coach of Kansas women's basketball. Her teams won 20 or more games 17 times and reached the NCAA Tournament 11 times. In 1996 she became the first Black woman to coach at the Olympic level as an assistant on the gold-medal winning 1996 team.

When Marian stepped into Kansas' Allen Fieldhouse for the first time in 1973, only one room in the arena was dedicated to women: the public restroom. Today the Marian E. Washington Women's Basketball Suite is among the finest facilities in the nation.

Marian has two grandchildren, Lauren and Ricardo, and two great-grandchildren, Cameron and Carter. She currently lives in St. Augustine, Florida with her Chihuahua, Bella.

About VICKI L. FRIEDMAN

Vicki L. Friedman was born in Washington, D.C., the younger daughter to Harry and Shirley Friedman. She has one sister, Penny L. Friedman.

Vicki fell in love with writing at a young age, starting with a series of stories about a fictional dog club. She graduated Phi Beta Kappa from The George Washington University with a Bachelor of Arts in Political Communications and earned a Master of Arts in Journalism from the University of Missouri. Vicki is the inaugural recipient of the Association for Women in Sports Media scholarship in 1990.

Vicki's sportswriting career spans more than 30 years and includes extensive newspaper coverage of collegiate women's basketball, including 15 years as the Old Dominion beat reporter. Among her honors is a third-place finish nationally in the 2008 Associated Press Sports Editors Awards for feature writing. She was a regular contributor to espnW.com for a decade, where her primary focus was volleyball, field hockey, lacrosse and feature writing. She is part of the Class of 2024 that will be inducted into the Hampton Roads Sports Media Hall of Fame.

Vicki resides in Chesapeake, Virginia, with her husband, Mike Holtzclaw. She is the proud mother to sons Harry and Ben Holtzclaw and four dogs, Lulu, Whiffie, Checkers and her Master Agility Japanese chin, Romeo.

FIERCE is her first book.

Discover more about the life and legacy of
Marian E. Washington at
www.marianewashington.com
Coach Washington is available for speaking
engagements and public appearances.